H. G. Wells:
Interdisciplinary Essays

Edited by

Steven McLean

CAMBRIDGE
SCHOLARS

P U B L I S H I N G

H. G. Wells: Interdisciplinary Essays, Edited by Steven McLean

This book first published 2008. The present binding first published 2009.

Cambridge Scholars Publishing

12 Back Chapman Street, Newcastle upon Tyne, NE6 2XX, UK

British Library Cataloguing in Publication Data
A catalogue record for this book is available from the British Library

ISBN (10): 1-4438-1126-2, ISBN (13): 978-1-4438-1126-2

To my Parents

TABLE OF CONTENTS

LIST OF ILLUSTRATIONS

ACKNOWLEDGEMENTS

This volume emerged from the conference 'H. G. Wells: New Directions', one of the annual symposiums hosted by the H. G. Wells Society each September. I would like to thank the delegates who attended the conference for their interest and enthusiasm. In their various ways, Bernard Loing, Patrick Parrinder, John Hammond, Mark Egerton and Paul Allen facilitated the organisation of this event and I record my appreciation here. I would especially like to thank the contributors to this book (most of whom were delegates at the 'New Directions' conference) for their patience and efficiency throughout the editing process. For advice on this project, I wish to thank Ann Heilmann, who gave generously of her experience and expertise. I would also like to thank staff at Cambridge Scholars Publishing for their interest in this volume.

Most of the essays included in this volume are fresh contributions, with the following partial and full exceptions. Patrick Parrinder would like to acknowledge the support of the European Thematic Network 'ACUME' and the Portuguese Comparative Literature Association, in whose journal *Dedalus* an earlier version of his chapter appears. My own 'Animals, Language and Degeneration in *The Island of Doctor Moreau*' first appeared in *The Undying Fire: Journal of the H. G. Wells Society, the Americas*, 1 (2002), 43-50, and I am grateful for permission to reprint this article. The H. G. Wells Society maintains an informative website at: http://hgwellsusa.50megs.com. Those interested in finding out more about the activities of the Wells Society should contact the Secretary at: secretaryhgwellssociety@hotmail.com.

The illustrations in Keith Williams's essay are reproduced by kind permission of the Trustees of the National Library of Scotland. In the case of individual illustrations which may still be in copyright, every effort has been made to trace the current copyright holders, who should contact the publishers to discuss further permission if required. The cover image is taken from the *Review of Reviews*, 17 (1898). Every effort has been made to trace all copyright holders, but if any have been inadvertently overlooked, the publisher will be pleased to make the necessary arrangements at the first opportunity.

Steven McLean, June 2008

INTRODUCTION

H. G. Wells was, as this volume demonstrates, a varied and prolific writer. Perhaps best known for his early 'scientific romances', which are generally acknowledged as the pioneers of modern science fiction, he also wrote science textbooks, journalism, short stories, utopias, social novels, futurist speculations, and works of popular history. From the very outset of his intellectual career, Wells was a polymath whose work invites the interdisciplinary perspective generated by the contributors to this collection.

As numerous commentators have noted, there was something of a scarcity of interest in Wells in the years following his death in 1946. The publication in 1961 of two important works, Bernard Bergonzi's *The Early H. G. Wells: A Study of the Scientific Romances* and W. Warren Wagar's *H. G. Wells and the World State*, is widely regarded as a pivotal moment in the emergence of modern Wells scholarship.[1] Since the publication of these now classic studies, a growing number of books and articles on Wells have appeared. The essays collected in this volume are intended to reflect something of the current range of interest in Wells.

Since the 1980s there has been an increasing concern with the scientific basis of Wells's writings, stimulated by a sustained critical focus on the interconnections between literature and science more broadly.[2] In the opening essay of this collection, 'What the Traveller Saw: Evolution, Romance and Time-Travel', Sylvia A. Pamboukian examines *The Time Machine* (1895) as a manifestation of a new late nineteenth-century genre immersed in discourses of evolution: the time-travel narrative. Pamboukian considers how earlier time-travel narratives such as William Morris's *News From Nowhere* (1890) and Edward Bellamy's *Looking Backward* (1888) restrict any radical scientific vision by limiting the evolutionary timescale and relying on romantic tropes. While she finds works such as Richard Jefferies's *After London* (1885) better represent evolutionary change, Pamboukian concludes that it is only with the publication of *The Time Machine* that this genre is truly able to represent evolutionary change and its dehumanising potential implications.

My own 'Animals, Language and Degeneration in *The Island of Doctor Moreau*' continues to investigate the scientific engagement of Wells's early work, and reveals how his second scientific romance responds 'to new theories of the relations between humans, animals and language'. I argue that the linguistic capacity of the Beast People partially endorses the view held by the American naturalist Richard Garner that simian language functions like a rudimentary form of human speech. In the course of my essay, I demonstrate how Wells in the novel resists any enduring distinction between human and animal language by 'showing human language to be subject to reversion' as 'its higher reaches turn into the same forms of gabble as that of the Beastfolk'.

While his rapid succession of scientific romances dominates Wells's early career, he was concurrently producing purely fantastical and social romances. Included among these non-scientific romances is *The Wheels of Chance*, a story inspired by the cycling craze of the 1890s and published shortly after *The Island of Doctor Moreau* in 1896. Simon J. James, in his 'Fin-de-Cycle: Romance and the Real in *The Wheels of Chance*', shows that, while apparently a peculiarity among the author's early works, the novel no less participates 'in the aesthetic and political debates that would come to shape, then dominate, Wells's career'. In particular, James investigates how *The Wheels of Chance* prefigures Wells's later emphasis on the need for art to instigate social reform. He examines how the romantic aspirations of the protagonists are partially indulged, as Hoopdriver is temporarily alleviated from his draper's existence. Yet, James argues, the inevitable conclusion of his bicycling adventures forces Hoopdriver – and by extension, the reader – to turn away from fantastic indulgences and towards more concrete political goals.

Having already articulated some of the prevalent scientific and aesthetic anxieties of late-Victorian culture in his fiction, Wells in *The War of the Worlds* (1898) makes a unique contribution to the proliferation of *Fin de Siècle* fictions expressing a fear of invasion. In the fourth essay in this collection, 'Alien Gaze: Postcolonial Vision in *The War of the Worlds*', Keith Williams examines Wells's alien invasion classic as an influential expression of the emergence of a critical 'postcolonial' vision. Optical technology was, Williams notes, instrumental to enforcing the imperial project. He demonstrates how the return of a technologically superior gaze by the Martians reverses the impact of visual technology, decentring the imperial subject and forcing the contemporary reader to consider the ethics of British foreign policy. A particular focus of Williams's analysis is Wells's fascination with the perception altering potential of visual technology, encapsulated in the descriptions of the Martian heat ray as 'camera' like. Williams draws intriguing parallels with other anti-colonial narratives featuring defamiliarised vision and optical devices, thus supporting his contention that *The War of the Worlds* was central to the emergence of a 'postcolonial' vision.

While his early romances brought Wells widespread critical acclaim – Joseph Conrad, for example, responded to the publication of *The Invisible Man* (1897) by terming him the ' "Realist of the Fantastic" '[3] – Wells himself was determined to become established as a *mainstream* novelist. In an early letter to Arnold Bennett, he protested: 'For me you are part of the Great Public, I perceive. I am doomed to write "scientific" romances and short stories for you creatures of the mob, and my novels must be my private dissipation'.[4] Bernard Loing, in his '*Love and Mr Lewisham*: Foundations and Sources for a First Social Novel', discusses how the composition of *Love and Mr Lewisham* (1900) functioned like 'a period of apprenticeship' for Wells in his determination to establish himself as a social novelist. He investigates how *Lewisham* elaborates situations and characters introduced in two of Wells's early short stories. The first of these is 'A Slip Under the Microscope' and the second, discovered by Loing himself, is 'How Gabriel Became Thompson'. By synthesising the ideas found in these narratives with the long tradition of the Bildungsroman in *Lewisham*, 'Wells the heirless author, was showing his credentials to enter an illustrious family where he intended to stay and become a legitimate member'.

As his confidence as a novelist grew, Wells experimented increasingly with narrative technique and methods of presentation. John R. Hammond, in his wide ranging study of 'Wells and the Discussion Novel', contends that Wells was a far more experimental writer than he is typically given credit for. While acknowledging that some of Wells's later novels bear the hallmarks of hasty composition, he argues that others have been unjustly neglected and deserve broader recognition. The scope of experimentation in the later fiction is such that in *Brynhild* (1937), 'the most Jamesian of all his novels', Wells is for once conforming to the standards of literary form prescribed by Henry James. Although novels like *You Can't Be Too Careful* (1941) contain didactic elements, Hammond finds that Wells is at his most effective as a novelist when his didactic intention does not interfere too much with his literary technique.

While Wells himself increasingly attempted to distance himself from his early fantasies in order to direct critical attention to his present work, some of his later fictions unmistakeably recall his scientific romances. *Mr Blettsworthy on Rampole Island* (1928), for example, works in the same tradition of island story as *Doctor Moreau*. However, as Partrick Parrinder points out in his 'Island of Fools: *Mr Blettsworthy on Rampole Island* and the Twentieth-Century Human Predicament', *Mr Blettsworthy* 'displays a quite different understanding of island biology, island psychology, and island symbolism'. Parrinder considers how *Mr Blettsworthy* supports a psychoanalytical reading, with England representing the Superego and Madeira and, to a greater extent, Rampole Island functioning as the Id. He concludes that the tension in the novel between the islands of Britain and Madeira – and between the hopeful but unreliable voice of Lyulph Graves and the prophetic despair of Arnold Blettsworthy – corresponds to the two voices of hope and despair that Wells wrestled with throughout his life.

Among his many influences, Wells himself repeatedly stressed the importance of Thomas Henry Huxley, who had of course lectured him during his studies at the Normal School of Science (now part of Imperial College, London).[5] In her ' "Buildings of the New Age": Dwellings and the Natural Environment in the Futuristic Fiction of H. G. Wells and William Hope Hodgson', Emily Alder discusses an important facet of Huxley's influence on Wells. She examines how the portrayal of the natural environment is integral to Wells's appropriation of Huxley's 'ethical' evolution, and argues that Hodgson – though influenced by Wells – offers an alternative interpretation of Huxley's ideas. For Alder, works like 'A Story of Days to Come' (1897) and *When the Sleeper Wakes* (1899) employ redoubts which secure the continuation of the 'ethically best' from the degenerative potential of the 'cosmic process' of evolution implicit in the 'wilderness' surrounding human dwellings. While she explores how Hodgson develops the notion of the redoubt in 'The Night Land' (1912), Alder demonstrates that both he and Wells simultaneously 'reflect Victorian beliefs that nature also has a positive part to play in human life'.

Though he periodically acknowledged the impact of Huxley in shaping his outlook, Wells was not always explicit regarding the influences on his work. In her 'H. G. Wells and William James: A Pragmatic Approach', Sylvia Hardy contends that the magnitude of William James's influence on Wells was comparable with that of Huxley. She identifies the nucleus of James's pragmatic method at the core of Wells's philosophical outlook, thus accounting for James's enthusiastic response to his work. Hardy detects the influence of pragmatism in a number of Wells's works, particularly *A Modern Utopia* (1905). In emphasising how James's distinction between different types of mind would have appealed to the author, Hardy proposes a fascinating explanation for Wells's repeated insistence that he did not regard himself as an artist.

In addition to assimilating various discourses in his work, Wells himself not only had an incalculable influence on popular literature and culture but also on significant political figures. In the final essay of this collection, 'H. G. Wells and Winston Churchill: A Reassessment', Richard Toye reveals that – despite their apparent differences – Wells had a definite intellectual influence on Churchill. While he acknowledges the need to remain tentative about this influence in certain instances, Toye shows that Churchill's indebtedness to Wells was most obvious during the Edwardian period, and more especially in his reaction to *A Modern Utopia*. For Toye, Wells's strong direct influence on Churchill during this period explains his decision to support Churchill in the 1908 North-West Manchester by-election. By establishing his influence on a 'doer' like Churchill, Toye reminds us of the material impact of Wells's status as a writer who imagines 'the shape of things to come'.

Notes

[1] Bernard Bergonzi, *The Early H. G. Wells: A Study of the Scientific Romances* (Manchester: Manchester University Press, 1961); W. Warren Wagar, *H. G. Wells and the World State* (New Haven: Yale University Press, 1961). For an analysis of the opposing approaches to Wells generated by these two studies – and of the possibility of reconciling them – see Robert Shelton, 'Locating *The Time Machine* within (and beyond) the Bergonzi/Wagar Debate', *The Undying Fire*, 1 (2002), 29-42.

[2] See Roslynn D. Haynes, *H. G. Wells: Discoverer of the Future, The Influence of Science on His Thought* (London: New York University Press, 1980) and my own *The Early Fiction of H. G. Wells: Fantasies of Science* (Basingstoke and New York: Palgrave Macmillan, 2009).

[3] Letter to H. G. Wells, dated 4 December 1898, *J. Conrad: Life and Letters*, ed. by G. Jean-Aubry (New York: Doubleday, 1927), pp. 249-50.

[4] H. G. Wells, Letter to Arnold Bennett (1901), cited in J. R. Hammond, *H. G. Wells and the Modern Novel* (New York: St Martin's, 1988), p. 6.

[5] In an appreciation of Huxley written in 1901, Wells recalls the enthusiasm Huxley inspired in him and his fellow students: 'we borrowed the books he wrote, we clubbed out of our weekly guineas to buy the *Nineteenth Century* whenever he rattled Gladstone or pounded the duke of Argyle'. H. G. Wells, 'Huxley', *Royal College of Science Magazine*, 13 (1901), 209-211 (p. 209).

PART I:

EARLY ROMANCES

WHAT THE TRAVELLER SAW:
EVOLUTION, ROMANCE AND TIME-TRAVEL

SYLVIA A. PAMBOUKIAN

Of all nineteenth-century scientific theories, evolution has received considerable attention from literary critics. George Levine, for example, persuasively argues that Darwinian 'ideas and motifs' such as observation, interdependence, abundance, scarcity, and chance were culturally so prominent that they 'helped shape late-century narrative form', especially the novel with its abundant characters, interconnected plots, and emphasis on inheritance.[1] In some late-Victorian novels, evolution underscores the fleetingness of human life, as in Olive Schreiner's *The Story of an African Farm* (1883) or Thomas Hardy's *A Pair of Blue Eyes* (1873), when the protagonist spies a trilobite embedded in a rock as he ponders his own death while dangling over a cliff. In others, evolution represents continuity with the past, as when George Eliot explains Maggie and Tom's contrasting natures by referring to each child's inherited Tulliver or Dodson traits in *The Mill on the Floss* (1860). Still others use evolution to examine individual and familial development over several generations, as when Samuel Butler traces the rising fortunes and waning emotional life of the Pontifex family in *The Way of All Flesh* (published posthumously, 1903). These texts deploy the epistemological power of evolution as a scientific theory to ground their social vision, which often encourages sympathy between classes by displaying the interdependence of supposedly unrelated communities (such as aristocracy and labour) and the commonality of human existence (shared by men and women, adults and children, masters and servants).

During the late nineteenth century, a new narrative form emerges which is also deeply invested in evolution: the time-travel narrative. A brief list of late-century time-travel narratives includes: Edward Bulwer-Lytton's *The Coming Race* (1871), Samuel Butler's *Erewhon* (1872), Richard Jefferies's *After London* (1885), W. H. Hudson's *A Crystal Age* (1887), Edward Bellamy's *Looking Backward* (1888), Grant Allen's 'Pallinghurst Barrow' (1892) and *The British Barbarians* (1895), H. G.

Wells's *The Time Machine* (1895) and *When the Sleeper Wakes* (1899), and Arthur Conan Doyle's belated *The Lost World* (1912). These texts integrate evolutionary theory with romance rather than with realism (as in earlier novels), since romance enjoyed a late-century resurgence in popularity. While certain critics attribute romance's popularity to imperialism and misogyny, Robert Fraser argues that 'for the advocates of romance, the esoteric and outlandish were newly worthy of attention, not simply because they permitted an escape from commonplace tedium, but because they opened onto the wilder excesses of fact'.[2] Just as Fraser distinguishes between mere escapism and engagement with the 'wilder excesses of fact,' H. G. Wells complains about the 'puerilities of romance' that 'prohibits anything but the superficialities of self-expression'.[3] To Wells, traditional romance offers only an escape into the 'bright, thin, gay excitements of a phantom world' while novels 'reflect and co-operate in the atmosphere and uncertainties and changing variety of this seething and creative time'.[4] Wells contends that the novel is 'an important and necessary thing indeed in that complicated system of uneasy adjustments and readjustments which is modern civilisation. I make very high and wide claims for it. In many directions I do not think we can get along without it'.[5] Since they interact with evolutionary theory, time-travel narratives participate in the 'uneasy adjustments' of a 'seething and creative' modernity rather than offering mere escapism, despite their romantic tropes.

This essay examines Wells's *The Time Machine* in the context of other nineteenth-century time-travel narratives. Many of these narratives incorporate aspects of nineteenth-century evolutionary theory in their depiction of characters, settings, and events; however, these narratives also offer a window into the changing view of evolution during this period. Peter Morton argues that during this period dominant evolutionary theories included a guiding intelligence responsible for development, increasing complexity of species, and the final goal of perfection for all species.[6] These dominant theories appear in a variety of forms and are often questioned by time-travel narratives. Examining this genre also illuminates the tensions between romantic forms, which tend toward escapism, and scientific theory. Each time-travel narrative must attempt to resolve this tension. Finally, this approach clarifies Wells's contribution to this genre. While he did not innovate in using time-travel or evolutionary concepts, Wells develops important tropes that open the genre to new possibilities. Wells introduces machinery to this genre and explores the role of technology in the genre. He also innovates in his presentation of tl

Traveller himself, which has far-reaching implications both in Wells's own work and in the genre as a whole.

In linking evolution and romance, several time-travel narratives appeal to evolution's epistemological authority as a way to ground a text dominated by romantic forms. For example, William Morris's *News From Nowhere* (1890) describes the experiences of an English gentleman, William Guest, in a quasi-medieval future where free love and communism are celebrated in an Edenic Thames valley. When he awakens in the future, Guest notes the beautiful weather, the clear Thames water, and the salmon nets, all of which seem unusual; however, Guest is more surprised by the 'fourteenth-century' dress of the inhabitants, the absence of industry, and the medieval-looking stone bridge which has replaced an iron bridge over the river.[7] The people are long-lived and youthful in appearance but speak English and appreciate familiar pleasures such as ginger-beer and lemonade (84). An old man, Richard Hammond, and his family orientate Guest to the social conditions of this new world, which is free of crime, poverty, discrimination and marriage. While several events indicate that a long time has passed, such as the oxidization of Guest's silver coins and the return of salmon to the now-clean Thames, the change is implicitly only a few hundred years because humanity and the landscape are very similar to nineteenth-century people and environments. Hammond recollects stories about the change from nineteenth-century social arrangements to the current formations, and familiar buildings, such as the Houses of Parliament, are still standing (49). Yet this Eden is static: as Hammond explains, social formations are ideal and do not change, as no change is needed. As a static Eden, this future is, as Morton argues in his reading of this text, 'free from the taint of evolutionism' because of its 'tight frame of a succession of sunny and placid days'.[8] In the end, Guest awakens in his own home and realises that his glimpse of the future was only a dream, implying that the wholesome social relations and beautiful landscape may truly exist nowhere, as the title suggests.

Similarly, Edward Bellamy's *Looking Backward* (1888) depicts Julian West falling into a trance-like sleep in his Boston home only to awaken about one hundred and thirteen years in the future to discover a communist society free of class, capital, and gender inequality. As his hosts, Dr Leete and his family, explain, this society boasts great technical innovations, such as the 'musical telephone' which is akin to a radio and credit cards, along with social innovations, such as universal, free health care. As in *News From Nowhere*, the political vision is indeed radical, but, as in *News From Nowhere*, *Looking Backward* does not present evolutionary change because of its limited timeframe. For example, Julian West identifies his home city of Boston by the familiar course of the Charles River and by the headlands of the harbour, 'not one of its green islets missing'.[9] The Bostonians of the year 2000 speak English and are, of course, physically identical to those of 1887, except for their better health due to better social arrangements. Where Morris depicts his utopia as only a vision, Bellamy toys with that convention by depicting West's horror at waking up back in the nineteenth century only to realise that his return is actually the nightmare and that he is still in the future, about to marry his old sweetheart's descendent. Bellamy's playful allusion to utopian dream-visions seems innovative in terms of narrative, just as the communist social vision seems politically radical; however, as static Edens, Morris's and Bellamy's texts do not innovate in terms of evolutionary theory. They limit depictions of biological and geological change by limiting the timeframe. In addition, their use of romantic tropes forecloses upon any radical scientific vision. The methods of travel, a magical sleep and a dream vision, hint at a purely fantastic reading of the story in which a magical sleeper awakens in a strange country peopled by strange natives. Even the strange natives are innocuous, since both men find sage guides, wise old men, who steer them safely through the new society, which presents no problems for the time-travellers. The helpful guide figures undermine evolutionary concepts such as competition, fitness, and extinction, and these harsher aspects of evolution play little part in a utopian vision of happy communism. While the concepts of the time travel and the betterment of society through rational living seems to owe a debt to evolutionary thinking, these romances fail to explore evolution in any serious way.

In *A Crystal Age* (1887), W. H. Hudson better represents the principles of geological and biological development by describing the experiences of a young man, Smith, who has fallen down a cliff and lain unconscious for thousands of years. When Smith awakens, he notices that the steep cliff has become a 'gentle slope', implying that erosion has altered the landscape, and that the birds, dogs, and horses 'did not look altogether familiar', alluding to biological evolution.[10] The people Smith encounters have also evolved: they are virtually asexual, have ethereal voices and function in a bee-hive society with one sexually active queen per house. They are clearly descendents of humanity since they speak English (22). The bee-people's sexless biology is understood by Smith as progress away from bestial sexual reproduction and reinforces the notion that development follows a route of continual progression. As a member of a primitive species, Smith shocks the inhabitants of the future with his sexual desire, his coarse voice (101), and his rough features (120). Just as in earlier utopias, the society is one of harmony, communism, and equality. Yet, the bee-people also illustrate evolutionary theories of the period, including the malleable nature of species, the progressive trajectory of development, and the great expanses of time involved in this paradigm. However, *A Crystal Age* falters when Hudson exploits the narrative devices of romance in a manner that undermines the scientific complexity. For example, Smith's mode of time travel (sleeping) appears magical rather than scientific. The magical reading is reinforced by the Cinderella plot: Smith is chosen as the mate for the next queen bee (although he accidentally drinks poison and dies before this happens). This undermines Hudson's evolutionary theory since it potentially locates the less-evolved Smith at the top of a more-evolved society. More importantly, just as in *News From Nowhere*, the Edenic setting undermines Hudson's earlier depiction of evolutionary change. Readers learn that the same family has inhabited the house Smith visits for over two thousand years without any natural disasters, changes in climate, developments in language, or new behaviours. Just as in earlier narratives, helpful guides attempt to fit Smith into the new social order; however, Hudson hints at this trope's inappropriateness for an evolutionary narrative. Since Smith is biologically unfit to live in this society, he cannot comprehend it fully and thus accidentally kills himself. On the one hand, the text offers a static Eden while on the other it endorses geology and biology as powerful and universal forces, a text in tension between science and romance.

Richard Jefferies's *After London; or, Wild England* (1885) manifests a similar tension in more concrete form: it is split into two sections. The former is replete with examples of evolutionary theory while the second section describes a hero's romantic adventures. In the first section, readers witness an accelerated version of events in which nature reclaims the English countryside. For example, after civilisation collapses, mice feed in the abandoned granaries and multiply until the hawks, owls, and weasels experience a related increase in numbers.[11] After the predators decimate the mice population, they experience a drop in their own numbers, so the rodent population swells again, and the cycle repeats itself (9). Such incidents recall Charles Darwin's *On the Origin of Species* (1859); for example, Darwin links the abundance of clover in a given region to the population of cats in the area since cats hunt mice, which destroy beehives, and bees pollinate clover. Jefferies also illustrates Darwinian concepts such as hybridity and extinction by describing the extinction of unfit domestic pets, such as poodles, and the interbreeding of the remaining dogs, leading to the survival of only three varieties (12). Like

Hudson, Jefferies speculates about geological changes to England's landscape, including the silting and flooding of the Thames and the Severn, the erosion of dams, and the blockage of canals by water plants, all of which create a vast inland lake. Conversely, the second half of the text depicts the quest of Felix Aquila, a young nobleman in a quasi-medieval society, to obtain enough wealth to marry his beloved. After numerous adventures in various courts around the large, central lake, Felix, who travels in a small boat, finally ventures into the swampy ruins of London, which are polluted to the point of toxicity, where he discovers the treasure that enables him to marry. In addition, his wanderings lead him to discover a new tribe who welcome him as a chief, allowing Felix to found a new English empire with his wealth and his technical innovations, simple, quasi-medieval machines and fences. Featuring a quest, a maiden, a forbidden marriage, treasure, court-life and derring-do, Felix's story seems to be a catalogue of romantic tropes, which contrasts sharply with the evolutionary material of the first section.

The two-part structure of the text highlights the tension between science and romance; however, the narrator's distinctive voice, which blends objectivity and legend, successfully unites the two. For example, the narrator, a sage guide to the new world, describes London as the place about which 'the old men say their fathers told them' (1). Such language mimics the opening of a fairy tale. The narrator describes trains as 'certain machines worked by fire, they traversed the land swift as the swallow glides through the sky, but of these things not a relic remains' (27). The words 'fire,' 'swallow' and 'relic' imply a magical mode of transport, although, of course, readers know that trains are technological. The narrator speculates that 'most of those who were left in the country were ignorant, rude, and unlettered. They had seen the iron chariots, but did not understand the method of their construction, and could not hand down knowledge they did not themselves possess' (33). Because readers know that the fantastic machines are quite real, these objects come to embody both science and fantasy, the commonplace facts of modern life and also the rarity and elusiveness of scientific knowledge. In depicting modern technology as the source of a future society's legends, Jefferies offers readers a sense not only of the fleeting nature of civilisation but of the malleability of cultures that other texts, such as *News From Nowhere,* do not offer. Rather than appealing to evolution's epistemological power as a way to explain or to stabilise cultural formations, Jefferies's blending of science and romance in the narrator's voice destabilises cultural formations by undoing binaries such as truth and fiction, science and superstition, fact and belief. The narrator's voice represents a synthesis of

...ie evolutionary section with the romance section and implies the limits of human knowledge, including scientific knowledge. While Felix does not travel in time per se, the text's representation of accelerated evolution over long periods of time present scientific knowledge as culturally bound, contingent, and ultimately futile before the power of evolution.

David Y. Hughes identifies Grant Allen as a major influence on Wells, noting that *The Time Machine* mentions Allen by name.[12] In *The Time Machine,* the Time Traveller awakens after his first nocturnal encounter with the as-yet-unknown Morlocks and believes that he has seen ghosts. He wonders what era they date from, imagines how the population of ghosts has increased since his own time, and calls this idea 'a queer notion of Grant Allen's'.[13] Allen's 'queer notion' originates in the short story 'Pallinghurst Barrow' (1892), in which a man walking on an ancient barrow one night encounters several ghosts dating from between the Stone Age and the sixteenth century, each of which conducts itself appropriately for its own era. Unlike the ghost story premise of 'Pallinghurst Barrow', Allen's *The British Barbarians* (1895) is a time-travel narrative that describes a twenty-fifth century, time-travelling anthropologist's adventures in nineteenth-century England. The time-traveller, Bertram Ingledew, attacks British assumptions of evolutionary superiority by equating nineteenth-century England with the so-called primitive cultures of Africa and the Pacific. As Nick Freeman notes, the novel's representation of British society 'is both part of the *fin-de-siècle's* love-hate relationship with suburbia and, in its use of anthropological investigative techniques, an attempt to hoist pseudo scientific complacency with its own petard'.[14] For example, Philip Christy, the first Englishman Bertram meets, is surprised and offended by Bertram's assertion that Britain ought to adopt coinage with printed, decimal denominations, unlike the idiosyncratic shilling, crown, florin, and guinea. Christy asserts that ' "you're [Bertram] in a civilised country, not among Australian savages" '.[15] Later, Bertram finds that he cannot wander the streets freely on Sunday wearing a tweed suit or rent rooms without suitcases because of the 'taboo' and 'poojah' of 'Respectability', a 'very great fetich [sic]' (29). Fearing arrest because of his tweed suit, Bertram wonders whether 'Respectability' is a ' "religious or popular, not an official or governmental taboo [...] Will the people in the street mob me for disrespect to their fetich [sic]?" ' (41). When Christy argues that there are no taboos or poojahs in England, Bertram concludes that 'it was one more proof to him of the extreme caution necessary in all anthropological investigations before accepting the evidence even of well-meaning natives on points of religious or social usage, which they are often quite childishly incapable of describing in rational terms' (50). Bertram compares the private ownership of land in Britain to customs of Samoa, Polynesia and West Africa, where given fruits are tabooed to the chiefs (62). He compares British mourning customs to Swaziland death taboos (85) and British courtship rituals to New Ireland practices of keeping girls in cages before marriage (92). Thus, Bertram's assessment of English taboo and poojah equates English customs with (to nineteenth-century readers) 'primitive' African and Pacific social formations, attacking the notion implicit in Philip Christy's conversation that British culture is more advanced than other nineteenth-century cultures.

Like other time-travel narratives, *The British Barbarians* represents evolution as progressive. A superior creature, Bertram deplores Victorian attitudes towards prostitution, divorce and child custody and argues that ' "if there is an injustice or a barbarity possible, I might have been sure the law of England would make haste to perpetrate it" ' (179). He claims that his society is governed by logic, reason and respect for others, whether in matters of property, family, or sexuality. This society is ' "a very, very long way off; and I can't even tell you where it is or how you get there" ' (175). The British people Bertram encounters recognise his 'distinct air of social superiority, [...] [and] innate nobility of gait and bearing' (2). Philip Christy is 'fascinated' by Bertram (25) and calls Bertram ' "a better man than me [...] higher and clearer and differently constituted" ' (126). Similarly, General Claviger claims that ' "He [Bertram] fascinates me" ' (123). Always graceful, Bertram easily picks up an angry landlord, Sir Lionel Longden, and carries him out of Philip Christy's sister, Frida's, path (76). Frida notes that Bertram 'regarded in very truth the Polynesian chief and Sir Lionel Longden as much about the same sort of unreasoning people – savages [...] to be treated with calm firmness and force, as an English officer on an exploring expedition might treat a wrathful Central African kinglet' (76). Frida describes Bertram as 'a civilised being in the midst of barbarians, who feel and recognise but dimly and half-unconsciously his innate superiority' (77). Conversely, Robert Monteith, Frida's Scottish husband, displays a 'savage thirst for vengeance' toward Bertram because 'his coarser nature was ill adapted to recognise that ineffable air as of a superior being that others observed in him' (191). Robert is 'pure Caledonian' (46) with the 'keen clear sight' of his 'highland ancestors' (187) and with the capacity for bitter jealousy, that 'lowest and most bestial of all the vile passions man still inherits from the ape and tiger' (192). Bertram calls Scotland 'a country exceptionally given over to terrible superstitions, fashioned by a race of stern John Knoxes', and he compares the Scots to the Africans as particularly fetishistic, another deliberate attack on British claims of racial superiority made all the more pointed since Robert's wealth derives from imperialist trade in African palm oil (54). When Robert Monteith shoots Bertram in a fit of jealousy over Frida, a blue flame exits Bertram's body instead of blood and takes Bertram's shape as his material body dissolves. The ghostly shape explains that Bertram must return to the ' "TWENTY-FIFTH CENTURY" ', leaving Frida with the hope that Bertram will return for her but in deep despair (195). Allen's use of block capitals reinforces the superiority of the future compared with the relative primitivism of Victorian England, Africa, the Pacific islands, and Scotland.

The British Barbarians is similar to *The Time Machine* in its depiction of technological, repeated time travel and in its central figure of the scientific traveller. Unlike time-travel narratives that describe only one journey, Bertram implies that he and others have travelled repeatedly in time. Indeed, Bertram's sudden appearance in suburban Brakenhurst implies a technological mode of travel that readers only later learn is from the future: initially, Bertram simply puzzles Christy because he appears seemingly out of nowhere. Bertram explains that he brought only one suit which he ' "was lucky enough to secure from a collector at home" ' (27) and that he forgot that shops close on Sunday because he ' "read it in a book on the habits and manners of the English people" ' but ' "one never recollects these taboo days" ' (31). Since Bertram often refers to customs of Africa and Oceania, he implies that he has travelled repeatedly in both time and space (42). Bertram's repeated travels in time differentiate between the ghost story pretext of 'Pallinghurst Barrow' and the time-travel narrative, without direct presentation of these other journeys or of time travel itself. Since Bertram's time-travelling is not revealed until the end of the text, time travel retains the mystery associated with earlier narratives. Just as in other time-travel narratives, readers compare the flawed nineteenth century and an ideal future through conversations between Bertram and his friends, Frida and Christy, in which Bertram obtains explicit instructions about mourning customs, chaperoning unmarried girls, trespassing, and marriage, while explaining his own advanced views on these subjects. However, this narrative inverts the usual pattern in which a nineteenth-century person visits the future, instead bringing a man of the future to the nineteenth century. Similarly, *The Time Machine* focuses on a traveller who makes repeated journeys in time, both backwards and forwards. Wells also reveals the mode of time-travel, the process of evolution, and the inherent mystery of futurity.

In *The Time Machine* (1895), Wells uses innovative tropes to resolve the tension between romance and evolutionary theory.[16] The time machine itself is a new trope that replaces earlier, supernatural time-travelling devices, such as sleeping, visions, and ghosts. While Allen's *The British Barbarians* mentions a technological time-travel device, Wells presents that device as simply another new technology. For example, the Traveller tinkers with his time machine like any owner of a mechanical gadget, such as a bicycle, which must be assembled prior to use: ' "when the putting together was nearly done, I found that one of the nickel bars was exactly one inch too short, and this I had to get remade; [...] I gave it a last tap, tried all the screws again, put one more drop of oil on the quartz rod, and sat myself in the saddle" ' (13). The sensations associated with riding the machine appear similar to other modes of transport: motion sickness, ' "switchbacks" ' and fear of a ' "smash" ' (14). As any new bicyclist might, the Traveller stops his machine too quickly at first and falls off (15).[17] When he encounters the child-like Eloi, the Traveller recalls that he has to remove the operating levers to prevent accidental activation, although it is the Morlocks who actually steal the machine, disassemble it, and clean it just as if it were any other machine (56). While the time machine's similarity to other modes of transport distances *The Time Machine* from earlier, supernatural stories, Wells also discredits supernatural narratives in his frame tale. For example, when the Traveller sends a small-scale model of the machine into the future, his guests initially treat the model's disappearance as if it were a magic show: the narrator wonders whether the whole thing is a 'trick' and the Traveller encourages his guests to ' "satisfy yourselves there is no trickery. I don't want to waste this model and then be told I'm a quack" ' (7). The narrator describes the model's disappearance as an illusion in a magic show: 'there was a breath of wind, and the lamp flame jumped. One of the candles on the mantel was blown out, and the little machine [...] became indistinct, was seen as a ghost [...] and it was gone – vanished!' (7). The flickering lights and allusions to ghosts and vanishing seem to imply that the disappearance is a trick, akin to the familiar disappearing tricks of a magic show. The Medical Man claims that he has witnessed magic shows and fraudulent séances before, and he attributes the machine's disappearance to the flickering candles (10). He alludes to the Traveller's own fraudulent séances when he calls the time-travel experiment a ' "sleight-of-hand trick" ' and asks, ' "are you perfectly serious? Or is this a trick – like that ghost you showed us last Christmas?" ' (9) The Medical Man is ready to credit modern technology with the power to trick him, but he rejects the notion of the supernatural. In the context of late-Victorian culture, the invention of a new machine that opens hitherto unknown territory appears not only possible but also plausible, and the time machine is introduced as yet another new invention that piques the bystanders' intellectual curiosity and excitement.

The time machine's mechanical nature also supports the evolutionary content of the text by allowing readers to visualise continual geological and biological change over a vast timeframe. After his adventures with the Eloi and the Morlocks in the year 802,701, the Traveller continues forward ' "stopping ever and again" ' until he reaches some point past the year three million before returning to his own age (59). At his first stop after leaving the Eloi and Morlocks, the Traveller notices that he is no longer in the England he recognises but on a strange beach thickly encrusted with pink salt under a twilight sun where lack of oxygen causes him difficulty breathing (58). This journey proves that the Eloi's lush Eden is necessarily short-lived because of the cooling of the sun, the erosion of the land, the extinction of many animals and plants, and the changes in the atmosphere. Without any trace of the Eloi or of the Morlocks (or of humanity in any recognisable form), this nightmarish landscape is occupied by a new species of giant crab, one of whom grasps the Traveller as a potential meal (58).[18] Any familiar elements of civilisation or of 'England' have disappeared, leaving only an unfamiliar landscape and ecology. The Traveller describes a final vista over thirty million years in the future: icy, dark, and barren (59). In the midst of an eclipse by an unfamiliar planet, the sun itself has become bright red, colder, and closer to the earth (59), and life appears to have become extinct except for some green slime and a football-sized shape that flops in the icy waves (60). As Morton claims, the dominant view of evolutionary theory during the nineteenth century includes the concept of continual improvement of species, but Wells undermines this view of evolution by depicting the flopping creature in the waves, who may indeed be the representative of a humanity that has regressed to simple form rather than progressed to greater complexity.[19] Since the time machine is a new sort of transportation technology, Wells (unlike Jefferies, Hudson, and Morris) is able to represent the continual state of flux inherent in evolution through repeated journeys in time. While the romance plot involving the Traveller's rescue of Weena and their subsequent relationship is certainly prominent in the middle section of the text, this relationship does not dominate the text as a whole. The journeys into the far future attach the awe and the wonder of romance to the sublime earth itself and to the power of evolution rather than to an individual traveller or to a particular group of characters, as is the case in earlier texts.

The sublime landscapes of the dying earth are not the only romantic elements in the text: the events of 802,701 include romance as well. As in other texts, the Traveller enters into a ' "miniature flirtation" ' with a denizen of the future, Weena, whom he saves from drowning (31). She affectionately gives him a garland of flowers (31), sleeps by his side (31), kisses him (37), waits for him while he explores the Morlocks' subterranean caves (37), and accompanies him on his journey to the Palace of Green Porcelain (42). When she faints in the Palace, the Traveller carries her to safety in his arms (51). He carries the flowers that she gives him back to the nineteenth century, and these dried petals are the final image of the frame tale. Examining them, the narrator concludes that, even if humanity evolves into unknown forms, 'gratitude and a mutual tenderness still lived on in the heart of man' (64). In this passage, the 'heart of man' seems to resist evolutionary change, and, if so, the entire Weena plot, like the romantic plots in earlier texts, seems to undermine evolutionary principles. If Weena and the Traveller are romantically linked, then humanity has not evolved into a new species but retains a kernel of unchanging compatibility throughout time. Wells, however, hints at a gap between the Traveller's and the narrator's sentimentalism about Weena and her actual nature. Although the Traveller (and perhaps some readers) cast Weena in a conventional damsel-in-distress role because of her repeated need for rescue, the Traveller admits that ' "she always seemed to me, I fancy, more human than she was, perhaps because her affection was so human" ' (45). When confronted by Weena's distress at his sleeping arrangements, he says ' "I was still such a blockhead that I missed the lesson of that fear" ' (31). His admission that he tends to see Weena through his own limited viewpoint serves as a warning to readers. For example, the Traveller speculates that the Eloi do not have different sexes, but he treats Weena as a woman nevertheless, uniformly calling her 'she' and treating her interest in him as romantic in nature (21). In addition, Weena's conversation is never represented directly, although the Traveller claims to speak a few words of her language. Because of this lack, her view of the Traveller is unclear, while his affection for her is very obvious. For example, after her death in a fire, he claims that he ' "was almost moved to begin a massacre of the helpless abominations [Morlocks] about me" ' because of his feelings of ' "intensest wretchedness" ' and loneliness (54). This desire for revenge represents his very human feelings of anger and loss, not hers, yet his strong feelings dwindle to 'mute enquiry' when he sees the dried flowers back at his home in the nineteenth century (62). The Traveller's focus appears to be the machine and time-travel rather than romance, which is far more prominent in other time-travel narratives such as in West's marriage in *Looking Backward* or Bertram Ingledew's love triangle in *The British Barbarians*. Where other time-travel narratives include a romantic relationship in order to settle questions about the future, Wells uses Weena's relationship with the Traveller to generate questions about the nature of humanity, allowing Wells to examine our ability (or inability) to comprehend evolutionary change due to its vast scale, its impersonality, and our own sentimentality.

Unlike earlier time-travel narratives, no ' "convenient cicerone in the pattern of the Utopian books" ' appears to explain the social formations of the future to the Time Traveller (36). Where Bertram Ingledew, West, Smith, and Guest have books and friends to guide them, Wells's unnamed narrator flounders as he tries to understand the future.[20] Just like Smith in *A Crystal Age* and Guest in *News From Nowhere*, the Time Traveller initially believes that he is in an Eden-like paradise created by superior creatures for the Eloi, if not by the Eloi. Like the bee-people and Bertram Ingledew, the Eloi are beautiful, a ' "pretty little people" ' with ' "graceful gentleness" ' and ' "child-like ease" ' (17). Like Smith among the bee-people, the Traveller fears that his voice is too ' "harsh and deep" ' for the ' "frail" ' and ' "consumptive" ' Eloi (17). Despite his disappointment that the Eloi have the intellect of ' "our five-year-old children" ' (17), the Traveller persists in viewing the future as a communist paradise, saying that ' "the whole earth had become a garden" ' (22) and that the Eloi's weakness and stupidity imply ' "a perfect conquest of Nature" ' (23). Yet, from the first the Traveller says that this theory is a ' "half-truth" ' (22) and ' "plausible enough – as most wrong theories are!" ' (24). He initially labels his second theory about the Eloi ' "the truth" ' (33) but later calls this theory ' "all wrong" '(41). According to the Traveller's second theory, humanity has not triumphed but has split into master and slave races based on the widening gap between capitalist and labour where the Eloi are masters and the Morlocks are slaves. After puzzling over the nature of the meat in the Morlocks' cave (41), he rejects his second theory and concludes that the Eloi are ' "fatted cattle" ' for the Morlocks (44). However, this third theory lacks the confidence of the previous two: ' "It may be as wrong an explanation as mortal wit could invent. It is how the thing shaped itself to me, and as that I give it to you" ' (55). Without guidance, Wells's Traveller is forced to theorise and re-theorise as evidence presents itself, mimicking the scientific method rather than a Utopian or romantic journey which offers definite information. As a result, Wells's future remains unclear and mysterious because of the limited power of humanity to comprehend evolutionary change.

As a result of his narrative innovations, including dispensing with a guide figure, undermining the romantic relationship and including a mechanical time travel device, Wells is able to present a more radical view of evolution than previous time-travel narratives. Where other texts employ evolution to argue for a given configuration of society, Wells downplays the power of humanity to comprehend, let alone influence, evolution. When he first discovers the Eloi's stupidity, the Traveller blames the softening influence of technology (48). He later blames technology for the division of society that results in the Morlocks' subterranean life, since he believes they are the descendants of underground workers. The Traveller's theories regarding degeneration and technology seem to assert the power of science to influence the process of evolution, an inference that gives great power to science and to humanity. However, this power is undermined by the journey to the year three million and by the Traveller's final thoughts about the Eloi and Morlocks. By the end of his adventures in 802,701, the Traveller admits that he has no real understanding of the Morlocks and the Eloi. As readers, we also doubt that any invention or human social formation could influence the course of evolution because of the grand scale represented in the text's concluding vision of the cooling sun. Moreover, the wisdom of the ancients reflected in the classical setting and in the Palace of Green Porcelain is utterly lost on the Eloi, proving that any advances in knowledge are time-bound and limited. Far from proving the instrument of evolutionary change, the Morlocks' and Traveller's technology offer only deceptive power, such as when the fire that the Traveller starts with his matches burns Weena instead of the Morlocks.[21] Although inventions such as the Traveller's matches and the time machine itself appear to bestow power and control, this power is ultimately an illusion. In this text, evolution itself dominates as the only inexorable and inescapable power before which knowledge, invention, and all human endeavours are futile.

Late-Victorian time-travel narratives often link romance forms and evolutionary theory in order to critique Victorian culture. Due to the expository nature of many of these texts, Victorian values are often explicitly attacked in long conversations on the evils of Victorian pollution, marriage and capitalism, and the depiction of future Eden-like landscapes, healthy people, and happy social groups attack these same values implicitly. Yet, many of these texts display tension between romance forms and evolutionary theory. While some simply avoid the radical implications of evolution by limiting the timeframe, romantic forms may undermine concepts such as the continual flux of nature and the long timeframe of evolution. Victorian evolutionary theory endorsed teleology; however, placing the end of evolution within only a hundred years or so undermines even this tenet. In *The Time Machine,* Wells uses romantic forms to explore evolutionary theory by introducing narrative tropes that depict the time-travel process itself and repeated journeys in time. His innovations render his text not merely a summary of earlier time-travel narratives but a radical commentary on science itself, which emerges as historically contingent and perhaps futile. The sublime landscapes of the future and the events of 802,701 highlight the vast sweep and power of evolution and the small, time-bound achievements of humanity, a somewhat distressing conclusion because it reverses the popular idea that science can influence evolution and produce a better society, a key concept of Social Darwinism, eugenics, and several earlier time-travel narratives. Despite the bleak outlook of *The Time Machine,* Wells himself indulged in hope that knowledge and science would eventually lead to a better world, if only temporarily. In a letter to James Joyce, H. G. Wells wrote that 'the frame of my mind is a mould wherein a big unifying and concentrating process is possible [...] a *progress* not inevitable but interesting and possible', but he nods to Joyce's pessimism by concluding that 'the world is wide and there is room for both of us to be wrong'.[22]

Notes

[1]   George Levine, *Darwin and the Novelists: Patterns of Science in Victorian Fiction* (Cambridge, MA: Harvard University Press, 1988), p. 11, 22.
[2]   Robert Fraser, *Victorian Quest Romance: Stevenson, Haggard, Kipling, and Conan Doyle* (Plymouth: Northcote, 1998), p. 14. Fraser cites Elaine Showalter's argument that romance developed in part due to male reaction against 'female' forms of writing, notably the novel, and also cites Edward Said's argument, which claims that romantic quests celebrated imperialism (p. 3). Fraser claims that both of these arguments contain 'the barely concealed note of postcolonial hubris' (p. 3).
[3]   H. G. Wells, 'The Lost Stevenson', *Saturday Review*, 81 (13 June 1896), 603-4, in *H. G. Wells's Literary Criticism*, ed. by Patrick Parrinder and Robert M. Philmus (Brighton: Harvester, 1980), pp. 99-103 (p. 102). Wells criticises Robert Louis Stevenson for wasting his talents on repetitious and conventional romances such as *The Weir of Hermiston* and praises authors as diverse as Jonathan Swift, Lawrence Sterne, and Charles Dickens.
[4]   H. G. Wells, 'The Contemporary Novel' (1911), in *H. G. Wells's Literary Criticism*, pp. 192-205 (p. 193; 199). This piece was also reprinted in *An Englishman Looks at the World* (London: Cassell, 1914), pp. 148-69 and appeared in various forms in periodical publication.
[5]   Wells, 'The Contemporary Novel', p. 192.
[6]   Peter Morton, *The Vital Science: Biology and the Literary Imagination, 1860-1900* (London: Allen, 1984).

---

[7] William Morris, *News From Nowhere* (1890), *News From Nowhere and Other Writings* (Harmondsworth: Penguin Classics, 1993), pp. 43-228 (p. 47). All subsequent references are from this edition and are cited in parenthesis in the text.

[8] Morton, *The Vital Science*, p. 98.

[9] Edward Bellamy, *Looking Backward* (1888) (New York: Dover, 1996), p. 19. All subsequent references are from this edition and are cited in parenthesis in the text.

[10] W. H. Hudson, *A Crystal Age* (1887), in *The Collected Works of W. H. Hudson* (London: J.M. Dent, 1922), p. 40. All subsequent references are from this edition and are cited in parenthesis in the text.

[11] Richard Jefferies, *After London; or, Wild England* (London: Cassell, 1885), p. 9. All subsequent references are from this edition and are cited in parenthesis in the text.

[12] Critics have claimed that Wells's *The Wonderful Visit* is plagiarised from Allen's *The British Barbarians*; however, David Hughes contends that this is incorrect because of the conventional nature of the 'plagiarized' plot elements and because of the relationship between the two authors during the summer of 1895 when both novels were composed. See David Y. Hughes, 'H.G. Wells and the Charge of Plagiarism', *Nineteenth-Century Fiction*, 21 (1966), 85-90; David Y. Hughes, 'A Queer Notion of Grant Allen's', *Science-Fiction Studies*, 25 (1998), 271-284.

[13] H. G. Wells, *The Time Machine* (1895) (New York: Barnes and Noble, 2006), p. 32. All references are from this edition and are cited in parenthesis in the text.

[14] Nick Freeman, 'British Barbarians at the Gates: Grant Allen, Michael Moorcock and Decadence', *Foundation*, 83 (2001), 35-47 (p. 36).

[15] Grant Allen, *The British Barbarians* (London: John Lane, 1895), p. 21. All subsequent references are from this edition and are cited in parenthesis in the text.

[16] Other critics examine the context of *The Time Machine*. J. R. Hammond argues that Wells draws upon 'an immense range of literature' in his novels and, because of this, acts as a transitional figure between Victorian realism and modernism. Stephen Derry claims that Wells parodies earlier time-travel romances in *The Time Machine,* and he calls this text Wells's 'summative fin-de-siècle statement'. Roslynn Haynes defends Wells's scientific credibility. J. R. Hammond, *H.G. Wells and the Modern Novel* (New York: St. Martin's, 1988), p. 18. Stephen Derry, 'The Time Traveller's Utopian Books and his Reading of the Future', *Foundation*, 65 (1995), 16-24 (p. 23). Roslynn D. Haynes, *H.G. Wells: Discoverer of the Future, The Influence of Science on his Thought* (London: Macmillan, 1980).

[17] See also Wells's *The Wheels of Chance* (1896) about a bicycling adventurer. *The Wheels of Chance* is the subject of Simon James's discussion in Chapter 3 of this collection.

[18] Wells's essay, 'A Vision of the Past' (1887) describes an encounter between a time-traveller and primitive lizards, which threaten to eat him.

[19] Wells himself examined the degenerative potential of evolution in his early article, 'Zoological Retrogression', *Gentleman's Magazine*, 271 (1891), 246-53.

[20] Where Bertram, West, Smith, and Guest are extraordinary, Wells's Time Traveller is, as Roslynn Haynes claims in her *H.G. Wells: Discoverer of the Future*, 'the epitome of ordinariness' (p. 198).

[21] In an essay entitled 'The Rediscovery of the Unique' (1891) originally published in the *Fortnightly Review*, Wells compares science to a lit match that illuminates only a very small patch, leaving the surroundings in darkness.

[22] H. G. Wells, letter to James Joyce, 23 November 1928, *The Correspondence of H. G. Wells*, ed. by David C. Smith, 4 vols (London: Pickering and Chatto, 1998), III, pp. 276-7 (p. 276; 277).

ANIMALS, LANGUAGE AND DEGENERATION IN *THE ISLAND OF DOCTOR MOREAU*

STEVEN MCLEAN

Published in April 1896, *The Island of Doctor Moreau* has often been explored in the context of scientific debates, which inform its historical moment. Specifically, the novel has been examined as an engagement with discourses concerning degeneration, and the presence of a notorious vivisectionist at its centre recalls heated contemporary debates surrounding the practice of vivisection and the treatment of animals. However, the critical privileging of discourses of degeneration has obscured a crucial context for extending our understanding of the novel. *The Island of Doctor Moreau* is responding to new theories of the relation between humans, animals and language which were threatening to overturn the existing dominant idea, popularised by Max Müller and C. Lloyd Morgan, that animals could not possess language. The American naturalist Richard Garner provided one of the most serious challenges to this view, and his initial experiments with monkeys appeared to reveal a simian language much like a simplified version of our own speech.[1]

Garner accepted the inextricability of language and reason: what he did not accept was that language belonged to humans only. With the aid of a modified phonograph, Garner conducted experiments with monkeys in his native America in 1884 and concluded he had found a number of Capuchin monkey words including those for food and drink.[2] For Garner, the importance of studying simian language was that it provided clues to the origins of speech. In 'The simian tongue [I]', the first of a series of three articles first published in the *New Review* between June 1891 and February 1892, Garner wrote that he was 'willing to incur the ridicule of the wise' and 'assert that "articulate speech" prevails among the lower primates'.[3] Furthermore, Garner thought his research significant because it revealed a close correlation between the uniformly progressive nature of evolution and the level of reason attained through language: 'To reason, they [simians] *must think*, and if it be true that *man cannot think without words,* it must be true of monkeys'.[4]   In order to validate his theories,

Garner next announced his plans 'to arrange for a trip to interior Africa to study the troglodytes in their native wilds'.[5] This, he hoped, would enable him to confirm his theories concerning the progressive scale of language and reason, allowing him to examine at close quarters what he considered to constitute the intermediate region of this scale. British readers first learned from a report in *Harper's Weekly* in December 1891 of Garner's plan to use a seven-foot square cage as the basis from which to conduct his research.[6]

Wells's awareness of the debates concerning animals and language is revealed in his 'The Mind In Animals', a review of Lloyd Morgan's *An Introduction to Comparative Psychology*, which appeared in the *Saturday Review* in December 1894.[7] In this review, Wells is critical of Morgan's 'perceptions of relations' which 'does not seem to give proper weight to the difference in mental operations that must exist' between, to use the example cited by Wells, the olfactory functions of man and dog. This may seem to imply that Wells makes a greater distinction between the human and animal mind than Morgan does. However, Wells makes such a distinction only in order to explore the possibility that the dog's enhanced powers of olfactory discrimination could provide the basis for something akin to rationality: '[the dog] may have on that basis a something not strictly "rational" perhaps, but higher than mere association and analogous to and parallel with the rational'.[8] Emphasising this point in a passage that does much to prepare us for the anthropomorphism of animals in *The Island of Doctor Moreau*, Wells intimates that his opinion of animal intelligence is higher than Morgan's. 'It may even be that Professor Lloyd Morgan's dog, experimenting on Professor Lloyd Morgan with a dead rat or a bone to develop some point bearing upon olfactory relationships, would arrive at a very low estimate indeed of the powers of the human mind', he writes.[9] I can find no evidence that Wells encountered the work of Garner. It is, however, a distinct possibility that, in the period of his apprenticeship as a journalist, the young Wells read 'The simian tongue' in the pages of the *New Review*, the same periodical that would later serialise his first novel, *The Time Machine*.

The narrator of *The Island of Doctor Moreau* appears to follow Morgan in identifying language as the distinguishing feature of humanity. In his early encounter with the Ape Man, Prendick identifies his interlocutor as 'a man [...] for he could talk'.[10] Yet, Moreau's imposition of a 'humanising process' on the Beastfolk seems to confirm Garner's conception of an unbroken chain of expression. Gradually, Prendick comes to accept that animals might reason: 'never before did I see an animal trying to think' (69). Rather like Garner in his African experiments,

Prendick is forced into an anthropological relationship with the Beastfolk following his initial inability to understand them from an observational distance: 'The speaker's words came thick and sloppy, and though I could hear them distinctly I could not distinguish what he said' (42).

Once among them, Prendick gains an understanding of the abilities and limitations of the Beastfolk in relation to their capacity to reason. Thus although the Ape Man had seemed perfectly human due to his use of speech, there remains a gulf between his speech and the higher levels of reasoning associated with humanity. His responses to questions are for Prendick highly unsatisfactory, being but 'chattering prompt responses [which] were, as often as not, at cross purposes with my question' (56). Later in the novel, the Ape Man himself creates a distinction which summarises much of the limitations of the Beastfolk's capacity for reasoning: 'He had an idea, I believe, that to gabble about names that meant nothing was the proper use of speech. He called it "big thinks", to distinguish it from "little thinks" – the sane everyday interests of life' (122). The Ape man's 'Big Thinks' are nothing but signifiers that have become dislodged from their referents or that have been conjured up from nothing. It would seem, then, that the Beastfolk conform to Garner's notion of an evolutionary chain – their communication only of relatively simple ideas reflects their comparatively lowly placing in a great chain of articulation.

Despite endowing the Beast People with the linguistic faculty that allows them to transcend what Morgan had considered to constitute an immutable barrier, *The Island of Doctor Moreau* is distinctly cautious concerning the possibility of these hybrid animals further developing that faculty to attain truly abstract reasoning. This cautiousness is foregrounded in the chapter 'The Sayers Of The Law' in which a somewhat perplexed Prendick is forced to participate in the recital of Moreau's Law:

'Not to go on all-Fours; *that* is the Law. Are we not Men?'
'Not to suck up Drink; *that* is the Law. Are we not Men?'
'Not to eat Flesh or Fish; *that* is the Law. Are we not Men?'
'Not to claw Bark of Trees; *that* is the Law. Are we not Men?'
'Not to chase other Men; *that* is the Law. Are we not Men?' (59)

The prohibitory nature of Moreau's law effectively binds his creations' imaginations, limiting them to little more than idiocy. This cruelly eliminates the potential for abstract reasoning that is created in the increased scope of the Beastfolk's intelligence. In their recital of the Law the Beastfolk do not employ anything which resembles abstract reasoning. Rather, they are subject to a 'kind of rhythmic fervour [which] fell on all of us; [as] we gabbled and swayed faster and faster' (59). Rather than substantiate Garner's theory that simian language 'contains rudiments from which the tongues of mankind could easily develop', the heavily ritualised nature of the Beastfolk's 'rhythmic fervour' tends to support Morgan's view that, although animals often display intelligent behaviour, abstract reasoning remains the sole property of the human species.[11] However, we should not overlook the parallels of the Beast People's recital of the Law with human religious practices.

The Island of Doctor Moreau's engagement with the debates concerning animals and language concurs with its overall suppression of the biological limen between man and beast. In this hybrid world of 'humanised animals' and 'animalised humans', the Beastfolk's recital of the Law functions as a comment on the status of those philosophical and religious activities considered to constitute the most advanced forms of human reasoning. To the anonymous author of an unsigned review in *The Guardian*, there is a definite hint of blasphemy in the novel: 'his [Wells's] object seems to be to parody the work of the creator of the human race, and cast contempt upon the dealings of God with His creatures'.[12] Moreau's Law is undoubtedly the most blasphemous element of the novel. Its recital by the Beastfolk recalls the prayers of a Christian Church: ' "*His* is the House of Pain. *His* is the hand that makes. *His* is the hand that wounds. *His* is the hand that heals" ' (59). The droning insistence that accompanies the Beast People's fearful worship of a mock deity reduces the metaphysical system of belief that is the Christian religion to a series of monotonous 'gabbles', which is entirely bereft of any conceptual dimension. The Ape Man's 'Big Thinks' similarly parodies what Frank McConnell has identified as 'the self-serving, metaphysical pretensions of the philosophical community'.[13]

The Ape Man is undoubtedly the most deliberately allegorical figure to appear in the text, and as such, his presence does much to emphasise the continuity between humanity and the animal species. At the time of his first encounter with this creature, the narrator is still, significantly, subject to the mistaken assumption that his interlocutor is another man, thus stressing a common heritage shared by all members of the species *homo sapiens*. Yet the Ape Man's use of speech is nothing like the 'true articulate speech' which Wells elsewhere identifies as the foundation of human society.[14] The 'artificial' education of the Ape Man falls distinctly short of the process of 'artificial' evolution or education which Wells would later advocate in 'Human Evolution, An Artifical Process', published six months after *The Island of Doctor Moreau* in the *Fortnightly Review*. In that article, Wells stresses the importance of the 'artificial' evolution of humanity as a method of escaping the biological pessimism of Natural Selection. For him, this artificial evolution constitutes the steady accumulation of what he terms 'the acquired factor', which consists of the morals, culture and traditions of human society. Rather than providing the basis of 'true articulate speech', the Ape Man's 'parrot-like' answers to questions function only for Prendick to identify him as a 'creature [who] was little better than an idiot' (56).

The one factor that does separate humanity from these hybrid animals is the capacity for untruths. In order to contain the Beastfolk following Moreau's demise, Prendick insists that Moreau has simply changed his state of being, and that the Law still applies. In Prendick's statement that 'An animal may be ferocious and cunning enough, but it takes a real man to tell a lie' (120), Wells offers a sardonic commentary on those powers of abstract reasoning that Morgan and others considered the exclusive property of the human species. As John R. Reed points out in his article, 'The Vanity of Law in *The Island of Doctor Moreau*', Wells seems to use the protagonist of his 1932 novel *The Bulpington of Blup* to identify lies as a universal fact of humanity's status as a 'the culminating ape'.[15] He states that the one gift that man, 'the poor ape' had as an aid to his development was that he could lie: ' "Man is the one animal that can make a fire and keep the beasts of the night. He is the one animal that can make a falsehood and keep off the beasts of despair" '.[16] Prendick's status as the sole remaining representative of humanity on the island therefore highlights the double function of mankind's ability to imagine what does not exist. Falsehood is construed as a negative aspect of humanity's supposedly enhanced evolutionary status but it is precisely the same capacity for mental inventiveness which enables the further development of the species as a whole.

It is in the 'Reversion of the Beastfolk' that *The Island of Doctor Moreau* makes its most explicit contribution to discourses of degeneration, thus marking a strong challenge to what Wells termed the 'excelsior' biology of the time. (In 'Zoological Retrogression' (1891), Wells used this term to describe the optimistic contemporary interpretations of evolutionary theory, which ignore the potential for degeneration contained in the process of natural selection). The lone human survivor on the island following the deaths of Moreau and Montgomery, Prendick witnesses the final degradation of the Beastfolk:

Of course these creatures did not decline into such beasts as the reader has seen in zoological gardens – into ordinary bears, wolves, tigers, oxen, swine and apes. There was still something strange about each; in each Moreau had blended this animal with that; one perhaps was ursine chiefly,

another feline chiefly, another bovine chiefly, but each was tainted with
other creatures – a kind of generalized animalism appeared through the
specific dispositions. (124)

To an anonymous writer in the *Review of Reviews*, the 'hybrid monsters'
of the story are 'loathsome' on the grounds that: 'the result in the picture is
exactly that which would follow as the result of the engendering of human
and animal'.[17]

With no means of escape from the island, Prendick is forced to lower
his anthropocentric conceptions and adapt, sharing both the Beastfolk's
food and living space. Prendick's comments on the initial suitability of
this arrangement read like an absurd parody of Garner's use of a cage in
Africa. 'We were in just the state of equilibrium that would remain in one
of those "Happy Family" cages that animal-tamers exhibit, if the tamer
were to leave it for ever' (124), he says. However, as the reversion of the
Beastfolk accelerates and his own increasingly fear-driven and violent
behaviour comes to mimic that of Moreau's creations, the 'cage' which
encloses Prendick actively renders him distinctly animalistic.

Revealingly, the acceleration of this reversion is accompanied by a
chronic degradation of the Beastfolk's use of language. 'My Monkey
Man's jabber', reports Prendick, 'multiplied in volume, but grew less and
less comprehensible, [and] more and more simian' (122). Others of the
Beast People seem to be 'slipping their hold upon speech', so that
language that was 'once clear-cut and exact' becomes 'mere lumps of
sound again' (122).

The Beast People's final reversion to a distinctly meaningless simian
tongue reveals that the status of their linguistic faculty is contingent upon
Moreau's Law and the perpetual engineering that occurs in the 'House of
Pain'. To this end, we should recall the Ape Man's comments regarding
the punishment he had received as the consequence of a lapse in his
linguistic capabilities: 'I did a little thing, a wrong thing, once. I jabbered,
jabbered, stopped talking. None could understand. I am burned, branded in
the hand' (60). The Ape Man's 'humanisation' was always bound to fail,
since Moreau can never entirely 'burn out' the Ape within him, and this
creature's mock human status was only ever achieved by the continual
application of violent means. The 'artificial' education of the Ape Man
could never be met with success, since there is no 'man' present in him for
Moreau to teach the power of *logos* to.

The ultimate collapse of the Beast People's use of language tends to
suggest that Moreau's distorted attempt to circumvent what T. H. Huxley
had called 'the cosmic process' of evolution is an act of coercion. (Briefly
defined, 'the cosmic process' refers to the uninterrupted way in which

Natural Selection has functioned in the animal and plant kingdoms. Huxley is at pains to emphasise that we should not advocate its imitation in constructing ethical frameworks for social interaction). Thus it would seem that, despite exploring the possibility that animals might be *temporarily* endowed with linguistic abilities, *The Island of Doctor Moreau* does not, in the final analysis, support the view that animals can reason through the use of language.

However, this would be to discount the impression on the reader of the excessively pessimistic ending of the novel. Fearing 'that presently the degradation of the Islanders will be played over again on a larger scale' (130), a deeply traumatised Prendick now observes that the whole of England is ripe for degeneration:

> I would go out into the streets to fight with my delusion, and prowling women would mew after me, furtive craving men glanced jealously at me, weary pale workers go coughing by me with tired eyes and eager paces like wounded deer dripping blood, old people, bent and dull, pass murmuring to themselves, and all unheeding a ragged tail of gibing children. Then I would turn aside into some chapel, and even there, such was my disturbance, it seemed that the preacher gibbered Big Thinks even as the Ape Man had done; or into some library, and there the intent faces over the books seemed but patient creatures waiting for prey. (131)

It is precisely those elements he had first encountered on Moreau's island space which an overwhelmingly fearful Prendick now identifies in his fellow human beings. Significantly, it is those who share the degenerate traits of those 'others' of Moreau's island – the prostitute, the proletarian –, who constitute central points of reference upon Prendick's return to contemporary England. Most poignantly, the entire species *homo sapiens* is subjected to the same retrogressive use of language as the Beast People, with even those of the religious order – 'the preacher gibbered Big Thinks even as the Ape Man had done' – unable to escape this form of linguistic damnation. The final juxtaposition of the bestial traits of *homo sapiens* – 'like wounded deer dripping blood' – with the reduction of its highest conceptual activities into a distinctly animalistic trait – 'there the intent faces over the books seemed but patient creatures waiting for prey' – not only underlines the allegorical intentions of the novel as a whole but also reinstates its overall suppression of any enduring distinction between man and beast.

We might conclude by stating that Wells creates a distinction between human and animal language, but then undercuts it by showing human language to be subject to reversion, or even more radically, its higher reaches turn into the same forms of gabble as that of the Beastfolk. Thus, the extreme pessimism of its ending can be attributed to the fact that *The Island of Doctor Moreau* represents the superiority of human evolution as a futile achievement. The final effect of the novel clearly reinstates Prendick's observation that the island of Doctor Moreau is a microcosm which implicates the entire human cosmos: 'I had here before me the whole balance of human life in miniature, the whole interplay of instinct, reason, and fate in its simplest form' (95).

Notes

[1]   See Gregory Radick's 'Morgan's canon, Garner's phonograph, and the evolutionary origins of language and reason', *British Journal for the History of Science*, 33 (2000), 3-23.

[2]   Radick, 'Morgan's Canon', p. 12.

[3]   R. L. Garner, 'The simian tongue [I]', *New Review*, 4 (1891), 555-62, collected in *The Origin of Language*, ed. by Roy Harris (Bristol: Thoemmes Press, 1996), pp. 314-21 (p. 314).

[4]   Garner, 'The simian tongue [I]', p. 320.

[5]   R. L. Garner, 'The simian tongue [II]' *New Review*, 5 (1891), 424-30, collected in *The Origin of Language*, pp. 321-27 (p. 325).

[6]   Radick, 'Morgan's Canon', p. 14.

[7]   H. G. Wells, 'The Mind In Animals', *Saturday Review*, 78 (1894), 683-4. This review appeared in the same edition (22 December) as one of Wells's articles, 'Another Basis For Life'.

[8]   Wells, 'The Mind In Animals', p. 683.

[9]   Wells, 'The Mind In Animals', p. 683.

[10]   H. G. Wells, *The Island of Doctor Moreau* (1896) (London: Penguin, 2005), p. 55. Subsequent references are to this edition and will be cited in the text.

[11]   Morgan's distinction between intelligence and reasoned action comes in his 'The limits of animal intelligence', *Fortnightly Review*, 54 (1893), 223-39. Due to the faculty of intelligence, which 'is ever on the watch for fortunate variations of activity and happy hits of motor response' an animal may appear to be reasoning abstractly, but truly reasoned action is always accompanied by powers of introspection concerning a particular action, with is not displayed by animals (p. 239).

[12]   Unsigned Review, *The Guardian*, 3 June 1896, collected in *H. G. Wells: The Critical Heritage*, ed. by Patrick Parrinder (London: Routledge and Kegan Paul, 1972), p. 53.

[13]   Frank McConnell, *The Science Fiction of H. G. Wells* (New York: Oxford University Press, 1981), p. 105.

[14]   H. G. Wells, 'Human Evolution, An Artificial Process', *Fortnightly Review*, 60 (1896), 590-5 (p. 593).

[15] John R. Reed, 'The Vanity of Law in *The Island of Doctor Moreau*', in *H. G. Wells Under Revision*, ed. by Patrick Parrinder and Robert M. Philmus (London and Toronto: Associated University Presses, 1986), pp. 134-43 (p. 142).

[16] H. G. Wells, *The Bulpington of Blup* cited in Reed, p. 142.

[17] Unsigned Review, *Review of Reviews*, 13 (1896), 374.

FIN-DE-CYCLE: ROMANCE AND THE REAL IN *THE WHEELS OF CHANCE*

SIMON J. JAMES

Even given the bewildering generic variety of H. G. Wells's output, *The Wheels of Chance* (1896) seems a peculiarity. At first glance a work of picaresque lower middle-class *fin-de-siècle* comic writing like Jerome K. Jerome's *Three Men in a Boat* (1889) or George and Weedon Grossmith's *The Diary of a Nobody* (1892), this comedy of manners rests slightly uneasily among Wells's other works of the 1890s and 1900s. In his Preface to the 1925 Atlantic Edition, Wells describes the book as one of a 'series of close studies in personality', adding Lewisham, Kipps, Mr Polly and Ann Veronica as further examples of 'personalities thwarted by the defects of our contemporary civilisation. [...] It is a very "young" book; indeed, in some respects it is puerile, but the character of Hoopdriver saves it from being altogether insignificant'.[1]

Like many of Wells's earlier romances, even *The Wonderful Visit* (1895), *The Wheels of Chance* consciously participates in the aesthetic and political debates that would come to shape, then dominate, Wells's career. Even this relatively slight work prefigures Wells's assault upon the canons of Victorian culture that is characteristic to his later representations of the artistic and imaginative. Wells revolted, most conspicuously in his debate with Henry James, against the valuing of art for its autonomy from society, increasingly emphasising the necessity for art to engage directly in creating the utopia that he saw as the only alternative to mankind's self-destruction.[2]

Often in Wells's writing, this antagonism towards a notion of a disinterested high culture that he sees as backward-looking and harmful is expressed in a satire of the practice of reading, in particular the reading of fiction (1914's *Boon* is perhaps the most striking example). Both hero and heroine in *The Wheels of Chance* are afflicted by false expectations generated from reading stories, a fault from which Adeline Glendower in *The Sea Lady* (1902) and Muriel in *The Wealth of Mr. Waddy* (an early version of *Kipps*, first published 1969) will also suffer. Jessie Milton's misguided plan for imaginative self-determination is inspired by a naïve reading of novels by George Egerton, Eliza Lynn Linton, Olive Schreiner and her own stepmother. Her 'motives are bookish, written by a haphazard syndicate of authors, novelists, biographers, on her white inexperience' (XVI); the narrator's ironic orthography mocks her desire ' "to write Books and alter things [...] to lead a Free Life and Own myself" ' (XXVIII).[3] In the world of *The Wheels of Chance*, such fictions are not to be confused with 'real life'. Hoopdriver's rescue of her takes place in an imaginary pastiche of 'world of Romance and Knight-errantry' (XXII), derived from 'Doctor Conan Doyle, Victor Hugo, and Alexander Dumas' (XVII), Walter Besant, Mrs Braddon, Rider Haggard, Marie Corelli and Ouida. Even the rascally seducer Bechamel attempts, like Manning in *Ann Veronica* (1909), to seduce with talk of ' "art and literature" ' (XXIV).

Although even books by high-cultural authors such as Emerson and the historian Motley also provide too limited a means of making experience intelligible, Wells's main target is the stereotyping and cheap appeal of popular fiction, for which his work as a critic for the *Saturday Review* shows a consistent dislike.[4] His own scientific and early romances aside of course, romance is for Wells an innately conservative genre. Hall Caine had claimed in 1890 that romance is the true genre of idealism, that the literary artist should depict the world as it should be, rather than as he sees it: 'Not the bare actualities of life "as it is", but the glories of life as it might be; not the domination of fact, but of feeling'.[5] In an early article protesting against the unreality of Victorian heroines, Wells parodies Caine as claiming that, 'If life is ugly [...] it is our duty to make it pleasant in fiction'.[6] For Wells, the reader's imagination only turns to romance out of dissatisfaction with the real world; romance cheaply amuses, and saps the desire to make the real world better instead:[7]

> The apprentice is nearer the long, long thoughts of boyhood, and his imagination rides *cap-à-pie* through the chambers of his brain, seeking some knightly quest in honour of that Fair Lady, the last but one of the girl apprentices to the dress-making upstairs. He inclines rather to street fighting against revolutionaries – because then she could see him from the window. (II)

Wells would later champion the kind of art that would fight alongside revolutionaries, by revealing possible alternatives to the existing order.

Wells's writing is very fond of the metaphor of knowledge as light: *The Time Machine*, for instance, regularly relies on this trope.[8] It is given literal substance in *The Wheels of Chance* in the opposition between deceptive, romantic moonlight and the revealing light of day.

There is a magic quality in moonshine; it touches all that is sweet and beautiful, and the rest of the night is hidden. [...] By the moonlight every man, dull clod though he be by day, tastes something of Endymion, takes something of the youth and strength of Endymion, and sees the dear white goddess shining at him from his Lady's eyes.   The firm substantial daylight things become ghostly and elusive, the hills beyond are a sea of unsubstantial texture, the world a visible spirit, the spiritual within us rises out of its darkness, loses something of its weight and body, and swims up towards heaven. This road that was a mere rutted white dust, hot underfoot, blinding to the eye, is now a soft grey silence, with the glitter of a crystal grain set starlike in its silver here and there.   Overhead, riding serenely through the spacious blue, is the mother of the silence, she who has spiritualised the world, alone save for two attendant steady shining stars.   And in silence under her benign influence, under the benediction of her light, rode our two wanderers side by side through the transfigured and transfiguring night.

Nowhere was the moon shining quite so brightly as in Mr. Hoopdriver's skull. (XXIV)

In the light of subsequently more accurate self-knowledge, such pseudo-lyrical delusions are revealed for what they really are. 'Beastly cheap, after all, this suit does look, in the sunshine' (XXVII), muses Hoopdriver after the romantic fantasy of his new suit making him look like an aristocrat is eventually deflated.

Hoopdriver's guidebook informs him that Guildford is the setting for Martin Tupper's historical romance *Stephan Langton* (1858), in which the low-born hero saves a maiden from villainous noblemen.   Tupper's narrator claims the authority of fact for showing even familiar and unexciting Surrey as home to stirring historical incidents, even 'romantic biography':

I will concentrate my pictured fancies in a framework of real scenery round characters of strict historic fame. [...] I will set before your patience rather reality than romance, drawing both landscapes and persons from the truth. [...] It may be possible [...] to make classic ground of certain sweet retired spots set among the fairest hill and vale county in South England [...] to invest familiar Surrey scenes [...] with their due historic interest; [...] to connect for your better entertainment our evident modern scenes (changed belike in such accidental features as culture brings about, yet substantially the same as to geography) with antique but actual incidents.[9]

In *The Wheels of Chance*, on the other hand, the mapping of romance onto the landscape, such as Hoopdriver's fantasy of 'pedalling Ezekiel's Wheels across the Weald of Surrey, jolting over the hills and smashing villages in his course' (XII) (prefiguring the destruction of Surrey in

Wells's later scientific romance *The War of the Worlds)* is made ironic by the humdrum nature of his environment in reality. In contrast to Tupper's assertion that romance might have occurred in the same place as contemporary real life, fantasy is undercut by present reality.

The Wheels of Chance's generic dissonance is sustained throughout by the device of a archly self-conscious narrator who deflates the central characters' romantically phrased aspirations to be a chivalric hero and the independent heroine of a New Woman novel. The narrator is alternately outside and inside the action of the plot and is not omniscient; he appears to be occasionally present as a character, like a Thackeray narrator. He is overt that he is relating a story – 'these things take so long in the telling' (IV), he pleads at one point, and repeatedly calls attention to Hoopdriver's misreading of his own story.

> You must not think that there was any telling of these stories of this life-long series by Mr. Hoopdriver. He never dreamt that they were known to a soul. If it were not for the trouble, I would, I think, go back and rewrite this section from the beginning, expunging the statements that Hoopdriver was a poet and a romancer, and saying instead that he was a playwright and acted his own plays. He was not only the sole performer, but the entire audience, and the entertainment kept him almost continuously happy. Yet even that playwright comparison scarcely expresses all the facts of the case. After all, very many of his dreams never got acted at all, possibly indeed, most of them, the dreams of a solitary walk for instance, or of a tramcar ride, the dreams dreamt behind the counter while trade was slack and mechanical foldings and rollings occupied his muscles. (X)

Like Mr Polly, Hoopdriver has juvenile taste in reading matter and fantasises about the 'gallant rescue of generalised beauty in distress from truculent insult or ravening dog' (X); as in the later novel, Wells's narrator mocks such conceit, but the fantasy is partly fulfilled, or rather temporarily indulged.

Romance traditionally privileges the singularity of its protagonist: this narrator repeatedly calls ironic attention both to the distinctiveness and ordinariness of his hero.

> Mr. Hoopdriver was (in the days of this story) a poet, though he had never written a line of verse. Or perhaps romancer will describe him better. Like I know not how many of those who do the fetching and carrying of life, – a great number of them certainly, – his real life was absolutely uninteresting, and if he had faced it as realistically as such people do in Mr. Gissing's novels, he would probably have come by way of drink to suicide in the course of a year. But that was just what he had the natural wisdom not to do.   On the contrary, he was always decorating his existence with

imaginative tags, hopes, and poses, deliberate and yet quite effectual self-deceptions; his experiences were mere material for a romantic superstructure. If some power had given Hoopdriver the 'giftie' Burns invoked, 'to see oursels as ithers see us,' he would probably have given it away to some one else at the very earliest opportunity. His entire life, you must understand, was not a continuous romance, but a series of short stories linked only by the general resemblance of their hero, a brown-haired young fellow commonly, with blue eyes and a fair moustache, graceful rather than strong, sharp and resolute rather than clever (Cp., as the scientific books say, p. 4). Invariably this person possessed an iron will. The stories fluctuated indefinitely. The smoking of a cigarette converted Hoopdriver's hero into something entirely worldly, subtly rakish, with a humorous twinkle in the eye and some gallant sinning in the background. [...] This day there had predominated a fine leisurely person immaculately clothed, and riding on an unexceptional machine, a mysterious person – quite unostentatious, but with accidental self-revelation of something over the common, even a 'bloomin' Dook,' it might be incognito, on the tour of the South Coast. (X)

If Hoopdriver were the hero of a naturalist novel (a school of which, rather unfairly, Gissing is the representative), determined entirely and predictably by his circumstances, he would be entirely predictable and thus fail to surprise the reader. Although Wells disapproves of late-Victorian romance in its most formulaic expressions, Hoopdriver's playful mental exploration of romance freedoms might allow the limitations of realism to be overcome. However his imaginative liberty may be curtailed in reality by economics and his poor education, the fact of Hoopdriver's possessing an imagination at all demonstrates his individuality.

The text's opening both employs and mocks the certainties of the late nineteenth-century literary naturalist, certainties that claim their epistemological certainty from the method of scientific enquiry.[10] The opening apes realism's presentation of outward surfaces ('nothing can be further from the author's ambition than a wanton realism,' the narrator later avers in Chapter VII) and the codes that may be read from them:

If you (presuming you are of the sex that does such things)—if you had gone into the Drapery Emporium — [...] you might have been served by the central figure of this story that is now beginning. [...] Under which happier circumstances you might – if of an observing turn of mind and not too much of a housewife to be inhuman – have given the central figure of this story less cursory attention.

Now if you had noticed anything about him, it would have been chiefly to notice how little he was noticeable. He wore the black morning coat, the black tie, and the speckled grey nether parts (descending into shadow and mystery below the counter) of his craft. He was of a pallid complexion, hair of a kind of dirty fairness, greyish eyes, and a skimpy, immature moustache under his peaked indeterminate nose. His features were all small, but none ill-shaped. A rosette of pins decorated the lapel of his coat. His remarks, you would observe, were entirely what people used to call *cliché*, formulae not organic to the occasion, but stereotyped ages ago and learnt years since by heart. [...] Such were the simple counters of his intercourse. So, I say, he would have presented himself to your superficial observation. [...]

But real literature, as distinguished from anecdote, does not concern itself with superficial appearances alone. Literature is revelation. Modern literature is indecorous revelation. It is the duty of the earnest author to tell you what you would not have seen – even at the cost of some blushes. [...] Let us approach the business with dispassionate explicitness. Let us assume something of the scientific spirit, the hard, almost professorial tone of the conscientious realist. (I)

The opening pretends to dramatise a process of scientific induction: because Hoopdriver is perceived as a shop assistant, he is expected to behave in a certain way. Such inductive certainty relies on observation and experience, however, and Wells's implied reader, here assumed to be female and of the leisure and shopping class, has paid insufficient attention beyond the limits of the counter for any such inductive judgement to be reliable. Karl Popper demonstrated in 1934 the weakness of the inductive method: 'no matter how many instances of white swans we have observed, this does not justify the conclusion that *all* swans are white'.[11] While Hoopdriver may be perceived as unremarkable, this does not preclude him from doing, or at least dreaming of doing, remarkable things.

The opening chapter alludes to late-Victorian realism's outstanding exponent of this technique of inductive observation, Sherlock Holmes. Holmes's 'method' depends on all individual members of a certain category behaving in an identical way.[12] Recent critical tradition has tended to read Holmes as a force for social order and thus, like romance as Wells views it, ultimately a maintainer of the status quo.[13] Hoopdriver's presentation as an identifiable 'type' is thus ironic. In 'The Novel of Types' (1896), Wells argues that typology in fiction should still accommodate individuality:

The peculiar characteristic of Turgenev's genius is the extraordinary way in which he can make his characters typical, while at the same time retaining their individuality. [...] Turgenev people are not avatars of theories nor tendencies. They are living, breathing individuals living under the full stress of this social force or that.[14]

Mrs Milton's aestheticist suitors are mocked for their reversal of this dictum:

> 'A novel deals with typical cases'.
> 'And life is not typical'. (XXI)

' "If I were a Sherlock Holmes," ' says Jessie later, ' "I suppose I could have told you were a Colonial from little things like that" ' (XXXIV): Hoopdriver, of course, is nothing of the kind. The rascally seducer Bechamel suggests to Jessie that 'men are really more alike than you think' (XXI), but the text encourages resistance to the notion that Hoopdriver's romantic aspirations are essentially the same as Bechamel's more 'Palaeolithic' ones. Wells's early journalism lays an obsessive emphasis on individuality, even down to, in the title of one essay, 'The Possible Individuality of Atoms'.[15] The status quo can be resisted by showing that the codes by which inductive judgements are made are arbitrary and unfair: indeed the plot depends on Jessie's misreading of Hoopdriver's clothing, language, culture and class:

> His English was uncertain, but not such as books informed her distinguished the lower classes. His manners seemed to her good on the whole, but a trifle over-respectful and out of fashion. He called her 'Madam' once. He seemed a person of means and leisure, but he knew nothing of recent concerts, theatres, or books. How did he spend his time? (XXIX)

In order to generate the plot, Hoopdriver has to behave against the expectations of the opening. In order to do so, he must escape being moulded by his economic role, and go on holiday. Crucial to this liminal change of conditions that is his holiday is Hoopdriver's opportunity to change his appearance, particularly his clothes.[16] Wells himself had been apprenticed as a draper when a boy, and his narrative eye always carefully discriminates in matters of clothing and cloth, a capability shared by his draper-hero.[17]

> Mr Hoopdriver, very uncomfortable, and studying an easy bearing, looked again at the breakfast things, and then idly lifted the corner of the tablecloth on the ends of his fingers, and regarded it. 'Fifteen three,' he thought privately. (XXXIV)

In his history of the late Victorian period, R. C. K. Ensor notes that, as mass-production made clothes cheaper, the working class began to abandon clothing distinctive to an individual and recognisable occupation.[18] Codes for reading appearance thus started to become less reliable; the barmaid even prophesies that Rational Dress, the cycling outfit for women, will make it too difficult even to distinguish between the sexes (XVIII).[19] Hoopdriver's cycling fashion of a brown chequered suit allows confusion between his read identity and Bechamel's; Bechamel is angry at this bounder's imitation of bourgeois fashion:

> 'Greasy proletarian,' said the other man in brown, feeling a prophetic dislike. 'Got a suit of brown, the very picture of this. One would think his sole aim in life had been to caricature me'. (VII)

The plot thus depends on the democratising effects both of new styles of clothing alongside another class-levelling, cheaply mass-produced technological innovation, the safety bicycle.[20] 1896, the year of the text's publication, marked the height of the cycling craze.[21] The narrator initially plays on Hoopdriver being caught in a machine (as an economic metaphor, he is);[22] but the 'shocking' or at least surprising fact of Hoopdriver's appearance in the first chapter is his legs, for the 'machine' that he has been caught in is a bicycle. When his health permitted in the 1890s, Wells himself was a very enthusiastic cyclist: his *Autobiography* recounts a touching story about teaching George Gissing to ride.[23] The bicycle is democratic technology available to all classes; as well as granting additional freedom of movement and of dress to women such as Jessie, it blurs class divisions as well (unlike segregated rail travel).[24] The priggish central character of Wells's story 'A Perfect Gentleman on Wheels' is insulted to be spoken to as an equal by a capable cycling 'bounder'.[25] George's tricycling Uncle from *Select Conversations with an Uncle* (who makes a brief re-appearance in *The Wheels of Chance*, XIV) is insulted by working-class cyclists asking him the price of his machine.[26] (Hoopdriver correctly guesses the value of Jessie's). The cheapness of the bicycle did allow the more affluent of the working class greater freedom of movement; for Wells this translates into corresponding freedom of thought.

> After your first day of cycling one dream is inevitable. [...] You ride through Dreamland on wonderful dream bicycles that change and grow; you ride down steeples and staircases and over precipices; you hover in horrible suspense over inhabited towns, vainly seeking for a brake your hand cannot find, to save you from a headlong fall; you plunge into weltering rivers, and rush helplessly at monstrous obstacles. (XII)

'The bicycle in its early phases has a peculiar influence upon the imagination,' Wells claims in 'A Perfect Gentleman On Wheels'.[27] The nature of learning to ride requires the correct exercise of the imaginative and romantic as well as physical capacities: 'To ride a bicycle properly is very like a love affair; chiefly it is a matter of faith' (IV).

While the text's presentation of cycling repeatedly makes ironic use of romantic motifs, realism again periodically intrudes, especially in the undermining presence of the body: 'talk of your *joie de vivre*! Albeit with a certain cramping sensation about the knees and calves slowly forcing itself upon his attention' (IV). The deformation of the body by material, especially economic, circumstances is a recurrent trope in Wells.[28] Hoopdriver cannot masquerade as a gentleman indefinitely because of the deforming effect on his body of the economic machine in which the book's opening has seen him trapped. Meeting Jessie, Hoopdriver's 'business training made him prone to bow and step aside' (V); later he bows 'over his saddle as if it was a counter' (VIII). (George Bernard Shaw accused Wells of the same kind of revealing posture when speaking in public).[29] Jessie claims to be, 'blessed or afflicted with a trick of observation', and eventually notices the draper's habits of 'bowing as you do and rubbing your hands, and looking expectant' (XXXIV), and of keeping pins in his lapel, a habit earlier called to the reader's attention that Hoopdriver had hoped to escape on holiday. Even Hoopdriver's language is deformed, since the narrator chooses to render his speech as phonetic cockney rather than in correct orthography.[30] Eventually Hoopdriver confesses to Jessie, 'Ay'm a deraper' (XXXV – though also of course he is a de-raper in the sense that he saves Jessie from rape). The romantic imagination can take the man out of the draper's, it seems, but not the draper out of the man.

Reality also asserts itself in reminders of the presence of money: Hoopdriver's wobbling bicycle imaginatively leaves 'a track like one of Beardsley's feathers' (V), but the track of Jessie's is 'milled like a shilling' (XX). Monetary metaphors serve as a reminder that the hero and heroine's romantic holiday adventures are underwritten by money, and are thus finite. Jessie's chastity is assailed by Bechamel as ' "If saving it is – this parsimony" ' (XXI); when abandoned by Jessie, he feels 'sold' (XXIII). The escapade in the moonlight leaves Hoopdriver with 'profit and loss; profit, one sister with bicycle complete, wot offers? – cheap for tooth and 'air brush, vests, night-shirt, stockings, and sundries' (XXVII). Finally the exhaustion of Hoopdriver's five-pound note and Jessie's £2 7s. ends their picaresque. 'Hoopdriver, indeed, was quite spent, and only a feeling of shame prolonged the liquidation of his bankrupt physique' (XXXVII).

Without money, the carnivalesque holiday, and the narrative, must end. Hoopdriver returns to un-narratable work, and Jessie her domestic imprisonment now at the hands of Widgery as well as Mrs Milton. For a comic romance, the conclusion is pessimistic. Jessie will lend Hoopdriver books, but the reader has already been told how little leisure for reading the life of a draper affords, and reminded of the gulf separating books from real life.

> 'Anyhow, if I'm not to see her – she's going to lend me books,' he thinks, and gets such comfort as he can. And then again: 'Books! What's books?' (XLI)[31]

That Wells thought the ending too pessimistic, for Jessie at least, is shown by his revisions of the ending for the 1901 fourth edition of *The Wheels of Chance* and the 1925 Atlantic Edition, volume seven of his collected *Works*. Wells could be an indifferent editor of his own work, but the *Wheels of Chance*'s prose style and a few typographical errors are revised. The Atlantic also acknowledges the inevitable lapse in time between the events narrated and their being read. The plot begins on the 14th August, 1895. The first edition has Sherlock Holmes 'now, after a glorious career, happily and decently dead,' 1925, 'now happily dead' (I).[32] In the first version, the ending appeals to the impossibility of a realist history of events that have not yet occurred: 'And of what came of it all, of the six years and afterwards, this is no place to tell. In truth, there is no telling it, for by a comparison of the dates you will readily perceive that the years have still to run' (XLI). The 1925 narrator claims ignorance instead, omitting 'by a comparison of the dates you will readily perceive that'.

Jessie's dream of succeeding as a New Woman shows more promise of being fulfilled in the Atlantic text, which rewrites the first half of chapter XXXIX. The clergyman whom Hoopdriver meets earlier proves to be connected to the pursuit.

> [Miss Mergle] had picked up the clergyman in Ringwood, and had told him everything forthwith, having met him once at a British Association meeting. He had immediately constituted himself as administrator of the entire business. Widgery, having been foiled in an attempt to conduct the proceedings, stood with his legs wide apart in front of the fireplace ornament, and looked profound and sympathetic. (1925, XXXIX)

In 1896 and 1901, Jessie is interrogated in chapter thirty-nine only by her stepmother and her schoolmistress Miss Mergle; in 1925 they are joined by Widgery and the clergyman. In the original text she admits to running away with Mrs Milton's friend Bechamel, and Jessie is interrupted too frequently to make any defence of her 'heroic mechanic' (1896, XXXIX). The latest text reads instead:

> She surprised herself by skilfully omitting any allusion to the Bechamel episode. She completely exonerated Hoopdriver from the charge of being more than an accessory to her escapade. [...] Her narrative was inaccurate and sketchy, but happily the others were too anxious to press opinions to pin her down to particularities.

In all versions, Miss Mergle's interruptions are ill-judged and ignorant; in the earlier text, Mrs Milton is equally hostile towards Jessie's desire to escape.

> 'Women write in books about being free, and living our own life, and all that sort of thing. No one is free, free even from working for a living, unless at the expense of someone else. I did not think of that. I wanted to do something in the world, to be something in the world, something vaguely noble, self-sacrificing and dignified'.
>   'You enlarge in the most egotistical way,' began Miss Mergle, 'on your own sentiments'. (1896, XXXIX)

The addition of two further interlocutors, however, disrupts the force of Miss Mergle's condemnation.

> 'I cannot understand this spirit of unrest that has seized upon the more intelligent portion of the feminine community. You had a pleasant home, a most refined and intelligent lady in the position of your mother [...] to cherish, protect, and advise you. And you must needs go out of it all alone into a strange world of unknown dangers –'
>   'I wanted to learn,' said Jessie.
>   'You wanted to learn. May you never have anything to *un*learn'.
>   '*Ah!*' from Mrs. Milton, very sadly.
>   'It isn't fair for all of you to argue at me at once,' submitted Jessie, irrelevantly.
>   'A world full of unknown dangers,' resumed the clergyman. 'Your proper place was surely the natural surroundings that are part of you. You have been unduly influenced, it is only too apparent, by a class of literature which, with all due respect to a distinguished authoress that shall be nameless, I must call the New Woman Literature. In that deleterious ingredient of our book boxes –'
>   'I don't altogether agree with you there,' said Miss Mergle, throwing her head back and regarding him firmly through her spectacles, and Mr. Widgery coughed.
>   'What HAS all this to do with me?' asked Jessie, availing herself of the interruption. (1925, XXXIX)

None of the four can agree in their response; the articulation of society's conventional disapproval by the others allows Mrs Milton to be comparatively more sympathetic. The revised text also allows Jessie to insist on saying goodbye to Hoopdriver, a scene elided in the earlier version, and not only suggests the possibility of Jessie's rapprochement with her stepmother, but even a future Woolfian independence:

> 'I want a room of my own, what books I need to read, to be free to go out by myself alone, Teaching –'
> 'Anything,' said Mrs Milton. 'Anything in reason'. (1925, XXXIX)[33]

In both versions, however, Hoopdriver is excluded from this final conference. The texts largely rejoin in the penultimate page of the chapter, with the paragraph beginning 'Meanwhile Mr Hoopdriver made a sad figure in the sunlight outside' (XXXIX). Later revisions serve to increase the distance between Jessie and Hoopdriver. The text of 1901 deletes Jessie's praise of Hoopdriver, ' "You have courage, you have chivalry – you have all the best' "; and her question ' "Need you be always a shopman?' " (XL); 'The value of a promise, a youthful promise' (1896, XL) is reduced to 'the value of a promise' (1901, XL); the sentence 'He recovered his balance and went on, not looking back' from 1896 is omitted in 1901 (although restored in 1925). In the Atlantic edition Jessie even 'looked at her watch ostentatiously'. The paragraph beginning 'She stood on ground a little higher than he,' in which Jessie is bathed in sunlight and looks down at him, is omitted entirely, as is the sentence about the value of a promise.[34] The adverb 'softly' is removed from Jessie's admonition for Hoopdriver to work; she also adds, ' "You are not a very strong man, you know, now – you will forgive me – nor do you know all you should" ' (1925, XL). Hoopdriver's speculation ' "Suppose a chap *was* to dress himself jest as hard as he could – what then?' " and repainting of his machine are both removed.

The *Wheels of Chance*'s narrator does, as in many of Wells's early pieces, make a claim for the value of lowly types such as Hoopdriver:

> But if you see how a mere counter-jumper, a cad on castors, and a fool to boot, may come to feel the little insufficiencies of life, and if he has to any extent won your sympathies, my end is attained. (XLI)

The author's choice of an unromantic, unhappy ending deprives his readers of the comfort of thinking that the underlings who serve them in shops all live contented lives. This form of ending forces the reader to confront the economic and class inequalities of such a relationship. As well as being a character, Hoopdriver himself is a reader, albeit one with less time for reading than the text's own implied reader, and the narrator hopes that Hoopdriver's disillusionment over the course of the narrative might turn his desires away from romantic fantasy towards more concrete political goals:

> To-morrow, the early rising, the dusting, and drudgery, begin again--but with a difference, with wonderful memories and still more wonderful desires and ambitions replacing those discrepant dreams. (XLI)

Notes

---

[1] *The Works of H. G. Wells: Atlantic Edition*, 28 vols (London: Unwin, 1924-27), VII, *The Wheels of Chance*, p. ix.

[2] See my own 'Pathological Consumption: Commodities and the End of Culture in H. G. Wells's *Tono-Bungay*' in *Consuming for Pleasure,* ed. by Nickianne Moody and Julia Hallam (Liverpool: Liverpool John Moores University Press, 2000), pp. 44-61 and *Henry James and H. G. Wells*: *A Record of their Friendship, their Debate on the Art of Fiction and their Quarrel,* ed. by Leon Edel and Gordon Ray (London: Hart-Davis, 1958).

[3] H. G. Wells, *The Wheels of Chance* (London: Dent, 1896). Since I will be referring to more than one edition of this text, the numbers given are for chapters, rather than pages.

[4] H. G. Wells, 'Popular Writers and Press Critics', *Saturday Review*, 81 (1896), 145-6, collected in *H. G. Wells's Literary Criticism*, ed. by Patrick Parrinder and Robert M. Philmus (Brighton: Harvester, 1980), pp. 74-7.

[5] Hall Caine, 'The New Watchwords of Fiction', *Contemporary Review*, 57 (1890), 479-88 (p. 488).

[6] H. G. Wells, 'The Sawdust Doll', *Pall Mall Gazette*, 13 May 1895, *Literary Criticism*, pp. 44-7 (p. 44).

[7] For an influential case against popular culture along such lines, see Theodor W. Adorno and Max Horkheimer, 'The Culture Industry: Enlightenment as Mass Deception', in *Dialectic of Enlightenment*, trans. by John Cumming (London: Verso, 1997), pp. 120-67.

[8] Michael Draper, *H. G. Wells* (Houndmills: Macmillan, 1987), p. 39.

[9] Martin Tupper, *Stephan Langton*, 2 vols (London: Hurst and Blacket, [1858]), I, pp. 2-6.

[10] See, for instance, Emile Zola, 'The Experimental Novel' (1880), collected in *Documents of Modern Literary Realism*, ed. by George J. Becker (Princeton: Princeton University Press, 1963), pp. 162-96.

[11] Karl Popper, *The Logic of Scientific Discovery* (London: Hutchinson, 1959), p. 27. On the decline of Baconian objectivity in nineteenth-century scientific thought, see Jonathan Smith, *Fact and Feeling: Baconian Science and the Nineteenth-Century Literary Imagination* (Madison: University of Wisconsin Press, 1994).

[12] Rosemary Jann, 'Sherlock Holmes Codes the Social Body', *English Literature in Transition, 1880-1920*, 57 (1990), 685-708.

[13] See Catherine Belsey, *Critical Practice* (London: Methuen, 1980), pp. 109-117.

[14] H. G. Wells, 'The Novel of Types', *Saturday Review*, 81 (1896), 23-4, *Literary Criticism*, pp. 67-70 (pp. 67-68).

[15] See throughout H. G. Wells, *Early Writings in Science and Science Fiction*, ed. by Robert M. Philmus and David Y. Hughes (Berkeley: University of California Press, 1975), but especially 'The Rediscovery of the Unique' (1891), originally entitled 'The Fallacy of the Common Noun', pp. 22-31 and the 1894 letter advocating 'individualism in ethics, socialism in economy', p. 180n. Cf. also 'The So-Called Science of Sociology', *Independent Review*, 6 (1905), 21-37, collected in *An Englishman Looks at the World: Being a Series of Unrestrained Remarks upon Contemporary Matters* (London: Cassell, 1914), pp. 192-206 (pp. 195-96).

[16] I owe to the unpublished PhD. of Yoonjoung Choi, 'Real Romance Came Out of Dreamland into Life: H. G. Wells as a Romancer' (Durham University, 2007) the insight into the importance to Wells of the carnivalesque, an inverting of hierarchies that often involves the exchange of clothes between classes.

[17] For Wells's narrative persona pretending to deny this, see H. G. Wells, 'The Shopman', *Certain Personal Matters* (London: Unwin, 1901), pp. 80-4.

[18] R. C. K. Ensor, *England 1870-1914* (Oxford: Clarendon Press, 1936), p. 168.

[19] See James McGurn, *On Your Bicycle: An Illustrated History of Cycling* (London: John Murray, 1987), pp. 100-07 on cycling and women's fashions.

[20] The bicycle manufacturer Sid Pornick in *Kipps* advertises the 'Best machine at a democratic price'. H. G. Wells, *Works, Kipps*, VIII, p. 140. 'In 1890, twenty-seven factories produced about 40,000 bicycles. Six years later 250 factories were producing 1,200,000 machines'. McGurn, p. 98.

[21] McGurn, p. 113.

[22] Cf. 'Dimly he perceived [...] how the great machine of retail trade had caught its life into his wheels, a vast, irresistible force which he had neither strength of will nor knowledge to escape' (H. G. Wells, *Kipps*, p. 50).

[23] H. G. Wells, *Experiment in Autobiography*, 2 vols (London: Gollancz: 1934), II, p. 568.

[24] McGurn, pp. 90-93.

[25] H. G. Wells, 'A Perfect Gentleman on Wheels', *The Humours of Cycling: Stories and Pictures* by Jerome K. Jerome, H. G. Wells, L. Raven-Hill, Barry Pain etc., (London: Bowden, 1897), pp. 5-14. See also Wells's 'Specimen Day [From a Holiday Itinerary]', *Science Schools Journal* , 33 (1891), 17-20.

[26] H. G. Wells, 'On a Tricycle', *Select Conversations with an Uncle with Two Hitherto Unreprinted Conversations*, ed. by David C. Smith and Patrick Parrinder (London: University of North London Press, 1992), pp. 54-57.

[27] H. G. Wells, 'Perfect Gentleman', p. 8.

[28] See, for example, H. G. Wells, *This Misery of Boots: Reprinted with Alterations from The Independent Review, December 1905* (London: The Fabian Society, 1907), pp. 12-13, or the Selenites in *The First Men in the Moon* (1901).

[29] George Bernard Shaw, *Bernard Shaw and H. G. Wells: Selected Correspondence of George Bernard Shaw*, ed. by J. Percy Smith (Toronto: University of Toronto Press, 1985), p. 66.

[30] See P. J. Keating, 'The Phonetic Representation of Cockney', in *The Representation of the Working Classes in English Fiction* (London: Routledge and Kegan Paul, 1971), pp. 246-68.

[31] Cf. ' "One book's very like another - after all, what is it?" ' wonders Kipps. ' "Something to read and done with [sic]. It's not a thing that matters like print dresses or serviettes." ' H. G. Wells, *Kipps*, p. 429.

[32] Conan Doyle killed Holmes off in 1893's 'The Final Problem', but bowed to public demand by resurrecting him in 1903's *The Return of Sherlock Holmes*.

[33] In Wells's unproduced dramatic version of the story, *Hoopdriver's Holiday*, ed. by Michael Timko (Lafayette: English Literature in Transition, 1964), the absence of the narrator reduces the farcical tone and emphasises political and sociological aspects. Jessie successfully escapes from her stepmother to a liberal-minded aunt, Mrs. Latham, and Hoopdriver is allowed a soliloquy to protest against social conditions.

[34] ' "Well?" she said, surprised and suddenly fearful. One thing he must say!' (1896)
' "Well?" she said, surprised'. (1901)
' "Well?" she said, surprised and abruptly forgetting the recent argument'. (1925)

ALIEN GAZE: POSTCOLONIAL VISION IN *THE WAR OF THE WORLDS*

KEITH WILLIAMS

O wad some Pow'r the giftie gie us
To *see oursels as ithers see us*![1]

This essay resituates *The War of the Worlds* (1898) as one of the most influential manifestations of the emergence of a critical 'postcolonial' vision in the science and culture of the late Victorian period.

Wells's writings are fascinated with advanced instruments of vision, not just for expanding the dimensions of scientific knowledge but the imaginative possibilities they offer for changing how humans think about themselves, their relations with Others and their place in the universe. David Y. Hughes and Robert M. Philmus note that Wells's early essays are 'exercises in dissolving the limits of human perception' through microscopic, astronomic or evolutionary lenses.[2] The first British book on Wells argued his distinctive vision was a corrective against conditioned 'mental astigmatism'. Wells developed a socially-critical way of seeing which played on the defamiliarising potentials of new optical media.[3] The study's American counterpart (also 1915) noted Wells's detached, yet penetrating anatomisation of presumptions, like a kind of X-ray vision, and the protean transformations of his narrative viewpoint. Like Bessel in 'The Stolen Body' (1898), his writing had 'that double quality' of being actively rooted in life while 'watching it from a great distance.' It stimulated the mind by 'telescoping […] suddenly' from a cellular to planetary perspective, 'expanding and contracting his vision of things at will'.[4]

A cluster of 1894 essays imagining the return of the human gaze by the disconcertingly cosmic is specifically connected with technological enhancement of vision. 'From an Observatory', on spectroscopic astronomy, is about the awe

> that comes with knowledge, when we see in its true proportion this little life of ours with all its phantasmal environment of cities and stores and

arsenals, and the habits, prejudices and promises of men. Down there in the
gaslit street such things are real and solid enough [...] but not up here, not
under the midnight sky. Here for a space [...] we may clear our minds of
instincts and illusions, and look out upon the real.[5]

'The Visibility of Change in the Moon' features a similarly cosmic
viewpoint.[6] Another, 'Through a Microscope', carried a suggestion of
humanity being scrutinised like oblivious animalcules, anticipating
TWOTW's ominous opening in detail:

And all the time these creatures are living their vigorous, fussy little lives;
in this drop of water they are being watched by a creature of whose
presence they do not dream, who can wipe them all out of existence with a
stroke of his thumb, and who is withal as finite, and sometimes as fussy
and unreasonably energetic as themselves. He sees them, and they do not
see him, because he has senses which they do not possess, because he is
too incredibly vast and strange to come, save as an overwhelming
catastrophe, into their lives.[7]

This reflexive gaze of the non-human is similarly imagined in Wells's
fictions. 'In the Avu Observatory' (also 1894) features the eruption of a
mysterious creature quite literally into an astronomer's face, as he
stargazes in an outpost of empire. 'The Crystal Egg' (1897) is a Martian
monitoring device, through which their world is reciprocally visible (their
astronomers observe earth in 'The Star' too, also 1897).[8] But 'Mr Cave'
cannot spectate this alien landscape with impunity, because

suddenly something flapped repeatedly across the vision, like the fluttering
of a jewelled fan or the beating of a wing, and a face, or rather the upper
part of a face with very large eyes, came as it were close to his own and as
if on the other side of the crystal. Mr Cave was so startled and impressed
by the absolute reality of those eyes, that he drew his head back from the
crystal to look behind it.[9]

TWOTW elaborated the possibility of this emerging 'alien gaze' to allow
contemporary Britain to look long and hard at itself and the ethics of its
foreign policy from the vantage point of another species, a nightmare
version of the colonial Other integral to its expansionist ideology.[10] Wells
did this by creating a kind of double perspective through his anonymous
first-person narrator, whose vision alternates between loyal British
subject's and the technologically-enhanced extra-terrestrial's. Before
invading, the Martians have 'scrutinised and studied' human affairs with
clinical detachment like humans observing microbes. In reverse
perspective, Wells's science journalist joins astronomer, 'Ogilvy',

scanning suspicious explosions on their planet's surface.[11] *TWOTW* also invokes the defamiliarising potentials of new mass media optical research was giving birth to, whose political and cultural consequences were barely imaginable. The futuristic heat-ray is repeatedly described as resembling a camera or projector (e.g. 63-4 and 111). Warwick Goble's 1897 serial illustrations highlighted this, showing a crippled tripod sending up steam, 'As the camera of the heat-ray hit the water'.[12] It is continuously visualised as a mobile optical device, zooming in or sweeping panoramically with devastating effect. Thus, as cinema would, it 'spectacularises' everything within its visual field. The Martian armoured vehicle is also suggestive of a portable camera mount, as well as Delphic Tripod, essential to prophetic visions.

TWOTW's visual dynamics, continually moving and refocused, make space seem as plastic as Wells did time in 1895. Indeed his narrator witnesses the rapid collapse of a whole imperial order's supposedly permanent structures with a 'sped-up' effect recalling *The Time Machine*'s telescoping of aeons of change into moments and with a viewpoint as chilling and detached as proto-cinematic: 'By ten o'clock the police organisation, and by midday even the railway organisations, were losing coherency, losing shape and efficiency, guttering, softening, running at last in that swift liquefaction of the social body' (*TWOTW*, 92). During the Martian occupation, normality and proportion are defamiliarised to the degree that 'I found about me the landscape, weird and lurid, of another planet'. Narrator and, vicariously, reader experience evolutionary 'dethronement' from atop the cosmic food-chain, as human scale is usurped. Whence everything tilts, as if seen microscopically 'under the Martian heel' (144).

The perception-altering alien invasion topos in late-Victorian 'scientific romance', with its attendant complex of themes, and the features of colonialism are synchronic in psychologically 'over-determined' ways. *TWOTW*'s fantastic scenario, as John Rieder argues, had roots in the real experience of 'enslavement, plague, genocide, environmental devastation, and species extinction' which followed from technologically superior Europe's first contact with the 'New World'.[13] Utopian and satirical depictions of encounters with other peoples form a major part of science fiction's prehistory, but colonialism's most fervid period in the 1890s also marks the emergence of its key tropes, predominantly in countries most involved in imperial projects, as Rieder points out.[14] These constitute a crucial flipside to imperial nations' official narratives of progress and the ideology subserving them. One particular mode – space literature – achieves a critical mass, as Karl S. Guthke notes.[15] Texts focused on Mars are most revealing in terms of colonial critique.

TWOTW is certainly a speculative response to the 'Mars fever' gripping the popular imagination, itself the sensational flowering of ideas and practices reaching back through Enlightenment to Renaissance.[16] Schiaparelli's 1877 discovery of an apparently geometric 'canali' system (suggestively translated as 'canals', rather than just 'channels') bolstered theories of fellow astronomers about alien intelligence. Carl du Prel's *Der Kampf ums Dasein am Himmel* (*The Struggle for Existence in the Heavens* (1873)) had already applied Darwinian theories about evolutionary competition and survival of the fittest to this possibility of life elsewhere, planting the idea of higher development on older worlds. If proven, it would administer a cosmic shock to human self-esteem, a second Copernican revolution decentring our place in the universal order and demoting us among 'the colonised primitives of the universe', as Guthke puts it.[17] This potential shock is reflected in fiction concerned with the superiority of a technological Martian gaze before *TWOTW*. For example, in Camille Flammarion's *La Fin du Monde* and George Griffith's *Olga Romanoff* (both 1894), Martian scientists used advanced telecommunications to warn Earthlings of a comet on collision course and supply instructions for survival.[18] Novels visiting Mars gave 'sneak previews' of a potentially superhuman future by anthropomorphic analogy (a tendency Wells criticised in his essay 'Intelligence on Mars' (1896)).[19] Percy Greg's *Across the Zodiac* (1880), Robert Cromie's *A Plunge into Space* (1890) and Gustavus W. Pope's *Journey to Mars* (1894) all literally take-off from colonial/frontier settings in America and the South Pole. While expressing anxieties about superseding of the human species, they provided degrees of reassurance. Earthlings might eventually overtake their neighbours, whose evolutionary cycle had already peaked, sliding from Utopia into post-human degeneration. Fictions of Martian invasion, however, suddenly envisioned the discomfiting reverse: alien colonial intervention (catastrophic or benign) would irrevocably change evolutionary conditions on our home planet. Previously, space travellers conform to the Victorian imperial adventurer, as Guthke notes, emerging from encountering extra-terrestrials with their 'sense of superiority triumphantly confirmed', since aliens were either not yet human or already degenerate. However, in Wells and Kurd Lasswitz (see below), the Martians come as conquerors of space to threaten the imperial subject itself.[20]

Percival Lowell's writings, based on observations from Flagstaff, Arizona were particularly sensational, even suggesting, like *TWOTW*, that

Martian survival was endangered by desertification. In order to develop their irrigation system, Martians must have long superseded terrestrial innovations such as electrophones and kinetoscopes and devised a single social organisation outgrowing nation states.[21] In human terms, Lowell's writings are revolutionary, as Guthke notes. Enlightenment writers compared potential encounters between humans and extra-terrestrials to European colonisation of primitive regions. However, in Lowell's thinking the tables were 'well and truly turned'.[22] He believed we should embrace our new found consciousness of immaturity as an opportunity for change, placing ourselves in an external perspective of cosmic 'humanism' with strong echoes in both Wells and Lasswitz.

Hence the emergence of a symptomatic 'postcolonial' alien gaze in contemporary science and fiction is by no means exclusive to Wells. Nevertheless, he gave distinctly powerful shape to it. I. F. Clarke describes *TWOTW* as 'the perfect nineteenth-century myth of the imaginary war'.[23] It combined key factors circulating in the contemporary psyche and, as Ingo Cornils argues, expressed them in a symbolic form 'that was immediately understood'.[24] Flashes observed by Ogilvy allude to contemporary reports of 'A Strange Light on Mars'. *Nature* noted the building expectation extra-terrestrials might be aware of our presence and were trying to communicate for some purpose: 'If we assume the light to be on the planet itself, then it must either have a physical or human origin; so it is to be expected that the old idea that the Martians are signalling to us will be revived.'[25] Wells, however, realised terrestrial technology and imperialism were especially linked along an axis of vision. Advanced ability to control visual time and space, was undoubtedly a factor in making Western nations 'serene in their assurance of their empire over matter', as *TWOTW*'s opening paragraph puts it. Alternatively, Wells plays on the perception-altering potentials of advanced technologies rather than simply endorsing their instrumentality for Britain's imperial project. Moreover, there were already signs this dominant technological gaze was being returned, indeed critically challenged from elsewhere on this planet. In December 1896 (the year before the serialisation of *TWOTW*), *Pearson's Magazine* featured 'An Electric Eye'. This was invented for detecting a newly-discovered radiation ranging beyond Röntgen's 1895 X-rays on the electromagnetic spectrum, by Jagadis Chunder Bose, professor at Calcutta's Presidency College.[26] Bose's apparatus calculated the refractive indices of non-transparent materials, from granite to the human body, through which these 'ether waves' could nonetheless pass. *Pearson's* science columnist, M. Griffith, noted how, despite India's educational and material deprivations, this development at the very frontier of physics countered colonial myths about a 'lotus-eating country', incapable of producing 'genius'. The article carried an 'artist's impression', because the invisible waves were unphotographable, showing a complex machine mounted on a tripod, operated by a metallic homunculus. The 'electric eye' itself sways cobra-like on a tentacular cable, seeming to emit radiation beamed intensely at the reader (see figure 1). The image's anticipation of the shape of *TWOTW*'s fighting machines, with their camera/projector heat-rays, and of its critical alien gaze focused back on the reader is striking.[27] The year of its serialisation, 1897, was also Victoria, Empress of India's diamond jubilee. Celebrations on the public mind would have increased the story's imaginative shock. Furthermore, analogous with unsuspected watching by artificially 'superhuman' vision in *The Invisible Man* (1897), Griffith described Bose's invention as a prosthetic or 'additional organ of sense', able to penetrate virtually anything and 'see the invisible'.[28] This led to speculations similar to the 'tele-vision' of 'The Remarkable Case of Davidson's Eyes' (1895) or the surveillance society of *When the Sleeper Wakes* (1899) about an alarming future, where such apparatuses might be ubiquitous: 'Invisible eyes peeping at us from every corner, ready to note down our every action, for ever tracking us down like sleuth hounds. An end to peace, rest, privacy, and all that makes home sacred.'[29] Hence the imaginative implications of an Eastern Professor's 'Marvellous Discovery' disturbed the once impenetrable superiority and self-belief of the imperial homeland.

Figure 1

Wells probably also read Griffith's earlier (July 1896) interview with venerable French Astronomer, Flammarion, 'The Christopher Columbus of Mars', (the interview was immediately followed by Wells's story 'The

Rajah's Treasure'.)[30] Griffith noted the possible impact of his hypotheses
on the arrogance of developed nations if verified:

> doubtless its denizens have among other conquests made electricity their
> chained slave, and by its aid travel in the air, or on sea, or land with
> incredible speed. Railways and steamboats must be toys of their long past.
> [...] we felt we should appear such undersized ignorant babies in the eyes
> of the advanced Marsians [sic] that we were glad to find ourselves back on
> the dear old earth, and to regain our lost self-esteem and importance.[31]

Figure 2

In August, Griffith returned to Mars in humorous anticipation of 'The
Paris Exhibition of 1900' (which Wells would visit on a cycling
holiday).[32] Griffith's 'Private View' of its coming marvels foreshadowed
TWOTW's ominous scanning of earth. In one of the earliest references to
possible alien invasion, Griffith suggested even the cutting-edge gaze of
human science might be faced down with sinister intent, through the
Exhibition's

> gigantic telescope, that will, we are promised, bring the moon within a mile
> of the earth. In this way planetary space will be annihilated. To spy upon
> the inhabitants of other worlds, to watch their movements, to prepare
> ourselves for possible invasion by these mysterious creatures, will be
> almost feasible.[33]

With tantalising proximity, the article preceded another Wells story about discovering unsuspected evolutionary competition, the ocean exploration tale 'In the Abyss.' This frames a visual close encounter with the mysterious inhabitants of a Piscean city through the portal of a bathyscape, with pictures by *TWOTW* illustrator, Warwick Goble.[34]

With even stranger synchronicity, the camera as medium of counter-imperial invasion featured in a November 1898 *Strand Magazine* photo-story, the same year Wells's book visualised Martian firepower on London locations. This anonymous narrative was also anti-colonial gothic and preceded Wells's story about decentred subjectivity and defamiliarised vision, 'The Stolen Body'. It concerned a 'mystic camera' sent back from Delhi, carved with Hindu figures.[35] Hence, if this was 'alien technology', like Bose's Electric Eye, it was specifically as an instrument of imperial world-view subverted and re-exported to its heartland. Significantly, the story puns on the slang expression 'camera fiend', referring not just to its snap-happy protagonist, but an apparently uncanny presence within the mechanism itself upsetting his control over a paradigm of representation, knowledge and subjectivity. He's previously 'fixed' the reality of everything from European beauty, to swallows on the wing, bullets in flight and celestial nebulae. Despite the highest technical skill, far from remaining the obedient 'photographic eye' of Western science,[36] the camera mercilessly distorts every subject, as illustrated in surreal plates.[37] The General Post Office's pillars, where 'The Imperial Penny Postage had just been introduced as a crowning memorial', buckle as if under Wells's heat-ray (see Figure 2). State-of-the-art ironclad, 'HMS Virago', explodes in flames like *TWOTW*'s 'Thunder Child', or news photos from the Spanish-American war, in which another empire would soon be eclipsed (see Figure 3).[38] New Oxford Street's emporia collapse into 'one long mass of common ruin'. Monuments to world power are systematically destroyed in the development process (see Figure 4). Finally, even the Imperial Institute, 'glorious testimony of [Britain's] high destiny, was struck down by celestial fire', and Parliament bulldozed by a 'Leviathan' from the Thames (Figure 5).[39] These might be more than malfunctions. Playing on photography's association with spiritualism, they could be psychic previews, time-travelling images of catastrophe.[40] That they are finally exposed as a hoax (the plates were defective, not haunted) does not disarm symptomatic parallels with Wells's anti-imperial imagery. The disclaimer foreshadows a similar reassurance by Orson Welles following his Hallowe'en *TWOTW* 'radio scare' of 1938, which shook another superpower's invulnerable confidence before World War II.

H.M. TORPEDO-DESTROYER "VIRAGO."

Figure 3

THE DEMOLITION OF TRAFALGAR SQUARE.

Figure 4

DOWN WITH THE HOUSE OF LORDS.

Figure 5

TWOTW's visionary method warns not so much about real danger of Martian invasion, as the delusions of a colonial civilisation radically mutated by technology to the pitch of potential self-destruction, as Liz Hedgecock points out.[41] Wells's narrator puts contemporary progress under his critical 'alien gaze', placing us under the external viewpoint of a different species. Hence the 'double-exposure' of his story,[42] which switches between the 'normality' of white, middle-class, imperial citizen and imagined Martian Otherness. *TWOTW* inflicted scientific terror on the complacent, bourgeois civilisation at the Empire's hub, inverting its relation to distant colonial subjects.[43] Escaping the first massacre, the narrator experiences a crucial dislocation of perspective which furnishes a commentary on the novel's paradoxical method of fantastic realism and its underlying satirical purpose:

> Now it was as if something turned over, and the point of view altered abruptly. There was no sensible transition from one state of mind to the other. I was immediately the self of every day again – a decent ordinary citizen. The silent common, the impulse of my flight, the starting flames, were as if they had been in a dream. I asked myself had these latter things indeed happened. I could not credit it. (31)

His sense of epistemological and discursive incongruity reflects the same defamiliarising potential of vision enhanced by technology Wells's own imagination was so fired by:

At times I suffer from the strangest sense of detachment from myself and
the world about me; I seem to watch it all from the outside, from
somewhere inconceivably remote, out of time, out of space, out of the
stress and tragedy of it all. This feeling was very strong upon me that night.
Here was another side to my dream. (32)

Simultaneously, Wells harnessed this alien gaze to a specifically anti-
colonial project by deliberately invoking a contemporary context of fear
and belligerence, especially the arms race between the Great Powers.
Clarke notes Wells was deliberately shifting the Victorian 'invasion novel'
to an interplanetary plane. This jingoistic genre dates back to Colonel G.T.
Chesney's *The Battle of Dorking* (1871). A propagandist wake-up call to
defend a somnambulantly over-confident Empire from its latest rival,
Chesney's text looks back, like *TWOTW*, from a near future in which
newly-unified Germany has used tactical surprise and superior technology
to conquer Britain through the Home Counties. Choice of location and
meticulous detail confirm Wells drew on Chesney.[44] Significantly, initial
reporting of the Martians fails to excite 'the sensation that an ultimatum to
Germany would have done' (*TWOTW*, 35). Both Chesney and Wells
realised British superiority was contingent, but drew very different
conclusions. As Rieder puts it, the abjection of Chesney's conquered
Britain 'never lay far from an ethical reflection' on its domination of other
nations. Wells drew out this latent potential.[45] Hence *TWOTW* differs from
most invasion fictions, because it is emphatically not jingoistic
propaganda, but an allegory of the 'Aliens "R" Us' variety.[46] It deconstructs
how racial Othering, coupled with technologies of communication and
destruction, alienated imperialistic humanity from its own species in moral
and psychological terms. Read alongside 'The Land Ironclads' (1903) and
The War in the Air (1908), this also makes *TWOTW* a 'prevision' of the
mechanised, total war of 1914-18, in which British anxieties about
subjection to colonial ambitions by others assumed concrete shape in
global conflagration.[47]

TWOTW makes no secret of its anti-imperial stance.[48] From chastened
retrospect, Wells's narrator opens with a pointed reminder of how
colonialists turned their sights on space, little suspecting their gaze was
reflected back with unimaginable intensity:

It is curious to recall some of the mental habits of those departed days. At
most terrestrial men fancied there might be other men upon Mars, perhaps
inferior to themselves and ready to welcome a missionary enterprise. Yet,
across the gulf of space, minds that are to our minds as ours are to those of
the beasts that perish, intellects vast cool and unsympathetic, regarded this
earth with envious eyes, and slowly and surely drew their plans against us.

And early in the twentieth century came the great disillusionment. (*TWOTW*, 7)

The novel turns the tables by making humans subject to the same ends, while drawing astringent parallels with terrestrial means:

> [...] we must remember what ruthless and utter destruction our own species has wrought, not only upon animals, such as the vanished bison and the dodo, but upon its own inferior races. The Tasmanians, in spite of their human likeness, were entirely swept out of existence in a war of extermination waged by European immigrants, in the space of fifty years. Are we such apostles of mercy as to complain if the Martians warred in the same spirit? (9)

The Swiftian irony is that at least Martian genocide is excusable, because we are not recognisably related and they are desperate to escape a dying planet. In contrast, by 1876 British settlers casually exterminated Tasmania's indigenous population by enslavement, murder and disease.[49]

Colonialism underpinned itself with the pseudo-science of 'Social Darwinism', claiming the right to exercise what Peter Fitting calls 'its evolutionary prerogative'.[50] This justified territorial expansion and subjugation through means of railways, telecommunications, Maxim gun and battleship, by naturalising one-sided conflict on grounds of evolutionary competition and racial 'superiority'. However, Wells's *Text-Book of Biology* (1893) warned against drawing mistaken conclusions from 'the book of nature' based on 'the triumphs of survival, the tragedy of death and extinction, the tragi-comedy of degradation and inheritance, the gruesome lesson of parasitism, and the political satire of colonial organisms.' Nevertheless, 'Zoology is, indeed, a philosophy and a literature' to those who could read its symbols more wisely.[51] *TWOTW* is thus 'political satire of colonial organisms' aggravated by the machine. The cult of technological progress was, of course, another key to both colonialism's methods and self-justification. Wells reviewed Rider Haggard's imperialistic adventure stories in a critical light and Herbert L. Sussman has argued his scientific romances are ironic adaptations of this genre to 'the problem of the machine'.[52] Hence, as Adam Roberts puts it, the Martians 'mechanised brutalities' symbolise 'a deeper set of concerns' exploring earthling violence and Othering.[53] *TWOTW* is a virtual exercise in projecting the experience of 'inferior races' back on the population of earth's most powerful empire. Despite appearing as cephalopods, the Martians are, what Hedgecock calls, 'hyper-evolved' parodies of our selves.[54] This is suggested by metafictional allusion to Wells's own 1893 essay about 'posthuman' mutation:

> To me it is quite credible that the Martians may be descended from beings
> not unlike ourselves, by a gradual development of brains and hands. [...]
> Without the body the brain would, of course, become a mere selfish
> intelligence, without any of the emotional substratum of the human being.
> (*TWOTW*, 127)[55]

Thus, as Frank McConnell puts it, they represent not just invasion from space, but 'from time', from the possible future of humankind itself.[56] Moreover, 'prosthetic' technology has played a key role in development of their species: 'it was in other artificial additions to their bodily resources that their great superiority over man lay. We men [...] are just in the beginning of the evolution which the Martians have worked out'. (*TWOTW*, 29) Rendered superhuman by donning different metal 'bodies', as well as artificially extending their senses, the Martians act, nonetheless, in *sub*human ways by ruthless violence against other sentient beings (although the narrator also makes it clear that they act no differently to the way humans treat animals, which is all we are to them). Wells confronts his readers with colonialism's true evolutionary implications. As so often in his narratives of Otherness, the play of difference and similarity gives way to shocking recognition the 'monstrous' alien is actually the secret identity of the self. Aptly, Niall Ferguson's new history takes *TWOTW* as its starting point for understanding how nations behaved with the inhumanity of Martians in twentieth-century genocides driven by ethnic hatred and militarised applied science.[57]

Nevertheless, from the sobering fragility of imperial power comes an imaginative potential for rethinking progress in terms of *inclusively* human values. The most radical shift from Chesney is this emergence of an ethical consciousness, cutting across racial divides and national interests in a common global agenda. Clearly, it foreshadows Wells's 'proto-postcolonial' concept of a cooperative and technocratic 'World State' developed in subsequent writings from *Anticipations* (1901) onwards: '[The Martian invasion] has robbed us of that serene confidence in the future which is the most fruitful source of decadence, the gifts to human science it has brought are enormous, and it has done much to promote the conception of the commonweal of mankind.' (179) In this way, Wells endorses the *re*-humanising conclusion of his mentor, T. H. Huxley, whose 1893 Romanes lecture tackled Social Darwinism's fundamental heresy:

> Social progress means a checking of the cosmic process at every step and
> the substitution for it of another, which may be called the ethical process;
> the end of which is not the survival of those who may happen to be the
> fittest [...] but of those who are ethically the best.[58]

Hence it is crucial to consider contemporary responses and parallels to understand how they enhanced or stifled *TWOTW*'s visionary method and themes.[59]

A contemporary complement appeared from the very epicentre of invasion novel anxiety, Wilhelminian Germany, by physicist and philosopher Kurd Lasswitz. That *Auf Zwei Planeten*, or *Two Planets* (1897), and the serialised *TWOTW* appeared without mutual awareness is more than explicable in terms of topical interest in Mars.[60] Both are visionary allegories about colonialism which cast Europeans as victims of the project of an 'advanced' species, to whom they become inferiorised Others. By their differing takes on this, they established what Guthke calls a 'dual paradigm' still influencing SF visions.[61]   Furthermore, as Patricia Kerslake points out, Lasswitz also employs a critical alterity of perception, between perspectives of superhuman coloniser and colonised, to transform the reader's outlook on their own species.[62]

Like Wells's analogy with Tasmania, Lasswitz's 'Grunthe' warns his fellow explorers when they stumble on the Martians' polar base against fatally underestimating the implications of first contact, as Aztecs and Incas did Cortez and Pisarro.[63] However, unlike *TWOTW*, Lasswitz's 'Nume' 'come in peace'. Their 'United Martian States' models a utopian community, prefiguring Wells's own thinking. Hence they appear an altruistic future humankind, guided by a cosmic version of Kant's categorical imperative. They wish to progress Earthlings beyond conflict and want, sharing benefits of social harmony, high-technology and cultural enlightenment, asking only earth's surplus oxygen and solar energy in return. However, this paternalistic mission goes awry. As Kerslake argues, the attempt to inculcate their ideology is 'inevitably subverted', resulting ironically not in 'pacification' of earth, but 'brutalisation of Mars' and near tragedy for both.[64]

TWOTW and *Two Planets* dealt with complementary aspects of colonialism. These can be identified with Gramsci's distinction between 'domination and hegemony': power by naked force or through ideas generating consent.[65] Wells's Martians exterminate, preserving only Earthlings necessary for nourishment, in the most dystopian imperial scenario imaginable. Lasswitz's superhumans espouse collaboration, effectively a Kiplingesque doctrine of 'little green man's burden'. Only when this fails, because, significantly, the British refuse to relinquish imperial pride, do they resort to violence. As in *TWOTW*, Britain becomes the focus for hamstringing humankind.[66] The Nume air fleet, mirroring 'gunboat diplomacy', blockade the island, demonstrating through bursts of atomic fission against the Royal Navy that resistance is futile. A planetwide 'protectorate' is established, forestalling Britain's rivals scavenging its colonies. However, erosion of respect for the existential dignity of Earthlings is 'justified' by the Nume's increasingly dehumanising view of them as a species incapable of rational behaviour.

Lasswitz's satire is therefore as much about empire's inevitably corrupting effect on the most high-minded colonisers, whose expedient ideology conceals atavistic motives even from themselves. This parallels Wells's Martians' unanticipated lack of immunities, symbolised by a psychosomatic 'Earth Rage' (*Erdkoller*), destroying their Zen-like equilibrium.[67] But it also anticipates the transformation of Conrad's missionary trader, 'Kurtz', in *Heart of Darkness*, as 'civilised' inhibitions give way to megalomaniac atrocity.[68] Hence both *TWOTW* and *Two Planets* caution against the hubris of a supra-rational, technologised humankind, capable of treating racial Others as lower life forms.

Crucially both also foreground and critique advanced visual intelligence as a form of imperialising 'power-knowledge'. Wells's narrator recalls the Martians' 'immense' staring eyes, 'at once vital, intense, inhuman, crippled and monstrous' (*TWOTW*, 22); by contrast, Nume pupils dilate to the lids as their main marker of genetic difference. But their vision is just as artificially boosted. Their pocket cameras capture earthly phenomena in perfect 'natural' colour. Their strategic views transcend the human's balloon: gazing down from the Nume space station, Lasswitz's awed protagonists share a perspective on the infinite littleness of their diurnal existence similar to Wells's narrator's.[69] The Nume scan earth with vastly powerful instruments, mastering optical space, but also time. Their 'Retrospective' (like *Lumen*'s viewpoint in Flammarion's 1866 light-speed physics fantasy and subsequent 'chronological telescopes', such as Eugène Mouton's 'L'Historioscope' (1883)) picks up images radiating from earth, to replay the past and dissect realities otherwise irrecoverable.[70] As in *TWOTW*, optical technology is in no way restricted to purposes of disinterested scientific understanding. Mediation is an increasingly politicised issue. Earthlings Saltner and Isma visit a virtual reality theatre in the anthropological 'Earth Museum'. This recounts the mutual misunderstanding between British destroyer and Martian airship, which escalates into conflict. The simulation zooms in from moving panorama to war dance by bloodthirsty 'savages', preparing their ambush. Hence Lasswitz satirises the chauvinism of European representations of other cultures which 'justified' punitive interventions and repression. The audience erupt into anti-Earthling hysteria, as 'By a switch of the picture which could hardly be followed', it transits into the warship's interior, where Nume explorers are menaced by their captors.[71]

Despite, or perhaps because of, the efforts of visionary anti-colonial writers, the British Empire quickly struck back and pressed space invasion spectacle into the service of Jingoistic values. Robert W. Cole's *The Struggle for Empire* (1900) introduced galactic rivalry with another humanoid Empire. As Edward James notes, it was a 'future war story writ large',[72] thinly disguising British and German navies as fleets from earth and Sirius. In this proto-*Dan Dare* yarn, London is capital of the Solar System. The errant US has reunited with the motherland. Other races have melted into the superior Anglo-Saxon gene pool, or 'naturally' withered away. Battles are fought between space Dreadnoughts, with wrap-round video screens instead of navigation bridges. Virtual reality theatre simulates colonised worlds for audiences to 'fancy themselves on the actual spot without any effort of imagination'.[73] Visionary technology features, ironically, to close rather than broaden the mind through unexpected perspectives. Readers are never prompted to imagine the situation from the Other's point of view. Instead, Cole's Anglo-Saxons inevitably defeat their treacherous enemies by innate moral superiority and inventiveness. His fantasy, unlike its Wellsian source, failed to understand that, far from spreading to the stars, Britain's terrestrial empire was doomed to decline.[74]

American responses were nonetheless caught up in a similar Grand Narrative of national power, most revealingly in priority given to flag-waving over Wells's reflexive vision, because they were themselves partly products of a cultural and economic expansion which superseded Victorian colonialism. The seductiveness of Nume imperialism sidelights the irony of US versions which promote a 'neo-colonial' hegemony in the process of liberating the world from Martian domination. Consequently, presumptions of moral immunity to *TWOTW*'s subtext inevitably foundered. At Hollywood's gung-ho extreme, Roland Emmerich's *Independence Day* (1996) deliberately omitted *TWOTW*'s humbling lesson (along with any explicit acknowledgement of it as a source), that the most 'advanced' nation emerge not as victors, but fortuitous survivors, though this is reinstated in Steven Spielberg's 2005, post-9/11 adaptation, which also implicitly questions the motivations and conduct of US foreign policy in the 'War on Terror'. Wells's Victorians face the future with a new sense of common human vulnerability. However, Emmerich's film shows no trace of this 'great disillusionment', nor unmasking of alien Other as disguised imperial self. It culminates instead a long tradition re-asserting confidence in specifically American 'manifest destiny', which evolved not from the 1938 broadcast, but a largely-forgotten response.

In 1898, popular astronomer, Garret P. Serviss, rapidly penned a sequel, for *Evening Journal* (12 January – 10 February). *Edison's Conquest of Mars* was more directly a response to pirated serialisations in New York and Boston newspapers and correspondingly switched Wells's location to the Eastern seaboard.[75] Such serialisations avoided Wells's reflexive critique by depicting the Martians as a purely external threat; the US military are portrayed heroically and their weaponry as more potent. In Serviss's sequel, the 'Wizard of Menlo Park' (as Edison became known for his patented inventions) makes SF motifs like anti-gravity and disintegrating rays into real devices, to carry the fight back to those alien varmints and whip them good. It was symptomatic of the Edisonian personality cult and American faith in the powers of applied science. However, Rudyard Kipling's 'The White Man's Burden' (1899) stereotypically associated with the Raj was in fact written to encourage America (which had just seized the Philippines from Spain) to take up the imperial baton for the new century. Effectively, Edison's fictional counterpart (in token coalition with British and German super-scientists, Lord Kelvin - pioneer of electrostatics and thermodynamics - and Röntgen) defeats Martian terror, at the price of achieving earthly supremacy for his homeland.

The prototype Edgar Rice Burroughs/Flash Gordon 'space opera', *Edison's Conquest* describes 'the avenging counterstroke that the earth dealt back at its ruthless enemy in the heavens',[76] envisioning American political championship as an ethically unproblematic given of modernity: 'The United States naturally took the lead, and their leadership was never for a moment questioned abroad.'[77] The mission presumes America's right to act on the planet's behalf, equating its interests with humankind's as a whole. Martian Otherness similarly differs sharply from *TWOTW*'s socio-biological satire. Their monstrosity is not explained by adaptation, but racist pseudo-science, phrenology. Anthropomorphic bipeds, but disfigured by evil, they combine superhuman intellect 'with some of the physical features of a beast, and all the moral depravity of a fiend.'[78] They are motivated not so much by survival (Mars is fruitful, albeit over-populated), as lust for conquest. Consequently, defiance of past overlordship is triumphantly invoked: Chapter 8, 'The Martians Are Coming', updates the War of Independence alarm call.[79] Nevertheless, when the Republic split away, it continued Britain's project of colonial expansion westwards on its own terms. This unquiet history resurfaces in Freudian slips displaced from a different popular genre – the Western: for example during a scouting party, ' "This affords good protection," said Colonel Smith, recalling his adventures on the western plains. "We can get close in

to the Indians – I beg pardon, I mean the Martians – without being seen."
'[80] Conquering the Red Planet is also justified, ironically, as liberation from racial bondage, when Edison's scouts discover humans, whose Earthling ancestors, Aryans like themselves, were abducted into slavery.[81] Despite such equivocations, the novel concludes by foreshadowing the universalisation of American values across a grateful earth in Emmerich's film. As *Independence Day* puts it, 'And should we win the day, the Fourth of July will no longer be known as an American holiday', but celebrated across the globe. Edison's victorious return begs the question of how our own planet has also changed, as 'new New York' towers resurgent from the ruins of the original attack as 'capitol of the world'.[82]

Despite such 'partial derivatives' (to borrow Gary Westfahl's phrase),[83] through its imagined alien gaze, *TWOTW* still provides a renewable template, a critical method for looking at ourselves and at how science, unyoked from ideology, might assist, not threaten the collective human project. Its visionary value persists in helping reveal the dangers posed in that project's direction by neo-colonial interests rather than those of the planet as a whole.

Notes

[1] Robert Burns, 'To a Louse' (1786), in *The Canongate Burns*, ed. by Andrew Noble and Patrick Scott Hogg (Edinburgh: Canongate, 2001), pp. 130-2 (p. 132).

[2] David Y. Hughes and Robert M. Philmus, 'A Selective Bibliography (with Abstracts) of H.G. Wells's Science Journalism 1887-1901', in *H.G. Wells and Modern Science Fiction*, ed. by Darko Suvin and Robert M. Philmus (Lewisburg: Bucknell University Press; London: Associated University Presses, 1977), pp. 191-222 (p. 195).

[3] J. D. Beresford, *H.G. Wells: A Critical Biography* (London: Nisbet, 1915), pp. 10-11 and 31-33.

[4] Van Wyck Brooks, *The World of H.G. Wells* (New York and London: T. Fisher Unwin, 1915), pp. 25-8. For the cinematic mobility of *TWOTW*'s virtual gaze, see my *H.G. Wells, Modernity and the Movies* (Liverpool: Liverpool University Press, 2007), pp. 139-41.

[5] H. G. Wells, 'From an Observatory', *Saturday Review*, 78 (1 December 1894), 594-5; repr. in H. G. Wells, *Certain Personal Matters* (London: Lawrence and Bullen, 1898), pp. 262-6 (p. 264).

[6] H. G. Wells, 'The Visibility of Change in the Moon', *Knowledge*, 18 (October 1894), 230-1.

[7] H. G. Wells, 'Through a Microscope' (1894), in Wells, *Certain Personal Matters*, pp. 238-45 (p. 244).

[8] See H. G. Wells, *The Complete Short Stories*, ed. by John Hammond (London: Phoenix Press, 1998), pp. 281-9 (p. 289).

[9] Wells, *Complete Short Stories*, pp. 267-280 (p. 274).

[10] The classic examination of the importance of the cultural construction of 'the Oriental' in European imperialism, 'as one of its deepest and most recurring images of the Other', remains Edward Said's *Orientalism: Western Conceptions of the Orient* (1978) (Harmondsworth: Penguin, 1995), especially introduction, pp. 1-26 (p. 1).

[11] H. G. Wells, *The War of the Worlds* (1898) (London: Penguin, 2005), pp. 7 and 10-11. Henceforth all page references to *TWOTW* will be given in brackets in the text.

[12] H. G. Wells, *The War of the Worlds*, *Pearson's Magazine*, July 1897, p. 113. The Martians' invisible beam may also owe something to X-rays, which could also not be seen, but whose impact was revealed in burns caused by prolonged exposure. The 1953 film of *TWOTW* (dir. Byron Haskin) shows it rendering victims' skeletons visible, before they vanish altogether, in what has become a cliché of alien weaponry sent up in Tim Burton's *Mars Attacks!* (1996).

[13] John Rieder, 'Science Fiction, Colonialism, and the Plot of Invasion', *Extrapolation*, 46 (Fall 2005), 373-394 (p. 373).

[14] Rieder, 'Science Fiction', 375.

[15] Karl S. Guthke, *Imagining Other Worlds*, trans. by Helen Atkins (Ithaca and London: Cornell University Press, 1990), p. 367.

[16] Growing controversy about intelligence on Mars between 1895 and 1910, roughly speaking, 'set the whole world agog'. Guthke, *Imagining Other Worlds*, p.354. It was the logical culmination of the Copernican theory of the 'plurality of worlds'; Laplace's 'nebular hypothesis' about planetary cooling duly giving rise to organic life; contemporary Kirchoffian spectroscopy, establishing the presence of elements on other planets which might support it.

[17] Guthke, *Imagining Other Worlds*, p. 353.

[18] See Camille Flammarion, *La Fin du Monde* (Paris: Ernest Flammarion, 1894), pp. 131-36 (the Martians' 'photophonique' dispatch, projected by 'téléphonoscope' in a vast hall, is illustrated by Saunier on 133); also Martian 'photo-telegraphy' in George Griffith, *Olga Romanoff* (London: Tower Publishing, 1894), pp. 289-302.

[19] See note 55.

[20] Guthke, *Imagining Other Worlds*, pp. 382-3.

[21] See Percival Lowell, *Mars* (1895) (London and Bombay: Longman's Green 1896), pp. 202 and 209-10.

[22] Guthke, *Imagining Other Worlds*, pp. 357 and 358.

[23] I.F. Clarke, *Voices Prophesying War* (1966) (London: Panther, 1970), p. 94.

[24] Ingo Cornils, 'The Martians Are Coming! War, Peace, Love and Scientific Progress in H. G. Wells's *The War of the Worlds* and Kurd Lasswitz's *Auf Zwei Planeten*', *Comparative Literature*, 55 (Winter 2003), 24-41 (p. 26).

[25] Anon., 'A Strange Light on Mars', *Nature*, 50 (2 Aug. 1894), 319.

[26] X-rays, which caused a sensation that year even greater than the Lumières' cinematograph, were discovered by German scientist, Wilhelm Konrad von Röntgen.

[27] M. Griffith, 'An Electric Eye', *Pearson's Magazine*, December 1896, pp. 749-56 (p. 749).

[28] Griffith, 'An Electric Eye', p. 754.

[29] Griffith, 'An Electric Eye', p. 756. Bose's later work foreshadows Norbert Wiener's cybernetics.

[30] M. Griffith, 'The Christopher Columbus of Mars', *Pearson's Magazine*, July 1896, pp. 30-7. Wells's 'The Rajah's Treasure' follows on pp. 39-47. Flammarion's monumental study, *La Planète Mars*, had been published in 1892.

[31] Griffith, 'Christopher Columbus of Mars', pp. 31-2. The article also mentioned Flammarion's latest fiction, the 25th century, *La Fin du Monde.*

[32] 'I have been prowling about the North of France on a bicycle and paying a visit to the Exposition'. Letter 'To Elizabeth Healey' (24 May, 1900), in *The Correspondence of H .G. Wells*, ed. by David C. Smith, 4 vols (London: Pickering and Chatto, 1998), I, 355.

[33] M. Griffith, 'The Paris Exhibition of 1900', *Pearson's Magazine*, August 1896, pp. 140-9 (p. 144). Illustrations were by Albert Robida, France's 'Jules Verne of the cartoon', famous for futuristic inventions.

[34] Wells's 'In the Abyss' followed on pp. 154-66.

[35] Anon. 'The Tragedies of a Camera', *Strand Magazine*, Nov. 1898, pp. 545-52 (pp. 545-6). ('The Stolen Body' followed on pp. 567-76.) Carlo Pagetti first spotted this parallel with the *TWOTW* (see his 'Change in the City', in *H. G. Wells's Perennial Time Machine*, ed. by George Slusser et al (Athens, GA., and London: University of Georgia Press, 2001), pp. 122-34 (pp. 129-30). Destruction of London was in vogue, as in Grant Allen's vision of volcanic disaster, 'The Thames Valley Catastrophe', *Strand Magazine*, December 1897, pp. 674-84, and many others. For a fuller discussion, see Patrick Parrinder 'From Mary Shelley to *The War of the Worlds*: The Thames Valley Catastrophe', in *Anticipations*, ed. by David Seed (Liverpool: Liverpool University Press, 1995), pp. 58-75.

[36] Victorian confidence in cameras and related visual instruments as handmaids of progress is typified by Richard Proctor's 1883 article 'The Photographic Eyes of Science'. Where the unaided eye was defective, one 'provided by science is practically free from fault.' Proctor celebrated the camera's 'panoptic' potentials for advancing knowledge: '[...] indeed with photography, spectroscopy, polariscopy, and other aids, science promises soon to be Argus-eyed.' *Longman's Magazine*, February 1883, pp. 439-62 (pp. 442 and 462); also repr. in *Literature and Science in the Nineteenth Century*, ed. by Laura Otis (Oxford: Oxford University Press, 2002), pp. 84-87.

[37] Both *Strand* and *Pearson's* ran regular competitions asking readers to submit photographs containing interesting or bizarre defects.

[38] Anon., 'Tragedies of a Camera', pp. 547-8.

[39] Anon., 'Tragedies of a Camera', p. 551.

[40] Anon., 'Tragedies of a Camera', pp . 550 and 552.

[41] Liz Hedgecock ' "The Martians are Coming!": Civilisation v. Invasion in *The War of the Worlds* and *Mars Attacks!*', in *Alien Identities*, ed. by Deborah Cartmell et al (London: Pluto Press, 1999), pp. 104-20 (p. 100).

[42] Richard Law also draws attention to this in his 'The Narrator in Double Exposure in *The War of the Worlds*', *Wellsian*, n.s. 23 (2000), 47-56.

[43] Wells famously spent days bicycling around the quarter of Surrey, where he then resided, getting facts right like a kind 'location shooting' to give utmost plausibility to scenes of fantastic devastation. Wells learnt to ride a bike while living at Maybury Road, Woking where he wrote *The Invisible Man*, *TWOTW* and *The Wheels of Chance*. See H. G. Wells, *Experiment in Autobiography*, 2 vols (London: Gollancz/Cresset, 1934), I, 543.

[44] See I. F. Clarke, *The Tale of the Next War* (Liverpool: Liverpool University Press, 1995), pp. 27-33. Clarke lists eight other topical 'terrestrial' invasion novels appearing in 1898, Virtually all imperialist 'wake-up calls' with racist overtones, such as *Anglo-Saxons Onwards! What Will Japan Do? The Yellow Danger*, etc. See Clarke, *Voices Prophesying War*, p. 233.

[45] Rieder, 'Science Fiction', 379.

[46] *TWOTW* plays a central role in this tradition. See introduction to *Aliens R Us*, ed. by Ziauddin Sardar and Sean Cubitt (London: Pluto, 2002), especially pp .6-7.

[47] Wells had already mooted the possibility 'of a sort of land ironclad', as well as the role of aeroplanes, in a chapter on future wars. See H. G. Wells, *Anticipations* (London: Chapman and Hall, 1902), especially   p. 189. A Second World War edition, extended *TWOTW*'s topicality by alluding to the Blitzkrieg, through the searchlighted skyline of the burning metropolis on its jacket, as recalled by Brian Aldiss in his introduction to the new Penguin *TWOTW* edition p. xviii.

[48] *TWOTW*'s anti-imperial satire is far from isolated in Wells's oeuvre. Arguably it was a pervasive subtext of his early fiction. It featured in the 'degenerative', posthuman ironies of *The Time Machine* (a notable influence on Conrad's *Heart of Darkness* (1902)) and as vivisective parody of civilising mission, *The Island of Doctor Moreau* (1896), itself invoking a whole tradition of imperial romance from *The Tempest* to *Gulliver's Travels*, Kipling's *Jungle Book*, etc. The theme returned in Wells's second extra-terrestrial novel, as China Miéville's recent interpretation emphasises (see his introduction to H. G. Wells, *The First Men in the Moon* (1901) (London: Penguin, 2005), pp. xiii-xxvii (pp. xx-xxiv)). Through its adventurist and self-justifying anti-hero, Bedford, and his philistine disregard for the indigenous Selenites and their sophisticated culture, Wells parodies ripping yarns like Rider Haggard's. Bedford effectively transforms Cavor's scientific mission into an intoxicated rampage of goldlust. Claiming the right of conquest for the Crown, he quotes Kipling's 'The White Man's Burden' (published in the *Times*, 1 Feb.1899); conversely, Wells drops frequent topical references to British colonialism's challenging during the Boer War. See for example Wells, *First Men in the Moon*, p. 78; the heavy defeat of the British at Colenso, Natal, is also mentioned specifically on p. 199. It is also possible Wells parodied a recent text in which the 'Luna Company, Ltd.' opens 'a new field [...] for British enterprise', by exploiting mineral rights on the moon, because the globe has already been carved up by the

Great Powers. See André Laurie, *The Conquest of the Moon* (London: Sampson, Low, Marston, Searle and Rivington, 1889), pp. 61-2.

[49] According to a 1920 interview, *TWOTW* germinated from a discussion about Tasmania on a stroll through rural Surrey. Wells's brother remarked 'Suppose some beings from another planet were to drop out of the sky suddenly [...] and begin laying about them here!' The first edition is consequently dedicated 'To [...] Frank Wells, this rendering of his idea.' H. G. Wells, abridged *War of the Worlds*, with illustrations by Johan Briedé, *Strand Magazine*, February 1920, pp. 154-63 (p154). Wells referred to the shameful episode again in *The Outline of History*, 2 vols (London: George Newnes, 1920), I, 521.

[50] Peter Fitting, 'Estranged Invaders: *The War of the Worlds*', in *Learning from Other Worlds*, ed. by Patrick Parrinder (Liverpool: Liverpool University Press, 2000), pp. 127-45 (p. 137).

[51] H. G. Wells, *Text-Book of Biology*, 8 vols (London: W.B. Clive/University Correspondence College Press, 1892-93), I, 131. Wells recalled that *'The War of the Worlds* like *The Time Machine*', with its dinner-party cross-section of smug late-Victorian professionals, 'was another assault on human self-satisfaction'. Preface to *The Scientific Romances of H. G. Wells* (London: Gollancz, 1933), p.ix.

[52] For Wells's reviews of Haggard, see *H. G. Wells's Literary Criticism*, ed. by Patrick Parrinder and Robert M. Philmus (Brighton: Harvester; Totowa, N.J: Barnes and Noble, 1980), especially pp. 55-7 and 98; also Herbert L. Sussman, *The Victorians and the Machine* (Cambridge, MA: Harvard University Press, 1968), p. 183

[53] Adam Roberts, *Science Fiction* (London and New York: Routledge, 2000), pp. 63-4. Ironically, those very colonialist attitudes, rendered some early reviewers blind to *TWOTW*'s 'deeper concerns', even when they applauded the dramatic power of its Home Counties setting. John St. Loe Strachey argued that 'A Martian dropped into the centre of Africa would be comparatively endurable,' because 'One feels that they are all mad and bad and awful there, or, if not, it is of no great matter.' 'Review of *The War of the Worlds*, *Spectator*, 80 (29 Jan. 1898), 168-9.

[54] Hedgecock, 'Martians Are Coming', pp. 106-08.

[55] Wells's 1893 essay, 'The Man of the Year Million', explains the stages of 'Martianisation':

'Clearly, then, man [...] will undergo further modification in the future, and at last cease to be man, giving rise to some other type of animated being.' '[W]it and machinery' will gradually replace shrinking bodily capacities and organs; conversely, brains and manipulative organs will enlarge. ('The Man of the Year Million', *Pall Mall Gazette*, 6 November 1893, p.3; repr. in H. G. Wells *Journalism and Prophecy*, ed. by W. Warren Wagar (London: Bodley Head, 1965), pp. 3-8 (p. 4). The face of Wells's medium future is already halfway to being extra-terrestrial: 'Eyes, large, lustrous, beautiful, soulful; above them, no longer separated by rugged brow ridges, is the top of the head, a glistening, hairless dome, terete [smoothly rounded] and beautiful; no craggy nose rises to disturb by its unmeaning shadows the symmetry of that calm face, no vestigial ears project; the mouth is a small, perfectly round aperture, toothless and gumless, jawless, unanimal, no futile emotions disturbing its roundness as it lies, like the harvest moon or the evening star, in the wide firmament of face.' ('Man of the Year Million', p. 6.) Besides loss of emotions, other Martian characteristics, such as atrophy of the digestive tract, replace solid food with 'nutritive fluid'. The essay continues to further evolutionary stages where our descendants hop, birdlike on their hands, bodies 'shrivelled to nothing, a dangling, degraded pendant to their minds' (p. 7). However, its tone darkens as these become increasingly 'less alluring', with posthumans exterminating other species on which they no longer depend. Finally, they retreat into the fully artificial environment of underground technocities, to escape the sun's heat death, leaving a chilling prospect of a fully "rationalised" future which makes 'contemplative man' shudder (pp. 7-8).

Wells speculated about extra-terrestrial life forms as far back as his student days in 'Mr Wells on the Habitability of the Planets', *The Science Schools Journal*, 15 (November 1888), 57-8. However, in 'Intelligence on Mars' (1896), his speculations assumed a very different trajectory to *TWOTW*: 'granted that there has been an evolution of protoplasm [...] there is every reason to think that the creatures on Mars would be different from the creatures of Earth, in form and function, in structure and in habit, different beyond the most bizarre imaginings of nightmare [...] No phase of anthropomorphism is more naïve than the supposition of men on Mars.' 'Intelligence on Mars', *Saturday Review*, 80 (4 April 1896), 345-6; repr.in H. G. Wells, *Early Writings in Science and Science Fiction*, ed. by Robert Philmus and David Y. Hughes (Berkeley: University of California Press, 1975), pp. 175-8 (pp. 176-7). This reinforces the idea that the novel's aliens, despite their apparent differences, are indeed allegorical versions of ourselves.

[56] Frank McConnell, *The Science Fiction of H. G. Wells* (Oxford: Oxford University Press, 1981), p. 128.

[57] See Niall Ferguson, *The War of the World* (London: Allen Lane, 2006), especially pp. xxiii-iv.

[58] *Evolution and Ethics* (1893), in T.H. Huxley and Julian Huxley, *Evolution and Ethics 1893-1943* (London: Pilot Press, 1947), pp. 60-102 (p. 81). In his 'Prolegomena', written as an introduction, Huxley also highlighted the Tasmanian genocide as an example of ruthless intervention with superior technology and alien flora and fauna species into the pre-existing balance of another environment. See Huxley, *Evolution and Ethics*, pp. 33-60 (pp. 42-3).

[59] Some responses reflected *TWOTW*'s themes of alien vision and Otherness from unexpected angles. *The War of the Wenuses* (1898) ('Translated from the Artesian of H. G. Pozzuoli') was an astute spoof of such motifs in Wells's work so far conducted as delightfully Popeian mockery of the issue of sex roles in modernity. The Wenuses (an affectation for 'Venuses') want to conquer earth, because their home planet has also become uninhabitable. Due to rising temperatures they are unable to wear the latest fashions, or to be reciprocally admired, since the male population have all become 'Invisible Men'. The authors, staff writers on *Punch*, poked fun at the gender limitations of scientific romance, but also picked up Wells's foregrounding of the power of the gaze, metaphorically condensing a heat-raylike effect with the viewpoint of the Other. The invaders emerge from their pink

spacecraft to turn male Earthlings to quivering jelly: 'a row of Wenuses with closed lids stood before the Crinoline. Suddenly they opened their eyes and flashed them on the men before them. The effect was instantaneous. The deputation, as the ray touched them, fell like skittles – viscous, protoplasmic masses, victims of the terrible Mash-Glance of the Wenuses.' Charles L. Graves and Edward V. Lucas, *The War of the Wenuses* (1898); repr. in *Sources of Science Fiction*, ed. by George Locke (London: Routledge/Thoemmes Press, 1998), p. 42.

[60] The serial appeared between April and December 1897, although Wells had been planning the novel since 1895 and his agent had seen the outline by January 1896. See *A Critical Edition of The War of the Worlds*, ed. by David Y. Hughes and Harry M. Geduld (Bloomington, Indianapolis: Indiana University Press, 1993), pp. 1-2. Although Lasswitz's novel sold in vast numbers, inspiring a generation of rocket scientists (notably Hermann Oberth, Willi Ley and Wernher von Braun) and was translated into many languages by the 1900s, the first English version was not published until 1971. Influence on Anglophone SF during Wells's lifetime is therefore largely speculative. See Mark R. Hillegas's 'Afterword' to Kurd Lasswitz, *Two Planets* (*Auf Zwei Planeten*, 1897), abridged by Erich Lasswitz and trans. by Hans. H. Rudnick (Carbondale and Edwardsville: Southern Illinois University Press; London and Amsterdam: Feffer and Simons, 1971), pp.397-405 (p.397); also Brian Aldiss, with David Wingrove, *Trillion Year Spree* (Thirsk and Poughkeepsie: House of Stratus, 2001), pp. 144-6.

[61] Guthke, *Imagining Other Worlds*, pp. 368-9.

[62] Patricia Kerslake, 'Moments of Empire: Perceptions of Kurt[sic] Lasswitz and H. G. Wells', *Wellsian*, n.s. 25 (2002), 25-38 (pp. 25-6).

[63] See Lasswitz, *Two Planets*, p.105.

[64] Kerslake, 'Moments of Empire', 26.

[65] See Antonio Gramsci, *Selections from the Prison Notebooks*, ed. and trans. by Quintin Hoare and Geoffrey Nowell Smith (London: Lawrence and Wishart, 1971), pp.12-13 and 57-60.

[66] See 'The Battle of Portsmouth', in Lasswitz, *Two Planets*, pp. 256-62.

[67] Lasswitz, *Two Planets*, pp. 361-3. Inter-species imperial contact also unwittingly revives the Martians' latent ancestral disease, 'gragra', for which, like Native Americans and smallpox, colonised humans have no natural immunity (pp. 294-5).

[68] The extremist 'Anti-Bati' party secretly draw up what is, effectively, a totalitarian 'final solution' to the earthling problem, which also anticipates Fotheringay's cataclysmic blunder in Wells's story 'The Man Who Could Work Miracles' (1898): complete extermination by arresting the earth's rotation and altering its climate (see Lasswitz, *Two Planets*, p. 389).

[69] See Lasswitz, *Two Planets*, p. 92.

[70] Lasswitz, *Two Planets*, pp.191, 214-15 and 216-19.

[71] Lasswitz, *Two Planets*, pp. 197-99

[72] See Edward James, 'Science Fiction by Gaslight', in *Anticipations*, ed. by Seed, pp. 26-45 (p. 43).

[73] Robert W. Cole, *The Struggle for Empire* (1900), in *Sources of Science Fiction*, ed. by Locke, p. 34.

[74] Cole reverted to terrestrial jingoism in *The Death Trap* (1907), another future war novel about German invasion and imperial wake-up call explicitly in the *Battle of Dorking* tradition.

[75] They included one in the William Randolph Hearst owned *Evening Journal* itself (15 December 1897-11 January 1898), possibly by editor, Arthur Brisbane, who commissioned Serviss. For details of pirate serialisations and Wells's protests about copyright infringements, see *A Critical Edition of The War of the Worlds*, ed. by Hughes and Geduld, Appendix II, '*The War of the Worlds* in the Yellow Press', pp. 281-89.

[76] Garret P. Serviss, *Edison's Conquest of Mars* (1898), in *Sources of Science Fiction*, ed. by Locke, p. 1. Rice Burroughs's first Red Planet potboiler, *Under the Moons of Mars*, was serialised in 1912. The *Flash Gordon* film serial began in 1936, adapted from Alex Raymond's comic strip. For further discussion of the genre's origins, see Gary Westfahl, 'Space Opera', in *The Cambridge Companion to Science Fiction*, ed. by Edward James and Farah Mendlesohn (Cambridge: Cambridge University Press, 2003), pp. 197-208 (p. 198).

[77] Serviss, *Edison's Conquest*, p. 12. It's tempting to think Serviss may have also have been rewriting Lasswitz. In *Two Planets*, 'the almighty dollar', coupled with American know-how and audacity, creates the fleet of carbon-copy airships by which the Martians are eventually defeated in a surprise rebellion (p. 381). However, this does not result in future American hegemony on Earth.

[78] Serviss, *Edison's Conquest*, p. 54. This anticipates *Independence Day*'s scene when American scientists find it impossible to reason with the implacable aggression of a captured alien.

[79] Serviss, *Edison's Conquest*, p. 64.

[80] Serviss, *Edison's Conquest*, p. 103.

[81] See Serviss, *Edison's Conquest*, p. 111.

[82] Serviss, *Edison's Conquest*, p. 160. Although Edison originally gave his blessing, he denounced the serial's crudity when it appeared. See Paul Israel, *Edison* (New York: John Wiley, 1998), p. 369. Perhaps regretting his chauvinistic sensationalism, Serviss returned to the subject of 'Mars, A World More Advanced than Ours' in more scientifically-informed vein in his *Other Worlds* (New York and London: Appleton, 1901), pp. 85-128.

[83] See Chapter 11, 'Partial Derivatives: Popular Misinterpretations of H. G. Wells's *The Time Machine*', in Gary Westfahl, *Science Fiction, Children's Literature and Popular Culture* (Westport, CN, and London: Greenwood Press, 2000), pp. 129-41.

PART II:

FROM ROMANCER TO NOVELIST

LOVE AND MR LEWISHAM:
FOUNDATIONS AND SOURCES
FOR A FIRST SOCIAL NOVEL

BERNARD LOING

When Wells began to work on *Love and Mr Lewisham* in July or August 1896, he was not only beginning to write another story; he was also deliberately opening a new period in his literary career. However, contrarily to a common hypothesis,[1] we cannot be sure that he had made up his mind from the start and decided, from the very first lines, to make of *Lewisham* the first great social novel of his career. And his decision to stop being 'a second Jules Verne' or 'a sort of literary page in the train of Caine, Zangwill and so forth',[2] and attempt to establish himself as a mainstream novelist probably took shape gradually during the writing of the novel. His first recorded allusion to it, in a letter to the publisher Dent, was indeed rather modest: 'a sentimental humorous story in hand. Title (in confidence) is Love & Mr. Lewisham. Expect 80 000'.[3]

The estimated length of 80, 000 words – more than double that of *The Time Machine*, and much longer than *The War of the Worlds*[4] – certainly shows that he intended to write a more extensive work than any of his others before. But at first he rather envisaged writing a light and mostly humorous comedy, in the vein of *The Wheels of Chance* (1896), or of Henri Murger's *Scènes de la Vie de Bohème* (1843) as he explained to J. B. Pinker in a note of presentation which is worth quoting at length:

> Love & Mr Lewisham is a humorous novel (darkening at times into absolute seriousness) having for its main theme the struggle between the natural impulse towards love & the worldly ambitions of a class & with educated youngsters of the lower middle class. The opening 12.000 words is idyllic & tells of a naïve love affair of the youngster at seventeen. The rest of the story lies in London & chiefly among the poor students at South Kensington, typewriters, struggling artists, coaches for exams & the like, a world largely unworked by novelists, of considerable humorous possibility & resembling in its poverty & high spirits, if not its easy morals, the Bohemia of Murger. The girl of the opening idyll, having become quite

lost to Mr. Lewisham, reappears startlingly as an accomplice in his attempt to expose a fraud medium at a spiritualistic seance & alters the direction of his whole life. This fraud medium is her father in law. To save her from her father in law Mr. Lewisham subsequently elopes with her & the fun & entertainment of the impecunious married life of these young people in London apartments is described in a vein entirely optimistic. Mr. Wells has not merely studied this [missing word, possibly aspect] of life he will describe in his novel – he has lived it. Of his previous work it will most resemble The Wheels of Chance, but it will be altogether a larger and more crowded work. The full length will be nearly 80. 000 words. The First Book is written. The rest is drafted & being written. The whole novel will be shaped & sufficiently written to give a clear conception of the whole by Christmas 1896. The novel can certainly be completed by April 1897 – if not before.[5]

We know that the finished work – which he completed more than two years later than the date announced here and after a long and difficult period of writing – is in many respects quite different from this initial description. Far from being only a light comedy, *Lewisham* appears as a serious novel, in which humour has a rather limited place. Thus an evolution took place as he was writing, leading the writer into new directions which he had not fully anticipated. As the novel was taking shape, and especially as he was writing the Second Part – 'Lewisham at South Kensington' – much more intricate with its numerous characters and elaborate urban scenery, Wells began to realise the novelty and the difficulty of his task, and probably felt the need of a period of apprenticeship. Such a feeling of uncertainty can be detected in a letter of November 1896 to his friend Elizabeth Healey where he first mentions to her his new endeavour:

I'm very glad indeed you liked the S.K. story.[6] Even now I'm engaged on the same (or similar) stuff. But this time it is to be an ample novel, and the museum and the schools and the streets, Clapham and Chelsea and so forth, are all to come in. Heaven knows when it will get done, for writing fantastic romance is one thing, and writing a novel is quite another.[7]

The decision to become a 'serious' writer and the sustained effort devoted to the writing of this first novel over a period of more than three years, now well-known and documented in Wellsian research, shows indeed that when published, *Lewisham* could be considered as an 'initial' work in the production of Wells, somehow as initial and new as *The Time Machine* had been five years before. This position as a new gateway to Wells's literary career does not mean that *Lewisham* is devoid of foundations and sources; on the contrary, it makes it all the more interesting to have a closer look at them.

Among the foundations, the most obvious one, which did not exist at the time of his very first attempts at scientific romancing, is Wells's new proficiency in literary criticism. When he began writing *Lewisham* in 1896, Wells had been engaged for more than a year as a literary critic for the *Saturday Review*, thus exploring from the outside the mechanisms of literary creation, and gathering elements for his own theory of literature. The extent of Wells's literary criticism and its influence on his work has been extensively presented and analysed by Patrick Parrinder and Robert Philmus among others,[8] and it is not our purpose here to add further comment on this issue – except perhaps to remark that Wells had claimed long before a vocation for literary criticism, 'hankering' – according to his own words, after a more intellectual approach to literature.[9]

We shall rather explore the sources of *Lewisham* here. They illustrate the deep originality of the work for they appear to be, with very few exceptions,[10] entirely drawn from Wells's own writings and experience. Apart from autobiography and personal experience, the complex ritual of marriage, with its social and psychological codification, was a subject that Wells had always wanted to grapple with. Long before engaging in a literary career, and even before he himself got married, shortly after leaving South Kensington, he was confiding this to Elizabeth Healey: 'The code of rules whereby two young people have to meet each other, go through all sorts of ceremonial and finally pass under the yoke, which exists in that effete state of humanity, is one of the most ghastly difficulties that the ambitious writer of stories has to encounter'.[11]

Published twelve years later, *Love and Mr Lewisham* was the first answer of some scope to the literary challenge he had set for himself at that time. Other disquisitions on the same subject were to follow repeatedly, marriage becoming a prevalent theme in Wells's work for many years. Yet even before *Lewisham*, Wells had tried to deal with the process of marriage and the hazardous life of a married couple in its various stages, generally in a facetious mode, in several articles and particularly in his numerous contributions to the *Pall Mall Gazette*, thus building up a hoard of material to be re-used later.[12] One can also find the preliminary sketches of some situations or some characters of *Lewisham* in a few short stories: for instance, the final parting scene between the young man and Miss Heydinger seems directly inspired from a similar situation in 'In the Modern Vein'; [13] the character of Bingham in 'Mr Ledbetter's Vacation' shares some features with Chaffery, and the theme of spiritualism – not uncommon in those last years of the century – appears in

'The Stolen Body'.[14] Yet the analogy between those various stories and the text of the novel is never very close and remains rather limited in scope.

In his note to Pinker cited above, Wells mentioned similarities, even a sort of relationship between *Lewisham* and *The Wheels of Chance*. Yet in the end, there is a great difference between the light, humorous tone of the latter, and the more serious outlook of the former. For Jean-Pierre Vernier: '*The Wheels of Chance* exuded a great impression of liberty and joie de vivre, whereas *Love & Mr Lewisham* was going to reveal the price of that liberty.'[15] Indeed, one cannot find in it that prevalent atmosphere of joy and sprightliness that Wells had meant to create. When the book came out, some critics even found it rather gloomy. Having noticed the connection with the story of Hoopdriver, *The Daily Telegraph* added, not unfavourably: 'In *Love and Mr Lewisham*, however, he strikes a deeper note than heretofore, and though the book begins very brightly, it ends in a minor key'.[16] The anonymous critic of the *Saturday Review* (16 June 1900), by contrast, in an overdone and rather unfair condemnation, declared: 'a more morbid, sordid, hopelessly dull and depressing dissection of characters it were difficult to conceive. We wallow in gloom from cover to cover amid a succession of dreary episodes'.[17]

In fact the humorous tone of *The Wheels of Chance* can be felt again in the first part of the novel, where he often mocks his hero with a wink of ironical complicity at the reader, much in the manner of Sterne in *Tristram Shandy* (1759), and even more in *A Sentimental Journey* (1768), which Wells admired so much. There is indeed a similarity in the situations of Lewisham and Hoopdriver when developing from adolescence to adulthood during their respective life stories. But there is no future, even slightly outlined, for Hoopdriver whereas the story of Lewisham is treated as the first serious step of a young man into real life. In fact the true successor to Hoopdriver would be Kipps, whose transition to manhood was to be told all along in a sustained tone of light comedy. So even if one can find similarities between *Lewisham* and *The Wheels of Chance*, it is difficult to speak of a real affiliation.

Such is not the case for two short stories, written shortly before *Lewisham*, which can be considered as direct sources, even as early drafts of the novel. One of them, 'A Slip under the Microscope', already mentioned above, is a well-known source for the novel, as Wells himself had pointed out to Elizabeth Healey in a letter quoted above. Like the second part of the novel, the story takes place in the Normal School of Science at South Kensington, and Wells will largely draw upon the same sceneries, characters and situations when writing the novel: the

amphitheatres and laboratories, the Debating Society where Hill, the hero
of the story, brilliantly develops and defends the same unorthodox views
as Lewisham will later, the discussions among students about socialism,
religion and the future of mankind, the 'Gallery of Old Iron' where Hill
meets Miss Haysman, a wealthier and older girl student who admires him
and lends him volumes of poetry, the academic rivalries among students,
both texts obviously draw upon the common source of autobiography.

The other story, entitled 'How Gabriel became Thompson', was
published anonymously in *Truth* – 26 July 1894 – under the heading
'Queer Story'. The identification of this text was a lucky strike of the
researcher.[18] On examining *The Time Machine* manuscripts at the Wells
Archive of the University of Illinois, I discovered, scribbled at the back of
one of the sheets, a list of short stories by Wells including this one,
followed by the name of the magazine in which it was published. All the
other titles were well-known and had been published in 1894, which made
it easy to trace this one and make sure of its authenticity. As I read it for
the first time, with some excitement as can be imagined, it appeared that
this newly discovered text had nothing to do with the scientific romance,
but that it was a real blueprint for the future *Lewisham*. In this humorous
narrative of some 3,400 words, the writer's purpose, as stated in the
introduction, is to illustrate one figure of the post-matrimonial taxonomy
which, according to him, is composed of nine possible situations. [19] The
one chosen here shows how an idealistic young man sheds his glorious
dreams and high ambitions in 'a story of compromise, of the clipping and
shedding of the archangelic pinions by which he soared' (209). Even if
such a metaphor – as well as the hero's first name – may remind us of the
angel in *The Wonderful Visit* (1895), the story is built on a series of
situations which one can find again practically unaltered in *Love and Mr
Lewisham*.

Gabriel and the narrator are two students impatient to change the ways
of the world and posturing as great apostles of Human Reformation, the
former as Luther, the latter as Erasmus. But the new Luther has fallen in
love. He speaks in passionate terms of the girl he loves – using the same
words as Parkson will in Chapter XVIII of *Lewisham*, 'The Friends of
Progress Meet' – and will soon forget his idealistic engagements. He finds
her intelligent but rather uneducated and lends her books – Lewisham will
choose the same authors – Ruskin, Carlyle, Wordsworth, Browning, to
improve her mind. Gabriel also receives the addresses of a Miss Gowland,
an idealistic girl who keeps with him the same platonic relation as that of
Miss Heydinger with Lewisham, remaining 'his armour bearer in that fight
for the righting of the world which his soul craved for' (209). Then

Gabriel marries the girl he loves, a sort of middle-class Ethel, who considers his Socialism as a child's disease, 'a kind of intellectual measles', who thinks she will help him in his work – 'he is going to do all kinds of scientific researches, and I shall help him copy his things out and put his experiments out for him and all that' (209) – and who intends to straighten him up – 'you must see Gabriel after I have polished him for a year' (210) – as she proudly says to her best friend and confidante.

Soon after the wedding Gabriel realises that his wife does not share at all his ideas and high interests and that she has not even opened the copy of John Ruskin's *Sesame and Lilies* (1864) he had offered her.[20] Becoming very angry, he quarrels violently with her and goes to his friend the narrator to tell of his disappointment: 'He had imagined that his marriage was to be an idyllic episode, from which he was to return presently to his dream of a new Reformation – Gabriel well to the fore, wife inspiring, helpful and advisatory. He felt himself cut from all this at once' (210).

He thus decides to part from his wife whom he finds vain and superficial: 'Why should the error of three months dwarf and ruin a life?' (210) Returning home however, he finds her sick in bed, complaining of his cruel behaviour. Confronted with her insidious strategy of victimisation, he relents and repents, reconciles with her, and tamed by a spouse in a perpetual state of precarious health, he finally gives up his ambition of reforming the world. He will not pursue a brilliant scientific career, but settling down as little Mr Thompson in a suburban area, he will nevertheless become a minor inventor.

This brief summary of 'How Gabriel Became Thompson' is enough to show that the short story is constructed along the same series of episodes as the novel. In *Love and Mr Lewisham* the hero, an idealistic and ambitious young man, is also a science student who imagines himself as 'the Luther of Socialism' (chapter XI). He is pursued by the devotion of a sister soul Miss Heydinger, but he loves another girl. He courts and marries her, only to discover subsequently that she is vain and superficial, unable to understand his ambitions and share his ideals. After a violent quarrel, he threatens to leave her; then touched by her frailty and sorrow he becomes reconciled with her. But by accepting his matrimonial situation, he has to give up his ideals forever as well as his professional ambitions. If we add the similarities in literary references and narrative technique,[21] the two stories appear as practically identical, the latter being, on the whole, a development of the former.

By exposing in its stark nakedness the common skeleton of both stories, one is able to stress some of the essential qualities of the novel, conspicuously absent in the short story. The first and essential quality is obviously the sense of perspective and the narrative technique which enables the young author to manage the logical structure and sustain the reader's interest in a work of fiction twenty times longer than its first sketch. Such an achievement was not obvious if we consider the extended and often broken up period of writing. During that overall founding period of four years – 1894 to 1898 – Wells was to learn how to handle considerable amounts of fiction, especially during the simultaneous writing of such long works as *Love and Mr Lewisham* and *When the Sleeper Wakes* (published in 1899).

A second quality lies in the introduction of social considerations into the novel which makes it much richer and more authentic than the short story. For several critics the social element is even the major interest of the novel. Whereas the characters in 'Gabriel' belong exclusively to a stereotyped bourgeois background, the lower social status and difficult financial situation of Lewisham provide that story of 'dislocation and adjustment' with its real substance. [22] In fact since we are examining sources, this social dimension rather came from the other short story, 'A Slip under the Microscope' in which Hill the hero, even more than Lewisham, was the victim of social pressure and iniquity.

The third quality that cannot be found in 'Gabriel' – or in any other 'preparatory' text leading to *Lewisham* – is the ability to express the tenderness that can lighten up the drabness of everyday life. Irony is the prevailing mood of the first chapters, and then tenderness gradually finds its expression in the novel as a bonus added to the coming maturity of the hero and his discovery of real life. Ingvald Raknem had noted, rather too severely, that it was an infrequent feature in Wells's work: 'It is manifest, we think, that Wells lacked Dickens's blend of anger and tenderness. Actually, he very seldom displayed any tenderness, and the lack of this *does* detract much from his writings. Indeed the lack of tenderness makes him inferior to any *great* novelist'.[23] But he did stress the fact that, in spite of the lukewarm welcome of the early critics, that quality of infinite tenderness for everyday life had been acclaimed.[24]

Original as it is, *Lewisham* is not a meteorite fallen from nowhere, and in his self-initiation to the 'literary' novel, Wells modestly finds his way into the rich European tradition of the 'Bildungsroman',[25] where one can find some of the greatest works of the nineteenth century like *David Copperfield* (1850) and *L'Education Sentimentale* (1869). Like most of the great Victorian novelists, Wells reveals himself as a moralist, a 'social' moralist like Thackeray, an intimist and secular moralist like George Eliot, and a 'sentimental' moralist like Dickens. He joins the fight against social and religious hypocrisy by denouncing together the clergy and the school system, [26] just as Samuel Butler will jointly denounce, a few years later, the clergy and the family. After Thomas Hardy and George Meredith, he joins the line of the marriage novelists. Following Dickens in *Great Expectations* (1861), he explores the themes of illusion versus reality, and of self-discovery. Not to mention the more commonplace issue of feminine treachery with the numerous mythical examples where a woman, either vain or powerful, thwarts the great and generous vocation of her mate. In the wake of *Jude the Obscure* which he so much admired,[27] Wells also writes, with *Lewisham*, a 'comedy of unfulfilled aims'.[28]

This range of references is not intended to suggest that all those works are in any way sources for *Lewisham*, or even that they have had a direct influence on its composition and writing. They have just been gathered to show that with this novel, new for him but mostly traditional in its general approach, Wells the heirless author, was showing his credentials to enter an illustrious family where he intended to stay and become a legitimate member.

Notes

[1] Gordon Ray, for instance, writes that: 'Late in 1896 Wells set to work on his first novel along the lines that he had laid down for himself in his Saturday reviewing […] *Love & Mr Lewisham* was to be the real thing'. Gordon N. Ray, 'H. G. Wells Tries to be a Novelist', in *Edwardians and Late Victorians*, ed. by Richard Ellmann (New York: Columbia University Press, 1960), pp. 106-229 (p. 122).

[2] Letter to Heinemann, 8 July 1898, in Bernard Loing, *H. G. Wells à l'Oeuvre (1894-1900)* (Paris: Didier Erudition, 1984), pp. 438-9 (p. 439), letter 63.

[3] 12 September 1896, draft by Catherine Wells at the Wells Archive University of Illinois. Quoted in Bernard Loing, *H.G.Wells à l'Oeuvre (1894-1900)*, pp. 431-2 (p. 432), letter 51.

[4] Totalling around 60,000 words, *The War of the Worlds* was serialised in *Pearson's Magazine* from April to December 1897 and published in book form in January 1898.

[5] From the Wells Archive at the University of Illinois (probably October 1896). Quoted in Bernard Loing, *H.G.Wells à L'Oeuvre (1894-1900)*, pp. 432-3, Letter 53.

[6] A 'Slip under the Microscope' published in *The Yellow Book*, 8 January 1896, then republished in *The Plattner Story and Others* (1897).

[7] Cited in Geoffrey West, *H.G. Wells: A Sketch For a Portrait* (London: Gerald Howe, 1930), p. 119.

[8] *H. G. Wells's Literary Criticism*, ed. by Patrick Parrinder and Robert Philmus (Brighton: The Harvester Press, 1980).

[9] He concluded his long letter to his friend A. M. Davies, written in November 1887 after the accident at Holt when one of his kidneys had been badly damaged: 'My only chance now for a living is literature. I have done sundry things since I left Denbighshire but up to the present I have had little success. I think the groove I shall drop into will be cheap noveletteering – not with my entire approval though; I hanker after essays and criticism – vainly'. Quoted in Bernard Loing, *H. G .Wells à l'Oeuvre (1894-1900)*, p. 404, letter 1.

[10] For instance the spiritualistic episodes organised around the character of Chaffery, which may be derived from *Among the Prophets*, an unpublished novel by George Gissing. For an interesting commentary on this possible source, see Simon J. James, 'The Truth about Gissing', *The Wellsian*, n.s. 24 (2001), 2-21.

[11] 19 June 1888, quoted by Geoffrey West in *H.G.Wells: A Sketch for a Portrait*, p. 110.

[12] With reference to *Lewisham*, one can mention among others the following articles, published in 1894 and early 1895 in *The Pall Mall Gazette*: 'Concerning Lodging-house keepers' (12 February), 'The Joys of being engaged' (16 April), 'The Great Change, a Meditation upon Marriage' (2 June), 'The Trouble of Life' (2 August), 'The Pleasure of Quarrelling' (9 August), 'House-hunting as an Outdoor Amusement' (24 September), 'In the Library, Some Reflections on a Married Couple' (4 December), 'On the Choice of a Wife'(16 January 1895).

[13] First published as 'A Bardlett Romance', *Truth*, 8 March 1894, pp. 555-8.

[14] Those two stories were written at the same time as *Lewisham* and first published in *The Strand Magazine*: 'Mr Ledbetter's Vacation' in October 1898 and 'The Stolen Body' in November 1898.

[15] Jean-Pierre Vernier, *H.G.Wells et son Temps* (Rouen : Publications de l'Université de Rouen, 1971), p. 148.

[16] Unsigned Review, *Daily Telegraph* (6 June 1900), in *H.G.Wells: The Critical Heritage*, ed. by Patrick Parrinder (London: Routledge & Kegan Paul, 1972), p. 80.

[17] Unsigned Review, *Saturday Review* (16 June 1900), in *H.G.Wells: The Critical Heritage*, p. 82.

[18] Already mentioned by Bernard Loing, 'H. G. Wells at Work (1894-1900)', *The Wellsian*, n.s. 9 (1986), 23-26, with a short analysis of the manuscripts of *Love and Mr Lewisham*.

[19] 'After the pact matrimonial there are nine possible events. All post-matrimonial stories belong to one or other of these nine classes indicated by these possibilities; the characters, the accessories, may vary infinitely, but the tale is always to be classified under one of these heads. For each party to the marriage says one of these things. First: 'It is not as I expected, but it will do very well' (contentment). Secondly: 'It is not as I expected, but we must manage' (compromise). Or lastly: 'It is not as I expected, and I will not endure it' (catastrophe). The permutations of these three formulae taken two at a time are nine, forming the diapason of marriage.' 'How Gabriel Became Thomson', *Truth*, 26 July 1894, pp. 208-211 (p. 208). Subsequent references will be cited in parenthesis in the text.

[20] Ruskin's book is subject to the sarcastic comments of Lewisham and the narrator in chapter XVII of the novel.

[21] This remark refers to the manipulation of points of view. Like the short story, the novel in the early stages of its writing included an elaborate balance of points of views. For instance the manuscript of *Lewisham* included a chapter XXVII entitled 'Ethel', discarded later, and in which Lewisham's wife expressed her views and opinions.

[22] H. G. Wells, *Experiment in Autobiography*, 2 Vols (London: Gollancz, 1934), II, p. 488.

[23] Ingvald Raknem, *H.G.Wells and His Critics* (Oslo: George Allen & Unwin, 1962), p. 294.

[24] Also particularly mentioned by Patrick Parrinder in *H.G.Wells The Critical Heritage*, p. 78.

[25] Especially when he proclaims it (on the first page of the manuscript) 'The Story of an Adolescence' in a subtitle later discarded and replaced by 'The Story of a Very Young Couple'.

[26] Like Dickens in *Martin Chuzzlewit* (1844), George Eliot in *Middlemarch* (1871-72), S. Butler in *Erewhon* (1871) and in *The Way of All Flesh*, posthumously published two years after *Lewisham* but written twenty years before, W. Hale White in *Mark Rutherford* (1881), and later Edmund Gosse in *Father and Son* (1907). But Wells's exposure of hypocrisy is even more explicit and strong in the early drafts of the novel (Chapter XXV 'The Fighting Continues', later discarded).

[27] Wells's review of *Jude* was published in the *Saturday Review*, 81 (8 February 1896), 153-4. For Ingvald Raknem, Hardy's novel had a significant influence on *Lewisham*. See *H.G.Wells and his Critics*, pp. 303-4.

[28] In his preface to *Jude*, Hardy declared that his novel meant to be 'the tragedy of unfulfilled aims'.

WELLS AND THE DISCUSSION NOVEL

JOHN R. HAMMOND

> I suppose for a time I was the outstanding instance among writers of fiction
> in English of the frame getting into the picture [...] The important point
> which I tried to argue with Henry James was that the novel of completely
> consistent characterization arranged beautifully in a story and painted deep
> and round and solid, no more exhausts the possibilities of the novel, than
> the art of Velazquez exhausts the possibilities of the painted picture.
> —H. G. Wells, *Experiment in Autobiography* (1934).[1]

1

From the time of the First World War onwards, Wells began to experiment
more and more openly with the possibilities of the novel. Dissatisfied with
the rigid parameters of the novel as defined by Henry James, he widened
the scope of his fiction to permit a greater diversity of narrative technique.
Boon (1915), for example, is a conversational novel in which a group of
people engage in a series of dialogues on the nature and purpose of
literature. The form of the work is modelled on W. H. Mallock's *The New
Republic* (1877) and achieves a hybrid between a classical dialogue (such
as Plato's *Republic*) and a novel of ideas such as Wells's own *Ann
Veronica* (1909). Since Boon, the central character, is challenged by a
series of interlocutors who disagree with his views, he is continually
obliged to clarify and restate his opinions. The result is a work of unusual
intimacy, as if Wells is thinking aloud or conducting a debate with
himself. For this reason, *Boon* is an extremely interesting guide to Wells's
thinking in the early years of the twentieth century.

 The Undying Fire (1919) is a modernised version of the Book of Job in
which a group of people conduct a debate on human behaviour, a debate
fluctuating between a wholly pessimistic view of the future and a more
hopeful one. Again, there is an effect of looking into a room and
eavesdropping on a philosophical discussion. *Men Like Gods* (1923) is
essentially a speculation in which an imaginary future society is contrasted

with the present. In each of these novels, Wells is experimenting with methods of presentation and points of view.

During the final three decades of his life he produced some twenty novels, many of which have not stood the test of time. He was well aware of his tendency to write too much: 'I have to overwork, with all the penalties of overworking in loss of grace and finish, to get my work done'.[2] In such an immense body of work it would be too much to expect that all his fiction would be of the same standard. Some of his later novels, for example *The Secret Places of the Heart* (1922), *The Autocracy of Mr Parham* (1930) and *The Holy Terror* (1939) are decidedly inferior and need not detain us here. They bear the hallmarks of being hastily written and lack the literary and imaginative qualities of his finest work.

During this period he also wrote a lengthy, highly ambitious novel, *Joan and Peter* (1918) in which he tried to render 'some whole phase or aspect in the experience of a community'.[3] Despite Wells's high opinion of the novel and that fact that its heroine, Joan Debenham, is one of his most vital and convincing female characters, it has not found favour with the reading public. What could have been a novel worthy to stand comparison with *Tono-Bungay* (1909) or *The New Machiavelli* (1911) is marred by a tendency to *talk at* the reader, to pontificate on the war, on education, and a host of other topics. The high aspiration of Wells's overall design is obscured by these digressions which many readers would regard as a distraction from the main thread of the story. It remains a promising but flawed experiment.

Much of the fiction of Wells's later period is of considerable interest, however. This chapter focuses on five of Wells's later novels: *The Dream* (1924), *The Bulpington of Blup* (1932), *Brynhild* (1937), *Apropos of Dolores* (1938) and *You Can't Be Too Careful* (1941). My purpose is to illustrate how Wells was far more experimental than he is traditionally given credit for.

2

On its publication in 1924 *The Dream* was well received, selling 15,000 copies within a month, and one reviewer hailed it as 'the richest and most generous thing that Mr Wells has given us for years and years and years'.[4] Despite this initial reaction, the novel is today almost unknown and – along with *Joan and Peter* and other later works – seems destined to fade into oblivion. This is regrettable, for *The Dream* is an interesting experiment in literary form and marks a return to the accomplished narrative style of *Tono-Bungay* and *The New Machiavelli*. It is cast in the form of the autobiography of a typical twentieth-century man viewed from the standpoint of two thousand years hence. Sarnac, a citizen of the future, experiences a vivid dream in which he imagines himself to be a character named Harry Mortimer Smith and, on waking, relates the dream to his companions. The substance of the novel is the story told by Sarnac, which describes the life, adventures and death of Harry Mortimer Smith spanning the years 1895-1920.

Wells was clearly in an intensely autobiographical mood at the time of writing, for *The Dream* contains reminiscences of his mother and father, his childhood home at Bromley, his apprenticeship at a chemist's shop, and his Uncle Williams, who is memorable fictionalised as 'Uncle John Julip'. The description of the deaths of his father and mother (Chapter Four, Section 1, and Chapter Five, Section 11 respectively) are sensitive pieces of writing and cannot be far from a direct account of his own reaction to the deaths of Joseph and Sarah Wells. Joseph had died in 1910 and Sarah in 1905; Wells was deeply affected by both events and had obviously reflected upon them extensively in the intervening years. In *The Dream* there are carefully written portraits of both his parents and of the home background of his early years. Especially memorable is the picture of the underground room at Atlas House in which he had spent so many years of his childhood:

> [...] the little fire-place with the kettle on a hob, the kettle-holder and the toasting fork beside the fire place jamb, the steel fender, the ashes, the small blotched looking-glass over the mantel, the little china figures of dogs in front of the glass, the gaslight in a frosted glass globe hanging from the ceiling and lighting the tea-things on the table.[5]

Mingled with his feelings of sorrow for the poverty of his upbringing there is an evident nostalgia for the London of his youth (Chapter Four, Section 3) with its streets and shops, its river embankment, its ever-changing lights and atmosphere. London never lost its fascination for Wells and for the larger part of his life he regarded it as his home.

For a brief period during January 1881 Wells was apprenticed at the chemist's shop of Samuel Evan Cowap of Church Street, Midhurst. His indentures were cancelled on his own initiative when he realised that his mother could not possibly afford the fees involved, but it is clear that although the experience was brief, lasting only one month, it made a strong impression on him,[6] and figures prominently in *Tono-Bungay* as 'The Wimblehurst Apprenticeship'. Harry Mortimer Smith becomes a 'boy in general' at a chemist's shop in Pimlico,[7] and here again Wells draws on his Midhurst memories – not only describing the shop with its coloured bottles in the window and its jars with abbreviated Latin inscriptions, but also in recounting his efforts to learn Latin and the genuine appetite for education stimulated by this endeavour.

All his life Wells had been fascinated by the meteoric career of the newspaper magnate Alfred Harmsworth, later Lord Northcliffe. In sketching the life and career of Edward Ponderevo in *Tono-Bungay* he appears to have been inspired, at least in part, by Northcliffe's example and to have embodied some of his 'Napoleonic' mannerisms in the novel. He returned to this preoccupation once again in *The Dream*, and in the description of Thunderstone House, the headquarters of the publishing enterprise of Crane & Newberry, conveys vividly a picture of such organisations as Newnes, Pearson and Harmsworth as they were in the opening years of the twentieth century. Northcliffe himself, whom Wells had known for many years, is caricatured as one of the central characters, Richard Newberry. Northcliffe had died in 1922, and it may well be that with his passing Wells felt able to write about him and his enterprises in a way that would not have been possible during his lifetime.

Judged simply as a piece of storytelling *The Dream* must be regarded as Wells's finest piece of writing for more than a decade. The novel is rich in characters drawn skilfully, including not only the narrator's parents, Martha and Mortimer Smith, and also Martha's friend Matilda Good, Harry's sister Fanny, his wife Hetty Marcus, and his uncle John Julip. These are notable creations and that fact that some, at least, were drawn from Wells's experiences provides the story with verisimilitude. The novel has to carry a large (some would say excessive) amount of authorial comment but this is not unduly obtrusive. Seen in retrospect it is not difficult to understand the enthusiastic welcome *The Dream* was accorded on publication. It represents not so much a fresh departure as a return to the strong narrative line and vivid characterisation of his earlier novels and romances, and as such it deserves a high place within the conspectus of his work. At the same time it is an interesting experiment in narrative technique which merits careful study.

Wells gave *The Bulpington of Blup* the sub-title 'Adventures, Poses, Stresses, Conflicts, and Disaster in a Contemporary Brain'. This phrase aptly summarises the novel: a sustained and remarkably consistent study of any acutely divided individuality. Robert Bloom, in his perceptive study *Anatomies of Egotism* (1977), has pointed out that the novel is in reality an anti-Bildungsroman,[8] and it is fascinating to compare the literary technique employed here with that adopted in earlier works such as *Kipps* (1905). In this long and elaborately conceived character study he produced one of his finest novels for many years and a work of considerable artistic merit.

Bulpington succeeds effectively in describing the leisurely, effete, cultured circles in which the wealthy intelligentsia moved during the closing years of the Victorian era and the opening decade of the twentieth century. Theodore Bulpington grows up in a comfortable, kindly, limited world shielded from all the coarser aspects of life and far removed from any contact with poverty or deprivation (In much the same manner as Arnold Blettsworthy in *Mr Blettsworthy on Rampole Island* (1928) spent his adolescent years). The account of Theodore's upbringing, his speculations about religion and science and his first experience of sexual love, is excellently done. Rarely did Wells achieve a more polished effect than in these chapters, notable for their ease of storytelling. It is the First World War with its implicit challenge to English manhood which provides the necessary shock to jolt Theodore from his daydreaming and present him for the first time with a direct assault on his secure private world. The description of the oncoming of war (see especially Chapter 6, Section 1, 'The Great Framework Cracks') conveys brilliantly the sense of foreboding as the façade of European stability crumbled and broke asunder. After much prevarication, Theodore reluctantly decides to enlist, but is only able to make his subsequent experiences tolerable by fabricating a web of falsehoods about his military career.

The novel is dominated by the image of the Delphic Sybil (at Wells's insistence Michael-Angelo's painting is reproduced as the endpapers in the first edition) which becomes for the hero a symbol of all that he desires in feminine companionship. He is haunted by 'that lovely being, with her sweet wide eyes, her awakening youth' and adopts her as his idealised picture of womankind.[9] Stephen Stratton in *The Passionate Friends* was also obsessed by the same image – clearly a powerful motif in Wells's imagination. The two central female characters, Rachel Bernstein and Margaret Broxted are both well realised – the latter recalling Joan Debenham (in *Joan and Peter*) in her manifest sincerity and integrity of purpose. Gradually Theodore identifies Margaret with the Delphic Sybil but becomes disenchanted with her when he realises ultimately that she embodies ideas and attitudes which he cannot share – scientific enlightenment, feminism and a concern for human betterment. At the end of the novel he deliberately defaces his painting of Sybil because she has come to stand for all those forces he refuses to face up to. The story ends, as it begins, with Bulpington living wholly in a world of the imagination, protected from reality by layer upon layer of illusions and pretences.

Some critics have seen *The Bulpington of Blup* as a thinly disguised satire of Ford Madox Ford (Ford Madox Hueffer, 1873 – 1939), with whom Wells had an uneasy friendship for some years. Ford had unkindly satirised him in *The New Humpty-Dumpty* (1912) and it may well be that Wells wished to pay off an old score. In his autobiography, Wells described the novel as 'a very direct caricature study of the irresponsible disconnected aesthetic mentality'.[10] What is so remarkable about the work, particularly in the light of his earlier fiction, is the unusual degree to which he succeeds in describing the mental world and attitudes of a character so totally alien to his own views. The fact that Theodore Bulpington engages the reader's sympathy and understanding even while deluding himself in a series of increasingly extravagant poses is testimony to Wells's skill in building up a portrait of a completely convincing personality. By the end of the book it is clear that he detests Bulpington as a type, yet page by page and chapter by chapter he has woven an elaborate tapestry of experiences which have helped to mould Theodore and make him what he is.

Brynhild, published in 1937, represents an interesting departure in Wells's work. In style and manner it is quite unlike any of his other novels – not least in its almost complete absence of either implied or overt didactic content. In its restrained language, carefully modulated structure and precise shaping of incident and conversation it resembles much more a novel by L. P. Hartley or Somerset Maugham. It is, moreover, the most Jamesian of all his novels in the sense that he appears for once to be subscribing to the Jamesian standards of form and to abandon the picaresque, discursive manner he had previously embraced as the mainstream of the English literary tradition.

That he intended it to be regarded as a major work is clear in the introductory note: 'If you like this story you will like *The Bulpington of Blup*, *Christina Alberta's Father*, *Kipps*, *Tono-Bungay*, and *The History of Mr Polly* by the same author'.[11] This selection is significant in that each is a novel which takes as its principal theme the exploration of an individuality. In the case of *Brynhild* there are two personalities whose character and psychology form the substance of the book: Rowland Palace, aesthete and writer, and his sensitive, beautiful wife Brynhild. The novel is concerned throughout with an examination of the way in which each impinges on the other and the impact of both upon a third personality, Alfred Bunter – the latter being apparently modelled on D. H. Lawrence. This is, for Wells, an alien world – the world of refined, aesthetic, art-conscious creative artists – and he now proceeded to explore it with penetrating relish and insight.

The book carries the subtitle 'The Show of Things', a phrase which reinforces the novel's concern with the theme of appearances and with the exploration of outward images. Rowland Palace is obsessed with the image of himself as a successful writer, and his search for an effective means of publicising his reputation provides Wells with ample scope for gentle mockery of the public relations industry. He himself cared deeply about his public image as a writer despite his protestations to the contrary, yet Palace is in no sense an alter ego. Wells does not seek to identify himself in any way with his central character but rather to demonstrate, through his use of a certain ironical detachment, the intrinsic shallowness of the aesthetic mentality. But the novel, significantly, takes its title not from Palace but from his beautiful, enigmatic wife; its thematic substance is concerned equally with her quest for fulfilment. Whereas he achieves his end in an increasingly diffuse mask of self-deception, Brynhild finds her completion in total honesty and integrity. In complete contrast to her husband (Brynhild appears to have been inspired by Moura Budberg, a close friend and intimate of Wells's during the final decade of his life) she remains steadfast throughout to her own ideals of candour and tenderness. Much of the novel's fascination lies in the way in which these differing personalities impinge upon each other and affect the lives and attitudes of their acquaintances. Moreover, underlying the surface narrative is a web of symbolic reference – seen at its height in the lengthy description of the charade at Valliant Chevrell – which reinforces the central preoccupation with the themes of image and reality, appearance and truth.

Brynhild looks back to earlier literary models – *The Portrait of a Lady* (1881) is an obvious and peculiarly apposite precursor – and at the same time in its extensive use of symbols and precise employment of language parallels the work of modernist writers. It is above all else a novel of *characterisation* – a novel concerned through and through with the delineation of individual character – in marked contrast to the bulk of his fiction which is concerned more typically with an examination of ideas and social forces. In exploring the mental and emotional world of Brynhild and Rowland Palace, Wells seems to have deliberately opted for a dignified, graceful style as if he is consciously seeking to make amends for his previous lapses and to demonstrate his ability to produce a polished and cohesive whole. (At one point in the narrative he even injects a comment apropos of himself: 'Wells was pinned down by his always being linked with "The Future of – this or that". But Wells at his best was a discursive intractable writer with no real sense of dignity. A man is not called "H. G." by all his friends for nothing'.[12] Behind the central theme – that of the shallowness of appearances and facades, and the contrasting reality of the true self – lies a wealth of observation and incident woven together in a tapestry of Jamesian complexity. The result is a wholly satisfying piece of writing which deserves broader recognition and merits considerably more critical attention than it has thus far received.

In a series of articles in *Time and Tide* (October 1934) which appeared under the title 'H. G. Wells – The Player', Odette Keun – who had been Wells's close friend and companion throughout the previous decade – strongly criticised him for his alleged inconsistency and disingenuousness and asserted that *Experiment in Autobiography*, which was then being published, was 'an enormous reel of self-justification'.[13] For ten years Wells and Madame Keun had enjoyed a turbulent friendship from which both no doubt gained much – his warm appreciation of her may be seen in the dedications of both *The World of William Clissold* (1926) and *The Bulpington of Blup* – but by 1934 the relationship had deteriorated. Instead of replying to the *Time and Tide* articles Wells bided his time and, four years later, expressed his mature reflections on the affair in *Apropos of Dolores*, a bitingly amusing novel in which Keun is caricatured as Dolores Wilbeck. This is not to say that Dolores is merely a fictional portrait of Odette Keun, but rather that Wells drew on many of her distinctive characteristics and mannerisms in sketching this wryly malicious vignette. He was careful to state in the Preface that: 'If a character in a book should have the luck to seem like a real human being that is no excuse for imagining an "original" or suspecting a caricature [...] Nothing in this book has happened to anyone: much in this book has happened to many people'.[14] Several publishers declined to accept the book, presumably because they felt that the fictionalisation was too recognisable and they feared a libel action. The novel was finally published in 1938 by Jonathan Cape. In looking back on his years of friendship with Odette, Wells recalled their association not with rancour or bitterness, as might have been expected, but a resigned whimsicality – in much the same manner as George in *Tono-Bungay* looked back on his marriage to Marion. The result is that *Apropos of Dolores* is one of Wells's happiest creations. The story is told throughout with an ease of style he was never to recapture. The novel is cast in the form of a journal kept by the narrator, Stephen Wilbeck, who reflects on his past life and in particular Dolores and the impact of her unique personality on his philosophy and outlook. The journal is saturated with sociological comment on a wide range of issues on which Wells in his own person had frequently written – racial intolerance, the teaching of universal history, the insidious effect of nationalism and so on – but in *Dolores* his touch is so light and accomplished as to render the book an exhilarating intellectual and emotional experience.

The novel is rich in episodes of enduring humour. The opening chapter, 'Happy Interlude', is written with benign goodwill which recalls the happy mood of *The History of Mr Polly* thirty years earlier. Wilbeck confides to the reader that he has a 'Boswell Self':[15] moods in which he is contented with life and looks charitably on all around him. The mood comes upon him all too rarely but under its influence he begins to describe himself and his world and the way in which he first met Dolores, who comes at last to exercise a dominating influence on his life.

Some of the finest incidents occur in the chapter entitled 'Dolores at Torquestol'. There is, for example, the scene in which she and Wilbeck arrive at the hotel and demand lunch; the hilarious sequence at the dinner tables when Dolores' dog, Bayard, becomes involved in an amorous encounter with the pet of the Baroness Schenitzy; the conversation with the English fisherman, culminating in the profound observation that one never sees a woman fishing. After the death of Dolores – which comes as a total surprise to the reader – there is an amusing description of the funeral, with Wilbeck wearing ill-fitting formal clothes so that he looks like 'an unmitigated scoundrel [...] the villain in a Victorian melodrama'.[16] He imagines Dolores remonstrating with him for his lack of chic. Each of these episodes is written with felicity and an infectious good humour.

The entire novel is in reality a sustained analysis of egotism, using Dolores as a case study in obstructiveness and resistance to ideas. *Dolores* is a characteristically Wellsian novel in that the narrator is not content to describe his personal experiences but speculates whether his story might not have a wider relevance to humanity. Could it be, he asks, that humanity is not one species but a mixture: that some people are 'Homo Doloresiform, a widespread, familiar type, emphatic, impulsive and implacable', and that others are 'Homo Wilbeckius, probably a recent mutation, observant, inhibited and disingenuous?'[17] The question, once posed, leads on to much intriguing psychological and biological comment, but this is not obtrusive. In this respect, as in others, Wells's literary technique is skilful and self assured: more so than in some of the earlier novels. Much of the artistry of *Dolores*, moreover, lies in the fact that Stephen Wilbeck is truly an invented personality, and Wells succeeds to a considerable degree in portraying the mind of a completely imaginary personality.

Although *Apropos of Dolores* was written at a time when the clouds of world war were clearly visible on the horizon, it is on the whole a refreshingly cheerful work. Wilbeck speculates on the probable shape of the future but, for all his caution, concludes that:

> [...] there were no biological precedents to guide us to a prophecy of the outcome, because man's limited but incessant intelligence makes his case unique [...] Stoical agnosticism is the only possible religion for sane adults. Accept and endure what happens to you, from within just as much as without [...] Go on without either absolutes of believing or disbelieving. Without extremities either of hope or despair.[18]

So it is that at the conclusion of one of his most humorous stories, undeservedly neglected today, Wells returns to the stoicism of Edward Prendick and Arnold Blettsworthy. The novel ends, as it began, with a visit to Rennes – where Wilbeck had found much happiness – and, in forgiving Dolores for all her implacabilities and exasperating behaviour, he concludes on a note of 'complacency and benediction'.[19]

With the publication of *You Can't Be Too Careful* in 1941 Wells's career as a novelist, which had begun nearly fifty years earlier with *The Time Machine*, came to an end. His final novel, despite the fact it has never found favour with literary critics, is in many ways one of his most remarkable and embodies Wells's characteristic approach to the art of fiction.

The novel, which is subtitled 'A Sample of Life 1901 – 1951', tells the life story of Edward Albert Tewler, a Pollyesque figure who blunders from one misadventure to another, and relates his gradual awakening into sexual and political consciousness. The story is told with a frankness which would have been unthinkable in Wells's early fiction, and which is strongly reminiscing of the George Orwell of *Keep the Aspidistra Flying* (1936) and *Coming Up for Air* (1939). The second and third parts, 'The Adolescence of Edward Albert Tewler' and 'The Marrying, Divorce and Early Middle Age', are brilliantly executed and are convincing evidence that Wells's ability to entertain and amuse the reader was undiminished even at the age of seventy-five. There are, for example, the cricket match (Book Two, section 2) in which it is not difficult to imagine reminiscences of his father on the cricket pitch at Bromley; the boarding house at Doober's (Book 2, section 11), an institution almost worthy of Dickens; and the description of his courtship and marriage to Evangeline Birkenhead. The latter is told with pitiless clarity and yet with freshness and insight.

Tewler himself is a pitiful figure who never at any stage accepts responsibility for his own actions, but in spite of his manifest shallowness and posturing he succeeds, like Theodore Bulpington, in holding the reader's sympathy. That Wells deliberately intended this effect is clear from his comment at the end:

> I have told this poor sordid story and that of the people whose lives he has helped to spoil; I have mocked at his absurdities and misfortunes and invincible conceit; but all the way along as I wrote something it has protested, 'This is not fair. Given a broader education, given air, light and opportunity, would he have been anything like this?' He is what our civilisation made of him, and this is all it made of him. I have told the complete truth about a contemporary specimen man [...] My case is that Edward Albert is not so much destable as pitiful [...].[20]

It is instructive to compare this passage with a similar admission at the conclusion of *The History of Mr Polly*:

> I have failed in presenting Mr Polly altogether if I have not made you see that he was in many respects an artless child of Nature, far more untrained, undisciplined, and spontaneous than an ordinary savage.[21]

Tewler is, however, a more complex (if less sympathetic) figure than Polly, because he sees life with fewer illusions. Whereas Mr Polly succeeded in transforming his life by escaping from an environment which had become intolerable, Tewler simply accepts life as it is. He reacts to external pressures but seems incapable of initiating change. The atmosphere of the two stories is similar in a number of ways but the later novel is told with a candour and bitterness altogether lacking in the former.

The essential theme of *You Can't Be Too Careful* is that humanity has not yet attained the status of *homo sapiens*, that all the human race is still *homo Tewler*, and that no advancement beyond the present stage is possible without a worldwide moral and intellectual revolution. Wells had been arguing much the same case for many years – most recently in a series of polemical works, *The Fate of Homo Sapiens* (1939), *The New World Order* (1940) and *The Commonsense of War and Peace* (1940) – but now he chose to illustrate and illuminate his thesis by telling the story of a 'contemporary specimen man' who grew to painful maturity during the years between the two world wars.

It is fashionable to dismiss *You Can't Be Too Careful* as a malicious, almost hopeless work of despair written by an elderly man who was tired and ill, but his son Anthony West has argued cogently that the pessimism which overtook Wells at the end of his life was not a final cry of despair but a reversion to deeply felt convictions he had felt from the outset of his intellectual career.[22] Indeed, the final impression of the novel is not one of hopelessness – as is the case with such early works as *The Time Machine* and *The Island of Doctor Moreau* – but a resigned stoicism.

> Yet a vista of innumerable happy generations, an abundance of life at present inconceivable, and at the end, not extinction necessarily, not immortality, but complete uncertainty, is surely sufficient prospect for the present. They (future generations) may be good by our current orientation of things; they may be evil. Why should they not be in the nature of our good and much more than our good – 'beyond good and evil'?[23]

Thus it is that at the end of his literary pilgrimage we find not the unrelieved pessimism of *Mind at the End of its Tether* but a serene impassivity: a refusal to be committed to any ultimate certainty regarding the future. His final novel, though flawed by unevenness and too overt didacticism, is still readable today for its abundant vitality and humour.

It follows from this discussion that Wells was at his most creative when his didactic purpose did not interfere too much and that it is when his imaginative power was at the forefront that he was at his best as a *novelist.*[24]

Notes

[1] H. G. Wells, *Experiment in Autobiography*, 2 vols (London: Gollancz, 1934), II, 495, 493.

[2] *The Book of Catherine Wells* (London: Chatto and Windus, 1928), p. 26.

[3] *The Works of H. G. Wells: Atlantic Edition*, 28 vols (London: Fisher Unwin, 1924-7), XXIII, *Joan and Peter*, i.

[4] Cited in John Hammond, *An H. G. Wells Companion* (London: Macmillan, 1979), p. 193.

[5] H. G. Wells, *The Dream* (London: Cape, 1924), p. 137.

[6] See Wells, *Experiment in Autobiography*, I, 138-9.

[7] Wells, *The Dream*, p. 155.

[8] Robert Bloom, *Anatomies of Egotism: A Reading of the Last Novels of H. G. Wells* (Lincoln: University of Nebraska Press, 1977), p. 83.

[9] H. G. Wells, *The Bulpington of Blup* (London: Hutchinson, 1932), p. 24.

[10] Wells, *Experiment in Autobiography*, II, 624.

[11] H. G. Wells, *Brynhild* (London: Methuen, 1937), ii.

[12] Wells, *Brynhild*, p. 79.

[13] Odette Keun, 'H. G. Wells – The Player', *Time and Tide*, 15 (October 1934), 1249, 1307-9, 1346-8.

[14] H. G. Wells, *Apropos of Dolores* (London: Cape, 1934), p. 8.

[15] Wells, *Apropos of Dolores*, p. 12.

[16] Wells, *Apropos of Dolores*, p. 265.

[17] Wells, *Apropos of Dolores*, pp. 215-16.

[18] Wells, *Apropos of Dolores*, p. 347.

[19] Wells, *Apropos of Dolores*, p. 349.

[20] H. G. Wells, *You Can't Be Too Careful* (London: Secker and Warburg, 1941), p. 285.

[21] H. G. Wells, *The History of Mr Polly* (1910) (London: Penguin, 1948), p. 223.

[22] Anthony West, 'H. G. Wells', *Principles and Persuasions* (London: Eyre and Spottiswoode, 1958), pp. 4-20.

[23] Wells, *You Can't Be Too Careful*, p. 293.

[24] The issues raised in the foregoing essay are discussed more fully in my critical study *H. G. Wells and the Modern Novel* (London: Macmillan, 1988) and again in my *H. G. Wells and the Short Story* (London: Macmillan, 1992).

ISLAND OF FOOLS:
MR BLETTSWORTHY ON RAMPOLE ISLAND AND THE TWENTIETH-CENTURY HUMAN PREDICAMENT

PATRICK PARRINDER

I

As John Donne wrote, 'No man is an *Iland*, intire of it selfe; every man is a peece of the *Continent*, a part of the *maine*'; [1] and islands themselves are not entire and self-sufficient in Donne's sense, despite their pinpoint status on maps of the globe. Geographically speaking, the existence of islands is manifest, but in human and in biological terms island status is relative rather than absolute. The ecology of islands depends upon the seas surrounding them and upon their proximity to other landmasses, while logically the concept of an island demands a mainland if it is to make any sense. Semantically and etymologically the word island is indissolubly linked to the ideas of *isolation* and *insulation*, but these can only be defined in relation to their opposites: communication, contamination, and so on. Another semantic peculiarity is that in Latin and all Romance languages the opposition between island and mainland is complicated by an in-between state, the peninsula or *presqu'île*, the almost-island. Thus Robinson Crusoe has to sail all round his island in order to be absolutely certain that it is an island. At least one fictional hero, David Balfour in Robert Louis Stevenson's *Kidnapped* (1886), thinks he is marooned on a desert island only to discover that it becomes a peninsula at low tide.

Not only are Crusoe's adventures presented as if they were the history of a real castaway, but Defoe does everything possible to suggest that his island is an actual and substantial place. Crusoe may have been its first inhabitant, but it later becomes a landing-place for tribes of cannibals, for various subsequent European castaways, and, in the volume of Crusoe's *Farther Adventures* (1719), for the returning Robinson Crusoe himself. David Balfour's island, by contrast, is doubly fictional. As a figment of

Balfour's imagination it has something in common with the other
imaginary and hypothetical islands of literature, islands that are 'lost' in
the sense that they cannot be revisited. The contrast between the merely
fictional island, and islands both fictional and hypothetical, may be seen
by setting Crusoe's story beside the work of Defoe's contemporary
Jonathan Swift, since the islands visited by Lemuel Gulliver (with the
single exception of Japan) are all hypothetical. *The Island of Doctor
Moreau* (1896), Wells's most famous island romance, is indebted to both
Defoe and Swift. The "Introduction' by the narrator's nephew (which
Wells deleted in several later editions) hints that the volcanic islet where
Dr Moreau set up his laboratory is 'Noble's Isle' in the Pacific,
supposedly visited four years after the events of Edward Prendick's
narrative by a party of sailors from H. M. S. *Scorpion*. The sailors found
no traces of Dr Moreau and his alleged menagerie, apart from 'certain
curious white moths, some hogs and rabbits, and some rather peculiar
rats'.[2] What if Moreau's island had been a true 'lost island' – a figment,
that is, of Prendick's traumatised imagination?   Wells explored a
possibility of this kind in his second island romance, *Mr Blettsworthy on
Rampole Island*, first published in 1928. This 'late exercise in satire and
allegory', as Roger Bowen has called it, remains rather little known. As
Bowen summarises, it 'looks back especially to the island setting and
themes of *Doctor Moreau*, retrieves a great deal of that early power and is
a reminder of the enduring, the essential Wells'.[3] But *Mr Blettsworthy* is
much more than a (somewhat eccentric) replay of *Doctor Moreau*. It
displays a quite different understanding of island biology, island
psychology, and island symbolism.
     The most famous of all 'lost islands' is not, in fact, a sunken island but
a sunken continent: the lost empire of Atlantis, described in Plato's
dialogues 'Timaeus' and 'Critias'. Atlantis was an immensely powerful
kingdom with a metropolis even more splendid than Plato's Athens, but
the story of Atlantis is one of a catastrophic fall, first political and then
geographical. Plato tells how Atlantis, once a rich and peaceful
civilisation, embarked on a ruinous policy of imperial conquest which
ended with it making war on the Greeks. Hubris led to nemesis, the latter
taking a physical shape with the onset of violent earthquakes and floods,
so that the continent itself disappeared into the sea.[4] (Many people have
speculated that some of the North Atlantic islands, including Madeira
where Wells's Arnold Blettsworthy is born, are all that is left of Atlantis.)
The Atlantis myth has a significant presence in modern literature,
especially in science fiction between 1885 and 1930,[5] which was the
period of Wells's fiction although he himself does not apparently make
use of it. Instead, he was fixated on a second Platonic image, that of the

utopian Republic.[6]

Atlantis according to Plato was once a real place, but his Republic is merely hypothetical. The Greek experience was one of city-states, so that the Republic is an imaginary city; but in Renaissance Europe the discovery of 'new worlds' across the seas made it inevitable for the utopian location to be figured as a hitherto unknown island, as part of the new maritime geography that was becoming known to European sailors. The Renaissance Utopia's 'offshore' status is further emphasised by the fact that, in Thomas More's work, the location is strictly speaking an almost-island since it has been artificially cut off from its nearest mainland. The utopian islands of More's *Utopia* and Bacon's *New Atlantis* are hypothetical places that no sailor, we may assume, has ever expected to find on a map.

The point of the fiction of hypothetical utopian islands is to record their difference from the 'mainlands' known to their readers. The island functions as a laboratory of human social organisation, and also as a kind of museum. It embodies a history of separate development, which may either be a model for the future or an illustration of the direction that humanity as whole might have, but has not, taken. It may be a blueprint or a conceptual dead end. The result of Charles Darwin's visit to the Galapagos Islands in 1835 was to extend this way of understanding the hypothetical utopian island – as laboratory, as museum, and as evolutionary paradigm – to all islands. Of course, it may be said that the biological aspects of island difference were largely known before Darwin, and certainly he did not need to go to the Galapagos to find them out, even as a naturalist. (For example, instead of studying the Galapagos finches he could have looked at the separate sub-species of the European wren, *troglodytes troglodytes*, to be found on the North Atlantic islands of St Kilda, the Hebrides, Fair Isle, Shetland, and the Faroe Islands.) But the voyage of the *Beagle* made the general and evolutionary aspects of island difference inescapable.

We would expect H. G. Wells, one of the first writers to emerge from within the Darwinian milieu (he was born in 1866 and took a B.Sc in Zoology in 1890), to incorporate the Darwinian island into his view of the human condition, and he does this initially in *The Island of Doctor Moreau*, in short stories such as 'Aepyornis Island' (1895), and in a brief *Saturday Review* essay on 'The Influence of Islands on Variation' (1895), which alludes both to Darwin and to Alfred Russel Wallace's evolutionary treatise on *Island Life* (1880).[7] Some thirty years later when he was writing *Mr Blettsworthy on Rampole Island*, Wells was also engaged with his son G. P. Wells and Julian Huxley in compiling the three volumes of *The Science of Life* (1930), an encyclopaedia of contemporary biology.

Here the discussion of 'island variation' and other biological aspects of island life plays a crucial role, especially in the first volume where the authors set out to establish 'The Incontrovertible Fact of Evolution'.[8]

In More and Bacon, the relationship of the utopian island to the mainland is one of absolute difference. Swift's dystopian islands, by contrast, draw their satirical effect from our growing awareness of blatant resemblances to the world with which we are already familiar. Grotesque as they are, Lilliput and Brobdingnag function all too clearly as representations of general nature. Similarly, in post-Darwinian biology island difference is chiefly significant for the evidence it conveys of the universal nature of the evolutionary process. In *The Science of Life*, Wells and his collaborators refer to the island biology of Darwin and Wallace for clinching arguments in favour of evolutionism against creationism. The Galapagos Islands, as Darwin had observed, closely resemble the Cape Verde archipelago off the coast of Africa in broad ecological terms:

> In a world deliberately planned and created they would be populated by the same kinds of creature; what suits one suits the other. But they are not. Their animal and plant inhabitants are totally different. [...] [I]f the distribution of living things is the result of evolution and migration, the reason is plain.[9]

The fact that 'isolation promotes divergence'[10] and contributes to the proliferation of species simply confirms the representativeness of the natural processes observed in the remotest and most insular environments. It follows, therefore, that, far from being planned and orderly, evolution is spectacularly wasteful. The greater the diversification of species, the more we must see evolution as a casual and accidental process involving not only continual new creations but continual extinction. Where the story of Atlantis told of a fall from an original, near-perfect state, and More's and Bacon's utopian islands implied the possibility of progress and human perfectibility, the Darwinian vision was one of apparently permanent mutability and disorder. This lesson from natural history was adapted to human history in a highly popular late nineteenth-century work, Winwood Reade's *The Martyrdom of Man* (1872), which helps to form the outlook of Wells's Mr Blettsworthy. As Blettsworthy reflects, 'Ten thousand pollen grains blow to waste for one that reaches a pistil; why should man be an exception to the common way of life?'[11]

II

On 12 February 1928 Wells wrote to Julian Huxley that 'I have done nearly half of my fantastic pseudo boy's adventure-story, which will be my *Candide*, my *Peer Gynt*, my *Gulliver*'.[12] We have already hinted at what *Mr Blettsworthy* owes to Swift; moreover, as Bowen remarks, Wells's curiously-structured narrative amounts to 'four chapters or, in effect, books, in the manner of *Gulliver's Travels*, each of the chapters defining a different area of the narrator's experience'.[13] This experience is a mixture of real and imaginary geography, taking in not only the fictitious Rampole Island but two other Atlantic islands, England and Madeira, as well as the continents of Europe and America which had featured in Voltaire's *Candide*. (Ibsen's *Peer Gynt* seems at first sight a somewhat surprising addition to the eighteenth-century *contes philosophique* of Swift and Voltaire, though it too is an episodic tale in which the hero's travels and misadventures bring him at last to a settled, though possibly deluded, understanding of the human predicament.) Wells called his hero Blettsworthy, meaning 'worthy to be blessed' and implying that human perfectibility is possible; and he dedicated Blettsworthy's story to the 'Immortal Memory of Candide', suggesting that the belief in evolutionary perfectibility may be a later but still recognisable version of the Panglossian belief that all is for the best in the best of all possible worlds. In Voltaire's tale Candide, accompanied by his tutor Dr Pangloss, wanders haphazardly across two continents suffering disaster after disaster. Arnold Blettsworthy, too, is shell-shocked by his experiences on three islands long before he joins the British Army in the First World War and is sent to fight in the trenches. In effect, Wells's novel becomes a debate about human perfectibility from three points of view represented by Madeira, England, and Rampole Island respectively.[14]

Blettsworthy is born on Madeira to a mother 'of mixed Portuguese and Syrian origin, with a touch of the indigenous blood of Madeira' (10). She dies when he is five and, says our narrator, 'my few memories of her are hopelessly confused with a tornado that ravaged the island' (11). Madeira is the land of tropical storms and tempests, just as the England to which the five-year-old Blettsworthy is taken is the land of calm. Similarly, Madeira is Catholic and female where England is Protestant and male. The fact that Blettsworthy retains so few memories of his storm-ridden infancy is doubtless due to the influence of his English uncle Rupert, an Anglican clergyman who serves as the novel's Dr Pangloss; Uncle Rupert represents the full glory of nineteenth-century English liberalism with its faith in human perfectibility and its ability to shut out unpleasant facts. Thanks to Uncle Rupert, Blettsworthy starts out in life 'with the completest confidence in myself, mankind and nature' (88); but Rupert dies, and his young nephew is cheated out of his inheritance and then suffers a complete nervous breakdown. Recommended by his new guardian to leave England and take a long sea voyage for the sake of his health, he witnesses scenes of brutality, mutiny, and shipwreck in the South Atlantic before being set adrift and left to die. He survives but, as we later learn, becomes insane. Five years later he comes out of his dementia in an apartment in Manhattan, having spent the intervening time (so he thinks) on Rampole Island among prehistoric beasts and primordial savages. Roger Bowen sums up the symbolism of Blettsworthy's brutalising sea voyage and his island landfall in the following manner: 'the entire sea journey is in fact a return to the origins of life, a journey which moves progressively closer to that origin. The island and what transpires there will demonstrate how inadequate was that first attempt to establish human evolution on land'.[15] It will be noted that in *The Island of Doctor Moreau* also, Prendick's horrifying experiences as a castaway preceded his arrival at the island where Moreau was attempting to establish a new process of 'human evolution'.

The disclosure that Rampole Island is a mere hallucination has been carefully prepared for by Wells, though it is cleverly hidden from the reader. Ultimately we learn that the demented Blettsworthy was found drifting in the South Atlantic and rescued by the crew of an American survey ship, who put in for a few hours at Rampole Island – described as a 'bleak desert' (221) off the coast of Patagonia – before taking him back to New York, where he is at first confined in a psychiatric clinic. But Blettsworthy believes he has been picked up by savages in a rowing boat and taken to their island, whose harbour is guarded by a 'rock in the shape of a woman with staring eyes and an open mouth', with a 'splintered pinnacle [. . .] like an upraised arm and hand brandishing a club' (138); this, he is told, is the 'Great Goddess welcoming her slaves'. Not only is the rock of the Great Goddess an ironic distortion of the Statue of Liberty, which the survey ship must have passed as it entered New York harbour, but Blettsworthy's life in a savage village in a deep gorge between overtowering cliffs on Rampole Island is a skewed reflection of his life in the streets of Manhattan. (Occasionally, indeed, his deep reverie of Rampole Island is penetrated by the sounds of city traffic.) Blettsworthy vividly recollects being adopted as the 'Sacred Lunatic' of the primitive tribe, whose chief, a brutal warrior called Ardam (a name suggesting the primordial Adam), is preparing to make war on a neighbouring village.

The meaning of his imaginary island has to be unravelled by the recovering Blettsworthy, aided by his New York psychiatrist Dr Minchett. Superficially his is a case of what Minchett calls 'Interpretative Reverie' arising out of the traumatic experiences of the sea voyage and shipwreck; unable to accept that he is in safe harbour in New York, Blettsworthy constructs a much grimmer reality. At a deeper level, his hallucinations are connected to his earlier nervous breakdown, caused (as already hinted) by the loss of the Panglossian progressivist faith inculcated by his English Protestant upbringing. It is Dr Minchett who notes that the sub-tropical landscape of Blettsworthy's lost island, so different from the bare rocks of Rampole Island off the coast of Patagonia, can only come from repressed memories of his patient's Madeiran childhood: ' "You lost all touch with Madeira, yes. But—something eager, stormy, self-centred and intense, pessimistic, lay hidden beneath your English self, formless and indefinite, outwardly forgotten" ' (220). The savages who people this sub-tropical fantasy island represent the ship's captain and his crew, with the Captain as Ardam, the terrifying warrior chief. But Blettsworthy remains a child of nineteenth-century liberalism to the extent that he identifies 'savagery' with tribal warfare and cannibalism, and regards the lives of modern primitive peoples as a survival from humanity's prehistoric past. This, it will emerge, is part of his defence-mechanism against the full horrors of modern life, with its advanced scientific civilisation blundering towards a catastrophic war. Rampole Island may have been a hallucination, but it was also, he eventually concludes, 'the real world looming through the mists of my illusions' (222).

Cannibalism, tribal warfare, and the strange biology of his lost island are, of course, very much part of the 'pseudo boy's adventure-story' narrative that Wells had promised Julian Huxley. (One of his models was undoubtedly Conan Doyle, whose *The Lost World* (1912) is a boy's adventure story and little else.) It is in keeping with this aspect of *Mr Blettsworthy* that at one point the protagonist should find himself being stalked by a terrifying primordial beast, a beast which the more studious of his adolescent readers could have found illustrated in *The Science of Life*. The skeleton of a giant Megatherium, a prehistoric ground sloth 'bulky as an elephant', was among a group of South American fossils excavated by Darwin during his voyage on the *Beagle*.[16] Blettsworthy's pages on 'The Dreary Megatheria' are one of a number of excursions into fictitious natural history which constitute a remarkable, if slightly digressive, aspect of Wellsian scientific romance. (Compare 'The Reversion of the Beast Folk' in *The Island of Doctor Moreau*, the description of the Martians seen from the ruined house in *The War of the Worlds*, and 'The Natural History of the Selenites' in *The First Men in the Moon*.) Blettsworthy records that the Megatheria have survived on Rampole Island, although they became extinct on the South American mainland at the end of the last Ice Age. Nevertheless, these last surviving specimens are slowly dying out. The details of their size, habits, and (above all) the nauseous smell that Blettsworthy meticulously records go far beyond anything that could be justified by the actual fossil record.[17] In the retrospective light in which he eventually comes to understand his hallucinations,

Blettsworthy's Megatheria also take on a grotesque symbolic meaning. They represent the 'laws and institutions of mankind' (172).

III

If these are the raw materials of Blettsworthy's Rampole Island experience, what does that experience mean? One difficulty in answering this question arises from the nature of Blettsworthy's narrative, which is not only interpretative and retrospective but is written at a considerable distance from the supposed experience. He regains his sanity in the United States at the outbreak of the First World War. As a British citizen he is liable to conscription into the British forces, so he returns to England, undergoes army training, and is sent to the Front, where he is badly wounded. His story, told in the post-war period, is inevitably overlaid with memories of the war. For example, the brutal military training that he undergoes becomes mixed up with his earlier suffering, leading him to observe in retrospect that 'I cannot be sure how far my conception of Ardam is due to that life of insult and humiliation' (238). Prediction and retrospect have become confused when, eventually, he comes to write the narrative of his adventures. To the extent that these adventures constitute a hallucination or dream experience, we should remember that in Freudian psychoanalysis it is not the dream itself, which cannot be recovered, but the patient's explicit memories of the dream that constitute the material to be analysed. Blettsworthy's account of his Rampole Island experience is similarly written up from memory, and this is one of several features of the novel which suggest Wells's familiarity with, and interest in, some of the basic concepts of early psychoanalysis.[18]

To a certain extent it is possible to view *Mr Blettsworthy on Rampole Island* through a Freudian lens, with the England of Blettsworthy's childhood representing the Panglossian world of the Superego, while tornado-torn Madeira and, still more, Rampole Island represent the Id, the world of the Unconscious. (Wells himself does not use this terminology, although he describes the Anglican God of Blettsworthy's Uncle Rupert as a 'super-Blettsworthy' in control of the universe (19), a phrase which could clearly suggest the Superego.) Madeira, the maternal island of Blettsworthy's infancy, remains almost totally repressed, suggesting that the Superego represented by Uncle Rupert's English liberalism has done its job. Rampole Island, however, continues to haunt Blettsworthy long after he has recognised it as a dream-memory. Events in the contemporary world, such as the trial and execution in 1927 of the American anarchists Sacco and Vanzetti, can only be understood by reference to Blettsworthy's dream. The Freudian notion of a 'talking cure', represented by the sympathetic Dr Minchett, is threatened by Wells's disturbing insight that, in Bowen's words, 'only insanity or abnormality can bring about true vision of the modern predicament'.[19] Rampole Island thus serves a double function, since it mirrors the brutal realities of twentieth-century civilisation and at the same time – while Blettsworthy's hallucination lasts – insulates him against those realities.

In addition to psychoanalysis, Wells in *Mr Blettsworthy* draws on what Robert M. Philmus has called 'psychological anthropology', replacing the more purely biological view of humanity's links with the animal kingdom that lay behind the fable of Dr Moreau's island.[20] On Rampole Island Blettsworthy is threatened with execution by his savage captors, but manages to persuade them that he should, instead, be maintained as a Sacred Lunatic with a cherished position within the tribe. In his role as narrator he offers a scholarly gloss on the role of Sacred Lunatic, referring to a recent article on 'The Eccentric Individual in Primitive Society' by a member of the 'Smithsonian Institution of Washington'. Here, as Blettsworthy puts it, 'The writer connects the Sacred Lunatics of Patagonia – for it seems they are known on the mainland also – with the widespread worship of sacrificial kings, and so shakes down a mass of ripe and rotting fruit from [Sir James Frazer's] *The Golden Bough*' (187-8).[21] Wells's fascination with the idea of the 'sacrificial king' may be seen in several of his works at this period, notably *Christina Alberta's Father* (1925) where the modern protagonist, Albert Edward Preemby, becomes convinced that he is the reincarnation of Sargon I, King of Kings. The Sacred Lunatic or sacrificial king is an embodiment not of madness as disease, requiring therapy, but as madness as insight or prophecy. His insanity is a sign not of his own but of society's maladjustment.

Just as Rampole Island – itself something of a madhouse – confers on Blettsworthy his position as Sacred Lunatic, so a lunatic in general might be described as someone who is both confined to their own mental island and, as often as not, kept stranded in an institution with other lunatics. In fact, Blettsworthy spends the first part of his sojourn in New York at a psychiatric clinic, the Frederick Quinn Institute, although the clinic is never described since his time there is entirely consumed by his hallucination. Isolated by his state of 'Interpretative Reverie', Blettsworthy experiences Rampole Island as what Wells would later call 'a caricature-portrait of the whole human world'.[22] The island (or, if we prefer, the mental clinic) thus represents the 'mainland' of human experience in the early twentieth century, to which, after his 'cure', Blettsworthy will regain unconfined access. A conventional narrative would have ended with his reawakening in New York, testifying to the power of psychotherapy to heal the injured spirit; but for Blettsworthy this is only the end of one phase of his nightmares. In his dual role as Sacred Lunatic and as an ordinary citizen taking part in the First World War, Wells's protagonist represents a humanity in thrall to the Giant Megatheria and to the warrior leader Ardam. Is there any escape from his condition, or does it represent not only humanity's past and present but also its future?

Since Rampole Island is a hallucination, the problem is not one of physically leaving it behind but of exorcising it, of escaping from its memory and its control over the imagination. But this ultimately depends upon social and political change rather than upon anything within the reach of psychiatry. It is for this reason that the blameless Dr Minchett has a ghostly double in the figure of Chit, the tribal soothsayer of Rampole Island who acts as protector towards the Sacred Lunatic but is unable to share his vision. Chit listens to Blettsworthy's Gulliver-like disquisitions on the benefits of civilisation only to dismiss them:

> 'There is no such world,' said Chit. 'There never was such a world. There never could be such a world, for men are not made that way [. . .] The real world is about you here and now, the only real world. See it for what it is.' (161-2)

Blettsworthy respects Chit, but sees that he like all his fellows is infected by the diseased mentality of Rampole Island:

> His mind moved within the idea of war, as Kant says our imaginations move within the ideas of space and time. For him war was an inevitable feature of human life, a necessary form of thought. He could not imagine men strongly sane enough to conquer that ancient disposition. (184).

However well-meaning, Chit's mentality (and by extension Dr Minchett's) is the mentality of the Great War in which Blettsworthy will soon find himself taking part, the war that demonstrates that 'Rampole Island had indeed now spread out and swallowed all the world' (247). To overcome it is a task for visionary politics rather than psychotherapy, although (since 'jaw, jaw' is the only credible alternative to war) the possible cure at which the novel hints remains a talking cure. As is altogether typical of late Wells, this narrative that begins in popular adventure-story mode ends with open-ended and deliberately inconclusive philosophical dialogues.

Not only does the island presuppose the mainland, but a Rampole Island that has 'swallowed the world' may be felt to presuppose another, better world somewhere else – foreshadowing, as it were, a second and more successful attempt to establish human evolution on land. In this sense, the mundane reality of the Frederick Quinn clinic could be seen as gesturing towards a more utopian kind of mental institution – the ultimate clinic of a sane world in which humanity's inherent disposition to violence has been conquered and eradicated. Wells is aware, however, that the physician presiding over such an imaginary and utopian idea of the clinic might be no more than a revived Dr Pangloss. For this reason, the spokesman for optimism at the end of the novel is an already discredited figure from Blettsworthy's English past: Lyulph Graves, the false friend who has earlier cheated him out of his inheritance. Plausible as ever, Graves reappears not only as a reformed sinner but as Uncle Rupert's successor, the embodiment of an English liberalism reborn or, at least, uncannily resilient in the aftermath of the First World War. (There is more than a hint of the messianic Wells of the 1920s and 1930s – the Wells who described the Great War as the war that would end war – about Lyulph Graves.) Would (and will) humanity's long martyrdom at last bear fruit in the achievement of a better society? ' "Take my word for it" ', says Graves in the last words of the novel, ' "it is your Rampole Island that will pass away, and I who will come true" ' (288). Rampole Island is replaced by a once perfidious but now repentant and resurrected Albion, but Graves's Wellsian optimism is manifestly fragile, a faltering attempt to shake both Blettsworthy's and the reader's incredulity.

Is Blettsworthy, then, 'worthy to be blessed', and will Rampole Island pass away? Arguably the novel's final, Panglossian gesture is undermined by the fact that Graves, for one, seems unaware of the aspect of Blettsworthy's life on a sub-tropical island that was not hallucination but primal reality – his infancy on Madeira. The novel's final section detailing what it calls a 'Sanguine Interlude' in a recovering, post-war England is both historically precarious – since the peaceful context of the novel's publication in 1928 was, indeed, only an interlude – and deliberately amnesiac. The male, temperate, Protestant mentality of England presupposes its opposite – female, stormy, Catholic Madeira – but England is doubtfully affirmed during the 'Sanguine Interlude' while Madeira remains repressed. As represented in *Mr Blettsworthy* both England and Madeira are offshore islands, insulated and necessarily eccentric variants of the life of the human mainland. They are laboratories but also museums: possibly evolutionary dead-ends but also, no doubt, evolutionary signposts. Wells's 1928 novel balances different visions of the utopian and dystopian 'human island', reminding us how closely the imaginative form of utopia itself is linked to the symbolism and mentality of islands. The 'pseudo boy's adventure-story' is a work of muffled prophecy, torn between the obstinate (and possibly obtuse) voice of human hope – ' "Take my word for it" ', says the deeply unreliable Lyulph Graves – and Arnold Blettsworthy's prophetic despair. Wells wrestled with these two voices throughout his life, from the outer narrator's dissent from the Time Traveller's vision at the end of *The Time Machine* to the startling contrast in the titles of his two last books, *Mind at the End of its Tether* and *The Happy Turning*. In this divided sense, at least, *Mr Blettsworthy* is truly 'a reminder of the enduring, the essential Wells'.

Notes

[1] John Donne, 'Meditations xvii', in Donne, *Complete Poetry and Selected Prose*, ed. by John Hayward (London: Nonesuch, 1962), p. 538.

[2] H. G. Wells, *The Island of Doctor Moreau*, ed. by Patrick Parrinder (London: Penguin, 2005), p. 6.

[3] Roger Bowen, '*Mr Blettsworthy on Rampole Island*: "The Story of a Gentleman of Culture and Refinement" ', *Wellsian*, n.s. 2 (1978), 6-21 (p.6).

[4] See *The Dialogues of Plato, Volume 3: Timaeus and Other Dialogues*, trans. Benjamin Jowett, ed. R. M. Hare and D. A. Russell (London: Sphere, 1970), esp. pp. 231, 306-14.

[5] See John Clute and Peter Nicholls, eds., *The Encyclopedia of Science Fiction* (New York: St Martin's, 1995), p. 68.

[6] See for example Tom Miller, 'Wells's Mythological Republic', *H. G. Wells Newsletter*, 5: 11 (Summer 2006), pp. 4-7.

[7] H. G. Wells, 'The Influence of Islands on Variation', *Saturday Review*, 80 (17 August 1895), 204-05, reprinted in Wells, *The Island of Doctor Moreau: A Critical Text*, ed. Leon Stover (Jefferson, NC and London: McFarland, 1996), pp. 246-9.

[8] See especially H. G. Wells, Julian Huxley, G. P. Wells, *The Science of Life: A Summary of Contemporary Knowledge about Life and its Possibilities*, 3 vols (London: Waverley Book Co., [1930]), i, pp. 250-9. 'The Incontrovertible Fact of Evolution' is the title of Book Three of *The Science of Life*, in which this section appears.

[9] Wells et al., *The Science of* Life, i, 257.

[10] Wells et al., *The Science of Life*, ii, 411.

[11] H. G. Wells, *Mr Blettsworthy on Rampole Island* (London: Ernest Benn, 1928), p. 124. Subsequent page references in the text are to this edition.

[12] H. G. Wells, letter to Julian Huxley, *The Correspondence of H. G. Wells*, ed by David C. Smith 4 vols (London: Pickering & Chatto, 1998), iii, 258.

[13] Bowen, '*Mr Blettsworthy*', p. 10.

[14] Before we plunge into Blettsworthy's story, its ambiguous geography merits one further comment. During the 1920s and 1930s the age of sea travel was succeeded by the beginnings of the age of air travel, which not only changed the notion of the castaway but made the whole idea of the 'lost island' less plausible. Some novels set on hypothetical islands would still be written, but their human visitors, as in William Golding's *Lord of the Flies* (1954) and Muriel Spark's *Robinson* (1958),

tend to be survivors of plane crashes rather than shipwrecks. Wells adopts a different solution to the growing implausibility of the imaginary island.

[15] Bowen, '*Mr Blettsworthy*', p. 16.

[16] Wells et al., *The Science of Life*, i, 255.

[17] For example, according to *The Science of Life* (ii, p. 610) the Megatheria which evolved on Rampole Island should have gradually diminished in size as compared to those on the mainland. Blettsworthy's Megatheria, however, are elephant-sized.

[18] Dr Minchett, the psychiatrist in *Mr Blettsworthy*, is one of several Wellsian characters with interests in clinical psychology and psychoanalysis. An earlier example is Dr Martineau in *The Secret Places of the Heart* (1922). Prendick at the end of *The Island of Doctor Moreau* confides his case to a mental specialist, presumably an early psychotherapist or psychoanalyst. In *Experiment in Autobiography* (1934) Wells offers a Jungian analysis of his 'persona'. Later he was one of the principal subscribers to a fund to mark Freud's 80th birthday.

[19] Bowen, '*Mr Blettsworthy*', p. 20.

[20] Robert M. Philmus, *Visions and Re-Visions: (Re)constructing Science Fiction* (Liverpool: Liverpool University Press, 2005), p. 55.

[21] This article seems likely to be authentic although it has not been traced.

[22] H. G. Wells, *Experiment in Autobiography*, 2 vols (London: Gollancz and Cresset Press, 1934), ii, 501.

PART III:

WELLS AND HIS INTERLOCUTORS

'BUILDINGS OF THE NEW AGE': DWELLINGS AND THE NATURAL ENVIRONMENT IN THE FUTURISTIC FICTION OF H. G. WELLS AND WILLIAM HOPE HODGSON

EMILY ALDER

The relationship between human civilisations and their surroundings has always been a preoccupation of the utopian tradition, and H. G. Wells and William Hope Hodgson are among those writers who transform this fixation by placing it within an evolutionary paradigm. Writing in the late nineteenth and early twentieth centuries, Wells and Hodgson propose social structures and human futures that probe T. H. Huxley's ideas about 'ethical' evolution as a means of overcoming the potential for degeneration implicit in the evolutionary process. In *The Time Machine* (1895), 'A Story of the Days to Come' (1897), *When the Sleeper Wakes* (1899), and *A Modern Utopia* (1905), the portrayal of the natural environment, of gardens and wilderness, is an integral part of Wells's exploration of Huxleian principles, while Hodgson, drawing on Wells, offers an alternative interpretation of the implications of 'ethical' evolution in *The Night Land* (1912).

Huxley, who lectured Wells during the first year of his studies at the Normal School of Science, argued that it was possible for the human species to direct its own course against the relentless 'cosmic process' of evolution.[1] In the 'Prolegomena' to *Evolution and Ethics*, Huxley acknowledged that the popular understanding of 'evolution' had 'widened to include the phenomena of retrogressive metamorphosis, that is, of progress from a condition of relative complexity to one of relative uniformity'.[2] Retrogressive metamorphosis was one of the potential consequences of evolution against which humans could guard. For Huxley, 'Social progress means a checking of the cosmic process at every step and the substitution for it of another, which may be called the ethical process; the end of which is not the survival of those who happen to be the fittest [...] but of those who are ethically the best.'[3] Huxley called this proactive advancement 'ethical evolution', and saw 'no limit to the extent to which intelligence and will, guided by sound principles of investigation, and organized in the common effort, may modify the conditions of existence for a period longer than that now covered by history'.[4] Although there is no escaping the world's cosmological end, Huxley saw humanity as nevertheless capable of ensuring its extended survival and resisting the potential for degeneration contained in the cosmic process of evolution.

The engagement of Wells and Hodgson with Huxleian principles in their futuristic narratives can be discerned in the use of human dwellings and the forms of wilderness surrounding them. Put simply, in these texts, dwellings often represent the success of the 'ethically best', while the wild environment represents the 'tenacious and powerful enemy' of 'cosmic nature'.[5] Both authors explore some of the ideals of a successful human future, but in doing so they also articulate the anxieties in which their contemporary culture was entrenched. In particular, they address the discourses of degeneration, which grew out of the increasing recognition that evolution would not necessarily result in humanity's changing for the better.[6] Huxley noted that 'Retrogressive is as practical as progressive metamorphosis' for organisms adapting to changing conditions,[7] while Ray Lankester, in his *Degeneration: A Chapter in Darwinism* (1880), used the example of the marine ascidian, whose bodily sophistication declines over its life cycle, to argue against the 'assumption of universal progress [...] it is well to remember that we are subject to the general laws of evolution, and are as likely to degenerate as progress'.[8]

Retrogression, however, was not limited to bodily form; Lankester emphasised that 'we have to fear lest the prejudices, preoccupations, and dogmatism of modern civilisation should in any way lead to the atrophy and loss of the valuable mental qualities inherited by our young forms from primaeval man'.[9] Human mental, as well as physical, potential was at risk, and the germs of destruction, according to some theorists of degeneration, were contained in modern life. In *Degeneration* (1892), for example, Max Nordau identified degeneracy in 'the tendencies of contemporary art and poetry, in the life and conduct of men who write mystic, symbolic, and "decadent" works'.[10] Civilisation itself was deemed to be subject to the laws and trends of evolution and appeared, to many in the 1890s, to be declining rather than progressing.

Perhaps the most significant symbol of the declining condition of modern life was the city, specifically London. For many, London, which had seen dramatic population growth throughout the nineteenth century, had once seemed to epitomise modern civilisation. Its growth, however, had resulted in a pronounced gulf between slums in the East End and new suburban housing for the wealthier.[11] Furthermore, surveys such as

Charles Booth's *Life and Labour of the People* (1886-1903) uncovered
evidence that the Capital contained a vast population of poor and
undernourished citizens: degeneration was not merely a problem of the
future or of remote peoples, but was taking place here and now, in the
heart of the greatest city in the world.[12] Reflecting this mood, William
Delisle Hay's *The Doom of the Great City* (1880) depicts the degenerate
centre of London destroyed by a rampant plague, while the suburbs
survive.[13]

The Second Law of Thermodynamics, which appeared to reveal that
the energy of the sun was finite, accentuated contemporary fears of decline
and entropy. The future of the human species was seemingly limited by
the life of the sun, even if it was not curtailed sooner by physical and
moral degeneration. In *The War of the Worlds* (1898), the inhabitants of
the dying planet Mars represent a possible future for humanity. The
Martians' advanced evolutionary state, with sophisticated technology and
highly developed brains, is offset by their degenerate features: their ugly
physical appearance and their 'primitive method' of reproducing by
'budding off' the young from the parent.[14] As Wells has his narrator
observe, the Martians bear a close resemblance to his description of 'The
Man of the Year Million' (1893): a tadpole-like creature comprising a
giant brain supported by a single giant hands.[15]

The response of futuristic literature to these concerns is not merely to
address consequences of degeneration on the development of the human
body, but also its effects on civilisation, particularly centred on the fate of
London. A defensive dwelling, a bastion or redoubt often represents
human society; a motif frequently employed in utopian fiction. Burrell and
Dale argue that a common principle of utopia is the notion of 'the
"beastliness" of the outside and the "bestliness" of the inside'.[16] Since
Thomas More's *Utopia* (1516), in which fifteen miles of ground are
'digged up' to allow the sea to encircle the land fully, the ideal society is
often deliberately separated and protected from the rest of the world.[17]
Other writers have varied this distancing mechanism, using time, as in
Bellamy's *Looking Backward* (1888), or a dream-vision, as in Morris's
News From Nowhere (1890). In dystopian writing, by contrast, such a
separation often reflects negatively on the society inside, as is the case in
Zamyatin's much later *We* (1924), and the boundary may become
detrimentally breached, which is the fate of the smaller redoubt of
Hodgson's *The Night Land*.

By the latter decades of the nineteenth century, the motif of the redoubt
becomes indelibly inscribed with degeneration theory. The society within
the redoubt has escaped, or must be protected from, the ravages of the

cosmic process, which all too often results in the degeneration of human civilisation as the natural wilderness is restored. Huxley compared this reassertion of nature to the fate of a garden without 'the watchful supervision of the gardener'; the 'antagonistic influences of the general cosmic process' would lead to the decay of gates and walls, and the invasion of wild beasts and native plants.[18] Human society, by analogy, requires constant maintenance of both its walls and its structure. These protected societies often represent the modern city, both recognisably and indirectly, as writers extrapolate from the malaise of modern life or attempt to provide solutions. In the texts being discussed here, the city, represented either literally, or symbolically as a building or house, is opposed to the external 'beastliness' of a chaotic surrounding environment. This 'antagonistic' wilderness opposes the order and harmony inside the dwelling and has the potential to overwhelm it, but is kept at a distance, though not always permanently, by distinct barriers or boundaries.

Wells's texts contain some clear boundaries between dwelling and wilderness. In *When the Sleeper Wakes,* an immense wall protects the massive capital of 2100. For Wells, as Mark Hillegas notes, the 'giant mechanical city' represents 'the victory of the city over the land'.[19] Yet in *Sleeper*, the struggle between Graham and Ostrog suggests the ultimate down-fall of the vast future London, as does the characterisation of the landscape around the victorious city. Graham can see that nothing remains of the London suburbs but 'a waste of ruins, variegated and dense with thickets of the heterogeneous growths that had once adorned the gardens of the belt' (170). Nature has quickly regained a hold on the abandoned land, recalling Huxley's decaying walls and invading weeds, much as the rapid reclamation of England by swamp and forest in Richard Jefferies's *After London* (1885) prefigures them.[20] The splendour of the twenty-first century city is contrasted with a wasteland that seems hungry and alive: the vegetation 'undulated and frothed amidst the countless cells of crumbling house walls, and broke along the foot of the city wall in a surf of bramble and holly and ivy and teazle and tall grasses'.[21] Wild nature is lapping at the doorstep of this new but fragile edifice of civilisation, a reminder of the limits of humankind's control over the environment.

The balance between city and wilderness is highlighted by the nature of the barrier between them: it is a distinct line, but also a fine one. Graham observes that 'the boundary of London was like a wall, like a cliff, a steep fall of three or four hundred feet. [...] The city limits were indeed as sharply defined as in the ancient days when the gates were shut at nightfall and the robber foeman prowled to the very walls' (170). Graham's

comparison suggests a return to a primitive state of the world outside the
wall once the human hand has abandoned it in favour of the self-contained
city, and implies the fate of the city if the wall fell.

'A Story of the Days to Come' is set in a glass-covered London
virtually identical to that in *When the Sleeper Wakes*.[22] Elizabeth and
Denton, two lovers who marry in secret, idealistically seek a new life in
this primitive external world, again divided from the city by a cliff-like
wall: 'The towering buildings of the new age, the mechanical ways, the
electric and water mains, all came to an end together, like a wall, like a
cliff, near four hundred feet in height, abrupt and sheer' (741). The
absoluteness of this barrier not only emphasises the extent and the limits of
human control but is a literal symbol of the gulf between humans and the
environment.

Additionally, a semi-natural boundary lies between the city wall and
the free wilderness Elizabeth and Denton seek: the fields of the Food
Company. All weeds have been eliminated by a martial 'campaign of
extermination' rather than trouble with the expense and inefficiency of
continual weeding – paving the way, perhaps, for the overgrown but weed-
free Eloi future of *The Time Machine*.[23] The city requires some way of
producing food for the citizens, but this vast agricultural garden is more
than just a food supply. It provides a buffer between the wilderness and the
city. It is a location in which humans can assert mastery over nature, yet
also one in which the wilderness encroaches on the urban human world.
On their journey through this buffer zone, Elizabeth and Denton pass the
final barriers, indicated first physically by passing 'the clay and the root
crops and the single fence that hedged them in' and then legally by
reaching the point at which 'the prohibition against trespass no longer
held' (742). Now they are free to cross the open hillside. Crossing this
final legal boundary symbolises not only their freedom but also their
passing into (environmentally) lawless, unregulated land.

The life the lovers imagine leading there harks back to a romantic
ideal, recalling the pastoral world of *News From Nowhere*. They imagine
'flower-covered, diamond-windowed cottages of thatch and plaster, with
the sweet air and the earth about them, amidst tangled hedges and the song
of birds' (737) but, soon, 'through the long neglected ceilings of the
derelict home came noisy spouts of water [...] and now a mass of plaster
from the wall would slide and smash, and now some loosened tile would
rattle down the roof and crash into the empty greenhouse below' (747).
They are living the actual moment of nature reclaiming the land humans
deserted, and their experience drives them back to the comfort of the city,
unfit for the realities of life outside the wall. It is 'as if they were in some

other world, some disordered chaos of stress and tumult' (747). The unwelcoming and chaotic wilderness is contrasted to the warmth and safety of the city. The existence of a wall may protect humankind from the wilderness, but also creates, reinforces, and perpetuates human inability to sustain a life outwith the artificial dwelling – at least, without the return to barbarism described by Jefferies and predicted by Wells.[24]

'A Story of the Days to Come' and *When the Sleeper Wakes* figure the wilderness as a threat: its continued presence indicates that humans have not won the right to a permanent existence, despite their giant mechanical cities. The wilderness is a reminder that the biological laws of nature and evolution will eventually triumph over civilisations established by humans in the current conditions of the world. The wilderness is threatening because of its chaotic potential – the potential through Darwinian natural selection to produce species better suited to the environment, unless humans submit to evolutionary and environmental pressures and, like the Eloi, risk losing their identity as 'human'. The environment is inevitably going to change as the planet and the solar system age, and 'what is "fittest" depends on the conditions'.[25] In *The Time Machine*, the climate in the year 802,701 is noticeably warmer than in the 1890s, with a corresponding flourishing of plant life. Eventually, however, as the Time Traveller journeys forward again, the sun dies, with a corresponding cooling of the planet, and humans have been unable to adapt for survival in the bitter cold and growing darkness in any recognisable form.[26] In this way the 'disordered chaos' of the wilderness also represents the threat of bodily degeneration, the potential in the human body for retrogressive metamorphosis. Protecting human society from the wilderness, therefore, is also protecting the human form.

Despite the safeguard from a potentially destructive natural wilderness offered by a dominant city, utopian texts often reflect Victorian beliefs that nature also has a positive part to play in human life. Twentieth-century town planning was greatly influenced by the ideas of Ebenezer Howard, who inspired the garden city movement with his publication of *Tomorrow: a Peaceful Path to Real Reform* in 1898.[27] Howard saw both the country and the city as having beneficial and detrimental qualities, and envisioned the best of each being combined in his Garden City. He argued that 'human society and the beauty of nature are meant to be enjoyed together. [...] Town and country *must be married*, and out of this joyous union will spring a new hope, a new life, a new civilisation'.[28] Tomorrow's cities, therefore, could be used to combat the evils of modern life by a judicious combination of urban and rural life.[29]

While Wells's philosophy was not dissimilar to Howard's, David C. Smith notes that he 'thought Howard's plans too small – the railways were too close, the factories too oppressive. [...] In Wells's Utopian city, no-one would live near his work'.[30] *A Modern Utopia* is devised on a global scale with natural and urban regions balanced accordingly.[31] The World State regulates not only cities but also the landscape. Some regions are designated for industrial purpose, 'wide stretches of cheerless or unhealthy or toilsome or dangerous land with never a household; there will be regions of mining and smelting [...] with a sort of weird inhospitable grandeur of industrial desolation,' to which the people will come and 'work for spell and return to civilisation again, washing and changing their attire' (39). To compensate, there are 'beautiful regions of the earth specially set apart' (40). All forms of nature, both garden and wilderness, are subordinate to the needs of humans. Attractive regions of pinewoods and arable land are criss-crossed by many paths, a visible and significant mark of human ownership (38). The industrial regions are exploited, and are passive, posing no threat to human society. No walls are required, for travel is rapid and limitless.[32] The 'weird inhospitable grandeur' carries an echo of the Gothic experience of the sublime amongst wild mountains, as does the dark and fiery landscape of *The Night Land*, but the workers 'return to civilisation' from these regions untainted and unharmed; the effect of the desolate landscape is sloughed off with a change of clothes.

In Utopia, even the problems of the city of London have been addressed. The city is now a 'noble mansion', and contains a 'central space, rich with palms and flowering bushes and statuary. We shall look along an avenue of trees, down a wide gorge between the cliffs of crowded hotels [...] to where the shining morning river streams dawnlit out to sea,' and 'multitudes of people will pass softly to and fro' (165). This central space is very similar to Howard's Central Park which is 'within very easy access of all the people' and features a 'beautiful and well-watered garden' at its centre.[33] Utopian London has become a variety of garden city in clear contrast to the mechanical city of *When the Sleeper Wakes*, which is already starting to breed Morlockian workers in its underground levels.[34]

In *A Modern Utopia*, passive nature, kept under control and bound to serve human needs, becomes a positive aspect of a future society. Furthermore, the success of a 'modern' Utopia is founded upon the recognition that if the cosmic process is relentless, then utopia must be continually developing or 'kinetic'. Wells argued that Darwinian thought had fundamentally affected the traditional utopia by undermining its 'perfect and static' condition with the kinetic pressures of evolution (11). The Modern Utopia applies Huxley's principles of ethical evolution to attain its success: it 'must shape not as a permanent state but as a hopeful stage leading to a long ascent of stages' (11). For change and development to take place without adverse affects, Huxley's common effort of organisation is employed, and this means applying it to nature and social constructions alike.

As indicated, the modern city was considered to produce degenerative influences; the garden was one way of improving the conditions of the city, and thus of society. The presence and enjoyment of gardens, as Howard advocated, is a way of combating degeneration, but only if, Wells appears to be saying, like ethical evolution, the garden can be properly controlled and made to serve rather than dominate humans. To return to Huxley's analogy in which gardens represented the 'state of art' of human civilisation, the ' "horticultural process"[...] sets itself against the "cosmic process" '.[35]   The former must be sustained in order to resist the detrimental effects of the latter, as both *When the Sleeper Wakes* and 'A Story of the Days to Come' suggest. In Arcadian utopias, however, such as Hudson's *A Crystal Age* (1887), the wilderness is embraced on equal terms, and the human dwelling is fully harmonised with the state of nature, while evolution appears to have ceased.

In *A Crystal Age*, the relationship of the house to its surroundings is seamless. There is no buffer of domesticated environment between it and the 'wilderness'; there are no 'trim gardens, lawns, or hedges near it. The building simply rose like a rock, or a mass of rock and greenery combined, from the earth'.[36] The sloping sides of the platform on which the house sits are 'clothed with ivy, shrubs, and many flowering plants; and beyond, everywhere, flourished the unfailing grass' (31); even the edges of the structure are softened with leafy plants to eradicate any hint of the house functioning as an enclosure and emphasise the seamlessness of building and landscape. The overall effect is of 'a cloud reposing on the stony summit of a hill': what begins as a description of a house blends gradually into the natural background until the 'house' as we usually understand one to be is obscured completely (32).

Yet it is the presence of the house that leads the protagonist, Smith, to revise his first impression of a 'pretty, primitive wilderness' to 'Not quite a wilderness' (5). In fact, what he calls a wilderness more closely resembles a garden, which enables the seamless transition from house to nature. Smith wishes to define what he sees in terms of established divisions between houses, gardens and wild land, but the blend confuses him, destabilising the familiar categories of his own world. In this world, wilderness and garden are one and the same; this utopia does not acknowledge Darwinian principles, and is at no risk from degenerative tendencies. This is further indicated by a conversation between Smith and the 'father', which reveals the discrepancies in their respective understanding of the fundamental concept of the house. The ideas of building or of pulling down a house puzzle and even horrify the father. It is not a refuge built to keep the degenerate outside out, but is an organic part of the world; perhaps not even human-made. 'For are not all houses, like the forest of trees, the human race, the world we live in, eternal?', he asks (32). Evolution, either progressive or retrogressive, requires the passage of time to effect its changes. The crystal age gives the impression of being cocooned from time, a crystalline moment in which the world and the species will remain untouched.

Wells is adamant that this changelessness is fundamentally untenable, and *A Modern Utopia* criticises societies in which 'Change and development were dammed back by invincible dams for ever' (11). Krishan Kumar notes that the nineteenth-century utopia is characterised by being 'temporal and dynamic'.[37] Texts such as *A Crystal Age* and Morris's *News From Nowhere*, however, oppose this notion and depict a timeless moment of perfection. It is perhaps more accurate to call dynamism and temporality characteristics of post-Darwinian utopia, where it acknowledges the inevitable passage of time and the inexorable effects of evolutionary laws. Evolution means the future must be 'kinetic', as *A Modern Utopia* maintains. Huxley emphasised that 'If, for millions of years, our globe has taken the upward road, yet, some time, the summit will be reached and the downward route will be commenced'.[38] If *A Crystal Age* displays the species at (arguably) a social evolutionary pinnacle, *The Time Machine*'s vision of the year 802,701 reveals what must happen afterwards in a kinetic world, if ethical evolution is not implemented.

The Time Machine contains echoes of *A Crystal Age* and *News From Nowhere*. Much as Smith observes the single mansion visible amongst the lush countryside, so the Time Traveller from a similar vantage point notices that 'here and there among the greenery were palace-like buildings' (29). He continues, ' "There were no hedges, no signs of propriety rights, no evidence of agriculture; the whole earth had become a garden" ' (30). Again, this lack of boundaries recalls Smith's first impression of the great house of the crystal age. Furthermore, the Time Traveller observes the lack of sexual differentiation amongst the Eloi, who all have the ' "same soft hairless visage, and the same girlish rotundity of limb" ' (29). Similarly, Smith struggles to distinguish the men and women he sees in *A Crystal Age*, 'so much did they resemble each other in height, in their smooth faces, and in the length of their hair' (14).

Wells adopts the utopian model of *A Crystal Age* for his own purposes, undercutting the Arcadian utopia by insisting on the inevitability of Darwinian law and revealing the terrible potential inherent in the degenerative tendencies of non-'ethical' evolution. As the Time Traveller gradually learns the truth about the year 802,701 and the notion of an Edenic or Arcadian utopia is eroded, the Eloi's garden starts to look like a twisted, distorted reflection of the crystal age. In this light, the excessive natural integration and the Platonic affection of *A Crystal Age* assume a threatening aspect. Furthermore, the ruins the Time Traveller sees are not organic like Smith's house. They have been over-run by a wilderness the Eloi neither control nor harmonise with, ' "a tangled waste of beautiful bushes and flowers, a long-neglected and yet weedless garden" ' (36). The obscured ruins and neglected garden again parallel Huxley's vulnerable horticulture, except that no weeds remain to choke the ' "wholesome plants" ' (31). Instead, it is the carefully-bred plants themselves that cover the place with a lush, exotic wilderness, and with a double layer of irony. Not only has the art of the horticulturalist, the human civilisation, been literally over-run by its own success, but the elimination of weeds and gnats along with the enhancement of 'fruits and sweet and delightful flowers' has contributed to human degeneration by removing the struggle embedded in the production and protection of crops and vegetation. ' "Strength is the outcome of need" ', the Time Traveller realises; ' "security sets a premium on feebleness" ' (31). The return of the garden to wilderness and 'tangled waste' parallels the degeneration of the human species itself, and is a call to Wells's contemporaries to combat it, through the implementation of a process of ethical evolution.

William Hope Hodgson's *The Night Land* addresses many of the issues that Wells explores in these texts.[39] The setting of *The Night Land* is also centred on a human dwelling of the distant future, a redoubt built in a hostile landscape, millennia after the heat-death of the sun, fulfilling Huxley's prophecy that the conditions of existence could be modified to ensure extended survival of the human species. *The Night Land* owes more than a passing debt to *The Time Machine*. It is a vision of life within and beyond the moment of 'rayless obscurity' and 'the horror of this great darkness' experienced by the Time Traveller (85). All life is found deep below the frozen surface near the warmth of the planet's core. This is just as Wells had imagined would happen in 'The Man of the Year Million': 'The whole world will be snow-covered and piled with ice; all animals, all vegetation vanished, except this last branch of the tree of life. The last men have gone even deeper, following the diminishing heat of the planet'.[40]

Yet in their environmentally-ravaged world of geological violence and
degenerate monsters, the humans in *The Night Land* have survived long
beyond any Wellsian expectation, protecting their physical form, identity,
and spirit by barricading themselves inside a pyramid-shaped refuge called
the Great Redoubt.[41] The 'wilderness' of the surrounding Night Land takes
a Gothicised form, of monsters, geological activity, miscegenation and
spiritual corruption. A series of colossal, indescribable creatures keep a
watch on the pyramid and are a living part of the landscape. The 'Thing in
the South' is 'a living hill of watchfulness [...] It brooded there, squat and
tremendous' (327). Later in the story, a black 'Humped thing' climbs out
of the Vale of Red Fire and approaches 'like a Hill of Blackness in the
Land' (358). The land itself comes alive, as threateningly vital as any
botanical wilderness. The wilderness is kept out not merely by a wall, but
by 'a grey, metalled mountain going up measureless into the gloom of the
everlasting night, and from [the narrator's] feet the sheer downward sweep
of the grim, metal walls, six full miles, and more, to the plain below'
(331). In this way, degeneration is kept at bay. In his description of the
pyramid's situation, Hodgson takes Wells's glimpse of degenerate horror
at the end of *The Time Machine* to its visual and literal extremes.

With its grim metal walls and internal travelling roadways, the Great
Redoubt superficially resembles Wells's giant mechanical city, but
internally the dwelling has much in common with *A Modern Utopia* and
Howard's Garden City.[42] The geometric layout, like Howard's, is
systematic and orderly, and Hodgson evidently subscribes to Howard's
view that human society and the beauty of nature are supposed to be
enjoyed together.[43] The lowest and therefore largest levels of this giant
pyramid are the Underground Fields at its base; this society is literally
built upon its gardens. The fields are not a threat to the human dwelling;
together they form a utopian whole. There are 'long roadways, and hidden
methods to help travel; and constant temples of rest along the miles; and
groves; and the charm of water, falling' (360), while 'in the corn-fields
there was the sweet rustle of grain, and the glad, silken laughter of
poppies, all beneath a warm and happy light' (335). The use of this space
recalls the central space in the London of *A Modern Utopia*, in which
'millions walk and take excursion, and go orderly or not' (335). In this
way, nature can be enjoyed safely while degeneration is kept at a distance
beyond the walls of the pyramid. The art of the horticulturalist is
preserved, while the cosmic process is steadily resisted.

This compromise is effective, but in both *A Modern Utopia* and *The
Night Land*, freedom (or restrictions placed upon it), is symbolised by the
use of walls and gardens. In both, a proper garden is beautiful and

wholesome, representing a positive, safe variety of liberty. In Wells's Utopia the domination of nature is so complete that there is no wilderness except that which is also subordinated. The possession of private land and property, however, is seen as vital: 'The room or apartments or home [...] must be private and under his or her complete dominion; it seems harsh and intrusive to forbid a central garden plot [...] within the house walls' (34-5). The risk, however, is of 'the residential areas becoming a vast area of defensively walled villa Edens' (35). The only solution is strict regulation. For Wells, liberty is not practical unless it is restricted.

The Underground Fields of the Great Redoubt could well be described as a 'defensively walled Eden': a safe garden in which the threat of the land outside is never quite forgotten. The existence of such a place is dependent on its division from external nature, not on its connection or similarity to it. By its awareness and use of this fact, however, the Great Redoubt has both achieved the protection of the inner society from the threatening wilderness, and has combated the degeneration inherent in the city by having a garden as its literal and symbolic foundation. Hodgson's stance on the issue of freedom is almost as complex as that of Wells. The rules of *A Modern Utopia* reveal an integral concern for the 'welfare of the community as a whole' (29). In *The Night Land*, the loss of individual freedoms for the sake of the common good is not questioned, since each citizen 'must to his duty to the security and well-being of the Redoubt' (335). Neither the ancient practice of flaying anyone caught leaving the pyramid, nor the current one of flogging receive condemnation: the rationale that an individual is 'corrected to the best advantage for his own well-being' is upheld. As Kelly Hurley has pointed out, the Great Redoubt is an 'absolutely closed society with rigid internal controls', and this is essential for humanity's survival: its only defence against the cosmic process are its literal and figurative walls.[44]

In this way, however, *The Night Land* embodies a contradiction, countering Wells's condemnation of the 'invincible dams' of static utopias. The threat of miscegenation and spiritual corruption from the surrounding Night Land is so great that Hodgson's society cannot achieve Huxleian success as the ethically best ('kinetic') *without* employing an invincible dam ('static'). Ethics, therefore, is not sufficient. It may, perhaps, be and have been sufficient for humans in a younger age of the world, but the further into the future humanity survives, the harder it becomes to resist the cosmic process. *The Night Land* seems to support both the idea of a successful bastion and of ethical evolution. By the time of the story, the human race has evolved psychically to become quite different from contemporary humanity. The importance of the Great

Redoubt's social empathy to humanity's successful survival in the hostile Night Land suggests that for Hodgson this spiritual evolutionary step is necessary to achieve the common unity of effort that Huxley saw as key. Wells, on the other hand, saw social, scientific, and political organisation as the means to achieving this end. Although both authors recognise the need to understand and use evolution in order to resist its degenerative aspect, their treatment of the wilderness reflects their different approaches. For Wells, nature may, ideally, be integrated in the service of Utopia; for Hodgson, nature poses both a threat and a boon to social success.

Huxley concluded that 'the ethical progress of society depends, not on imitating the cosmic process, still less in running away from it, but in combating it'.[45] Futuristic novels have attempted extrapolations of all three of these routes to social progress. In the texts examined here, the human dwelling (which comprises both an architectural and a social structure) represents a claim by the species for the right to exist in a universe in which biological laws are inescapable. The dwelling structure imposes order on itself, and sometimes also on the environment around it. Both impositions are statements of human dominance and serve as a defence against degeneration as represented by the natural wilderness. In this way, late-Victorian anxieties about humanity's place in the universe are expressed through the tension between human-made dwellings and the surrounding natural environment. Nature is perceived as a threat, and therefore must either be regulated, as in *A Modern Utopia*, or kept at a distance, as in *The Night Land*, *When the Sleeper Wakes*, and 'A Story of the Days to Come', lest it should over-run civilisation, as in *The Time Machine*.

Nevertheless, these texts also express a degree of ambivalence about the relationship between nature and degeneration. The environment is figured both as a threat and a benefit to humanity, depending on how successfully and justly human societies make use of it. The human dwelling, like the modern city, can contain its own sources of degeneration. However, this can be countered, as *A Modern Utopia* does, by the judicious inclusion of controlled nature into the social structure and the acknowledgement of evolutionary inevitability, showing that only by admitting and combating the potential causes of degeneration can it be addressed. While the laws of evolution and entropy mean that even Hodgson's indomitable civilisation must one day come to an end, sufficient ethical vigour remains for humans to live as though this were not so, as they follow the Time Traveller into futurity.

Notes

---

[1] In his *Experiment in Autobiography*, 2 vols (London: Gollancz, 1934), Wells recalled that 'That year I spent in Huxley's class was, beyond all question, the most educational year of my life', I, 201.

[2] T. H. Huxley, 'Prolegomena', in *Collected Essays By T. H. Huxley*, 9 vols (London: Macmillan, 1894), IX, *Evolution and Ethics and Other Essays*, 1-45 (p. 6).

[3] T. H. Huxley, 'Evolution and Ethics' [the Romanes Lecture] (1893), in *Collected Essays*, *IX*, 46-86 (p. 81).

[4] Huxley, 'Evolution and Ethics', p. 85.

[5] Huxley, 'Evolution and Ethics', p. 85.

[6] For a more extensive discussion of degeneration and evolutionary theory see, for example, *Fin-de-siècle/ Fin-du-globe: Fears and Fantasies of the Late Nineteenth Century*, ed. by John Stokes (Basingstoke: Macmillan, 1992), William Greenslade, *Degeneration, Culture, and the Novel 1880-1920* (Cambridge: Cambridge University Press, 1994), and Gillian Beer, *Darwin's Plots: Evolutionary Narrative in Darwin, George Eliot and Nineteenth-Century Fiction* (London: Ark, 1985).

[7] T. H. Huxley, 'The Struggle for Existence in Human Society', in *Collected Essays*, *IX*, 195-236 (p. 199).

[8] E. Ray Lankester, *Degeneration: A Chapter in Darwinism* (London: Macmillan, 1880), p. 60.

[9] Lankester, *Degeneration*, p. 61.

[10] Max Nordau, *Degeneration* (1892) (New York: Appleton, 1895), p. 15.

[11] Linda Dryden, *The Modern Gothic and Literary Doubles: Stevenson, Wilde, and Wells* (Basingstoke: Palgrave Macmillan, 2003), p. 56.

[12] Booth's survey was conducted between 1886 and 1903. Two volumes of his findings first appeared in 1889, and by 1903 seventeen volumes were published under the title *Life and Labour of the People in London*. Booth's survey comprehensively mapped and classified living conditions in London in the late nineteenth century, identifying around a third of the capital's population as living below the poverty line.

[13] William Delisle Hay, *The Doom of the Great City; Being the Narrative of a Survivor, Written A.D. 1942* (London: Newman & Co, 1880). Hay's novel was one of a series of British disaster novels of the late-nineteenth century, which also included Chesney's *The Battle of Dorking* (1871), Jefferies's *After London* (1885), and M. P. Shiel's *The Purple Cloud* (1901).

[14] H. G. Wells, *The War of the Worlds* (London: Heinemann, 1898), pp. 209-10.

[15] H. G. Wells, ' The Man of the Year Million' (1893), reprinted in *H. G. Wells: Journalism and Prophecy*, ed. by W. Warren Wagar (London: Bodley Head, 1965), pp. 3-8. Wells's speculative essay was first published in the *Pall Mall Gazette*, and he built on some of its ideas in *The Time Machine*, *The War of the Worlds* and *The First Men in the Moon*.

[16] Gibson Burrell and Karen Dale, 'Utopiary: Utopias, gardens and organization', in *Utopia and Organization,* ed. by Martin Parker (Oxford: Blackwell, 2002) pp. 106-27 (p. 108).

[17] Sir Thomas More, *Utopia* (1516) (London: Dent, 1974), p. 50.

[18] Huxley, 'Prolegomena', p. 10.

[19] Mark Hillegas, *The Future as Nightmare: H. G. Wells and the Anti-Utopians* (New York: Oxford University Press, 1967), p. 107.

[20] Richard Jefferies, *After London; or Wild England* (1885) (Oxford: Oxford University Press, 1980). In Jefferies's novel, the reassertion of wild nature is illustrated by native plants which are stronger than the domestic crops: 'Year by year the original crops of wheat, barley, oats, and beans asserted their presence by shooting up, but in gradually diminished force, as nettles and coarser plants, such as the wild parsnips, spread out into the fields from the ditches and choked them' (p. 4).

[21] H. G. Wells, *When the Sleeper Wakes* (1899) (New York: Random House, 2003), p. 170. Subsequent references to this work will be cited in the text.

[22] H. G. Wells, 'A Story of the Days to Come' (1897), in *The Complete Short Stories of H. G. Wells* (London: St. Martin's Press, 1974), pp. 715-806. Subsequent references to this work will be cited in the text.

[23] Dryden, p. 152. Both 'A Story of the Days to Come' and *When the Sleeper Wakes* can be seen as stages on the evolutionary journey from the nineteenth century to the world of *The Time Machine*, resembling the civilisation that flickers past the Time Traveller on his first leap into the future.

[24] *The War in the Air* (1908) (Harmondsworth: Penguin, 1975) ends with Bert Smallways returning home to find England declining into peasantry; the countryside 'presented the strangest mingling of the assurance and wealth of the opening twentieth century with a sort of Düreresque mediaevalism' (p. 359). Dürer was a German artist known particularly for his medieval prints.

[25] Huxley, 'Evolution and Ethics', p. 80.

[26] H. G. Wells, *The Time Machine* (1895) (London: Penguin, 2005), pp. 84-5. Subsequent references to this work will be cited in the text.

[27] Standish Meacham, *Regaining Paradise: Englishness and the Early Garden City Movement* (New Haven, CT: Yale University Press, 1999), p. 53.

[28] Ebenezer Howard, *Tomorrow: a Peaceful Path to Real Reform* (London: Swan Sonnenschein, 1898), pp. 9-10. Republished in 1899 as *Garden Cities of Tomorrow.*

[29] In 1785 William Cowper wrote that 'God made the country and man made the town' (*In the Task,* Book 1, line 749): a distinction echoed by Howard's philosophy.

[30] David C. Smith, *H. G. Wells: Desperately Mortal* (New Haven: Yale University Press, 1986), p. 186.

[31] H. G. Wells, *A Modern Utopia* (1905) (London: Penguin, 2005). Subsequent references to this work will be cited in the text.

[32] W. Warren Wagar, *H. G. Wells: Traversing Time* (Middletown, CT: Wesleyan University Press, 2004). Wagar notes that in *Anticipations*, Wells describes how progress in transportation could lead to the expansion of London over the whole of England: 'the sharp division between city and country prophesied in *When the Sleeper Wakes* would virtually disappear' (p. 81).

[33] Howard, *Tomorrow*, p. 14.

[34] Wagar, *Traversing Time*, p. 67.

[35] Huxley, 'Prolegomena', p. 33.

[36] W. H. Hudson, *A Crystal Age* (London: Fisher & Unwin 1887; repr. 1906), p. 30. Subsequent references to this work will be cited in the text.

[37] Krishan Kumar, *Utopia and Anti-Utopia in Modern Times* (Oxford: Blackwell, 1991), p .45.

[38] Huxley, 'Evolution and Ethics', p. 85.

[39] William Hope Hodgson, *The Night Land* (1912) in *The House on the Borderland and other novels* (London: Gollancz, 2002). Subsequent references to this work will be cited in the text. Hodgson's published fiction started to appear in 1904, but there is evidence from his letters that much of his actual writing took place from 1898 onwards. Sam Gafford presents convincing evidence from Hodgson's letters indicating that his four novels were written in the reverse order to that in which they were published. This positions *The Night Land*, published in 1912, as having been written sometime between 1898 and 1905, which helps to account for the extent of the influence of *fin-de-siècle* culture on it. See Gafford, 'Writing Backwards: the novels of William Hope Hodgson' (1997) <http://alangullette.com/lit/hodgson/gafford.htm> [Accessed 2/05/2006] (originally published in *Studies in Weird Fiction*, 11 (1992), 12-15.

[40] Wells, 'The Man of the Year Million', p. 8.

[41] The narrator of Hodgson's novel lives in the 'Great Redoubt', but the plot centres on his rescue of his beloved from a second, smaller redoubt, which has succumbed to degeneration and the hostility of the Night Land and serves as a prophetic warning of the fate of the Great Redoubt if, and when, its defences fail.

[42] The Great Redoubt is laid out in the shape of a pyramid a hundred miles high, with a four-sided base. Its upper levels are mainly residential, and also house the Room of Mathematics, where the Monstruwacans, the society's scientific elite, work. The lower levels contain recreational space as well as the agricultural fields that support the population of many hundreds of millions.

[43] Howard, p. 9.

[44] Kelly Hurley, 'The Modernist Abominations of William Hope Hodgson', in *Gothic Modernisms*, ed. by Andrew Smith and Jeff Wallace (Basingstoke: Palgrave, 2001), pp. 129-49 (p. 141).

[45] Huxley, 'Evolution and Ethics', p. 83

H. G. WELLS AND WILLIAM JAMES: A PRAGMATIC APPROACH

SYLVIA HARDY

H. G. Wells and William James met only once, in 1909, the year before James's death, but they had been corresponding for several years, and were already familiar with one another's work. The younger man – Wells was forty-two at the time – was already a well-known novelist and thinker; James, twenty-four years older, was by then a philosopher and psychologist with a world-wide reputation, best known for his promotion of Pragmatism. After the publication of *The Principles of Psychology* in 1890, James concentrated on philosophy, and in the summer that Wells met him he was in England to deliver the Hibbert Lectures at Oxford.

His wife had presented Wells with *The Principles of Psychology* in November 1898, and the marginalia and copious underlining in the two volumes indicate that he had read them thoroughly.[1] James's initial training had been in medicine, and throughout his book he emphasises that mental life depends on physiology, an emphasis which Wells the biologist endorsed. *The Principles of Psychology* introduced him to James's philosophical views because, as Gerald E. Myers points out: 'Since psychology and philosophy were not distinctly separated in 1890, *Principles* is not only a textbook in experimental psychology but also a landmark contribution to the philosophy of psychology or the philosophy of mind'.[2] Wells's brief religious phase at the end of the First World War was very much guided by James's highly influential *The Varieties of Religious Experience* (1902) and probably, too, by the discussions they had in 1909. He attributes the central idea of *God the Invisible King* (1917) to the recent work of 'my friend and master, that very great American, the late William James'.[3] In 1930, Wells's biographer, Geoffrey West, wrote that James was a thinker 'whom Wells regards as an influence as important to his maturity as Huxley to his youth', and the use of the present tense indicates that this was a topic that he and the author had discussed.[4]

James reciprocated the admiration and was an enthusiastic advocate of Wells's writings. As early as 1902 he was recommending Wells's books to a number of friends and neighbours, praising him as a 'growing man' and one likely to influence the coming generation. In one letter he thanks a friend for sending him a copy of Wells's latest book (the title is unspecified but it was clearly *Anticipations*), and comments: 'He makes a sudden daylight break through innumerable old blankets of prejudice'.[5] In June 1905, James wrote to Wells for the first time. He had, he writes, read and admired *Anticipations* (1901) and *Mankind in the Making* (1903), together with 'numerous other lighter volumes of yours'. It is, however, his recent reading of the newly-published *A Modern Utopia* (1905) which has prompted this letter: ' "the summation of stimuli" reaches the threshold of discharge and I can't help overflowing in a note of gratitude'.

> You 'have your faults, as who has not?' but your virtues are unparalleled and transcendent, and I believe that you will prove to have given a shove to the practical thought of the next generation that will be amongst the greatest of its influences for good.[6]

James believed that Pragmatism was gaining converts, and the following year, he wrote in a letter to a friend that the world of thought was 'on the eve of a renovation no less important than that contributed by Locke', and amongst the band of 'pragmatic' and 'humanistic' philosophers leading this movement, says James, 'H. G. Wells ought to be counted in'.[7] It is interesting that even before the publication of his most overtly philosophical book, *First and Last Things: A Confession of Faith and a Rule of Life* (1908), Wells was being hailed as a fellow spirit by one of the world's foremost philosophers. When he had read the book, James wrote to Wells enthusiastically:

> *First and Last Things* is a great achievement. The first two 'books' should be entitled 'philosophy without humbug' and used as a textbook in all the colleges of the world. [...] This book is worth any 100 volumes on Metaphysics and any 200 of Ethics, of the ordinary sort.[8]

A few months later, James visited his next-door neighbour with a copy of the book exclaiming, 'Why can this Wells, without any philosophical training, write philosophy as well as the best of them?'[9]

It is true, of course, that H. G. Wells had no formal education in philosophy, and he began 'Scepticism of the Instrument', his address to the Oxford Philosophical Society in 1903, by admitting that his first title had been 'Metaphysics of an Amateur'. Nonetheless, since he had read more he found himself 'somewhere near to and parallel with what you are calling here Pragmatism and Humanism'.[10] The paper outlines Wells's belief in the uniqueness of all physical objects and organic beings. He argues that the limitations of the 'instrument', the human brain itself, which 'has only a limited number of pigeon-holes for our correspondences with an unlimited universe of objective uniques'[11] oblige it to seek resemblances and impose classifications.[12] In *First and Last Things*, Wells builds on these ideas and makes a clear statement about his personal philosophy – the book is, after all, subtitled 'A Confession of Faith and a Rule of Life'. He adopts certain beliefs, Wells claims, because he feels the need for them, and 'My belief in them rests upon the fact that they work for me and satisfy my desire for harmony and beauty'.[13] Although, he concedes, these are arbitrary assumptions they are not necessarily either original or idiosyncratic – other people may well have reached similar conclusions – and they are always subject to test and revision: 'each day they stand the wear and tear, and each new person they satisfy, is another day and another voice towards showing that they do correspond to something that is so far fact and real'.[14] This is the approach which William James sees as the core of the Pragmatic method. In *Pragmatism* he attacks the view held by both idealist and rationalist philosophers that truth is, or can ever be, 'an inert, static relation':

> *True ideas are those that we can assimilate, validate, corroborate and verify. False ideas are those that we can not.* […] The truth of an idea is not a stagnant property inherent in it. Truth *happens* to an idea. It *becomes* true, is *made* true by events. Its verity *is* in fact an event, a process: the process namely of its verifying itself, its veri-*fication*. Its validity is the process of its valid-*ation*.[15]

No wonder James responded so enthusiastically to *A Modern Utopia*, which starts from the premiss that 'the Modern Utopia must not be static but kinetic, must shape not as a permanent state but as a hopeful stage, leading to a long ascent of stages'.[16] It is easy, too, to see why Wells, the sceptical empiricist, finds himself in accord with Pragmatism which is, as he puts it, 'the abandonment of infinite assumptions, the extension of the experimental spirit to all human interests'.[17]

James's ideas feature in Wells's fiction, not only at this period but throughout his career. In *Pragmatism*, for instance, James inveighs against philosophers and scientists who assume that providing a name for 'God' or 'Matter' or 'Energy' provides an adequate verbal solution to a metaphysical problem. They feel that, 'You can rest when you have them. You are at the end of your metaphysical quest,' whereas:

If you follow the Pragmatic method, you must bring out of each word its
practical cash value, set it to work within the stream of your experience. It
appears less of a solution then than as a program for more work, and more
particularly as an indication of the ways in which existing realities may be
changed.[18]

This is the task Richard Trafford sets himself in Wells's 1912 novel,
Marriage. Despite being successful in his career, Trafford is dissatisfied
and restless and determined to find a worthwhile outlet for his energies.
He concludes that hitherto all assertions about aesthetics and ethics have
been meaningless because they lack an adequate means of expression: '
"All the religions," he said, "all the philosophies, have pretended to
achieve too much. We've no language as yet for religious truth or
metaphysical truth" '.[19] Trafford decides on a project, as he tells his wife:

'One cannot struggle at large for plain statement and copious and free and
courageous statement, one needs a positive attack'.
He designed a book, which he might write if only for the definition it
would give him and with no ultimate publication, which was to be called:
'The Limits of Language as a Means of Expression.' [...] It was to be a
pragmatist essay, a sustained attempt to undermine the confidence of all
that scholasticism and logic chopping which still lingers like the *sequelæ*
of a disease in our University philosophy. [...] His thought had come out to
a conviction that the line to wider human understanding lies through a huge
criticism and cleaning up of the existing methods of formulation, as a
preliminary to the wider and freer discussion of those religious and social
issues our generation still shrinks from.[20]

For a Pragmatist, language can never be regarded as fixed or static, and
both James and Wells are very much concerned with the ways in which
the language of scientific thought influences human understanding. In
First and Last Things, Wells stresses that empirical science has added
richly to the store of human knowledge during the last three hundred years
and has done much to clarify men's thinking, but there can be problems
when a scientist who is accustomed to working with technical terms which
have a fixed, precise definition within a specialised field, assumes that he
can apply the same standards to ordinary concerns: 'The man trained
solely in science falls easily into a superstitious attitude; he is overdone
with classification. He believes in the possibility of exact knowledge
everywhere. What is not exact, he declares, is not knowledge. He believes
in specialists and experts in all fields'.[21] George Ponderevo, the narrator of
Tono-Bungay (1909), is just such a man. His world view has been shaped
by his training in the physical sciences, and throughout the book he makes

'the error of excessive claims to precision' that Wells outlines in *First and Last Things*.[22] George, appalled by what he sees as the 'unmanageable realities'[23] of Edwardian capitalist society, goes back to 'the fine realities of steel'[24] of his Thames-side shipyard. The scientific truth he claims to have found proves to be a destroyer, and he neither knows nor cares about its purpose and utility. In search of an unachievable ideal he has retreated and, in James's words, taken refuge 'from the intolerably confused and gothic character which mere facts present'. Such a solution, James claims, provides 'no *explanation* of our concrete universe, it is another thing altogether, a substitute for it, a remedy, a way of escape'.[25] Idealistic, dogmatic, above all a rationalist, George is, in fact, the perfect exemplum of the Tender-minded temperament James outlines in *Pragmatism*. He is a marked contrast to the wise psychiatrist, Wilfrid Devizes, in Wells's 1925 novel, *Christina Alberta's Father*,[26] or the questioning, optimistic Gemini Twain in the 1939 *Babes in the Darkling Wood*,[27] both specifically categorised as Pragmatists, who mediate between the Tender-minded rationalists and the materialistic empiricists James characterises as Tough-minded.[28]

For the Pragmatist the issue of freewill is of central importance because moral responsibility depends on it. For James determinism and free-will are incompatible.[29] For him, as for most philosophers, since 'ought' implies 'can' there is no sense in holding that we ought to do what we cannot do, either psychologically or ethically. According to his biographer, it was William James's inability to resolve the problem of determinism through philosophical deliberation which led to a suicidal depression in 1870. He finally decided that, since the issue could not be resolved by argument or experiment, it had to be a matter of belief and choice: 'My first act of freewill,' he wrote in his diary, 'shall be to believe in freewill'.[30] For Wells, too, the issue is fundamental because, as T. H. Huxley had argued in 'Evolution and Ethics,' the exercise of freewill is the only means by which human beings can counter the otherwise inexorable processes of evolution and lead a moral life.[31] In *First and Last Things*, Wells acknowledges that most scientific work is based on the provisional assumption that the universe is 'orderly and absolutely predestined',[32] nevertheless, if he starts from the assumption that he and his fellow beings are free, his life works for him, whilst 'on a theory of mechanical predestination nothing works'.[33] For Wells, as for James, the will is bound up with commitment and purposive action and the closing words of *The Time Machine* reflect this view. After speculating about the Time Traveller's 'cheerless' and deterministic view of the future, the narrator comments, 'If that is so, it remains for us to live as though it were not so'.[34]

Revealing the influence of Huxley, Wells is interested throughout his work in the ways in which human beings can combat the evolutionary process and shape their own future. This not only predisposed him towards William James's Pragmatism and voluntarism, it also – perhaps most significantly – made him receptive to James's theories on reasoning. James's analysis of different ways of thinking not only affected Wells's approach to his writing, it also helped shape the way he saw himself. This is evident in the chapter in *Experiment in Autobiography* where Wells, looking back over his career, compares his ideas on style with those of Joseph Conrad and Ford Madox Ford, and describes what he sees as the fundamental difference between their minds and his. From his boyhood, Wells claims, he has tended to differ from many of his friends who saw and felt and heard much more vividly and emotionally than he did, but, he argues, although this has had its disadvantages, there were compensations, 'the very coldness and flatness of my perceptions gave me a readier apprehension of relationships', [35] and this, he believes, has had important effects on his subsequent development:

> My education at Kensington was very broad and rapid, I suggest, because I was not dealing with burning and glowing sense impressions – and when I came to a course where sense impressions were of primary importance, as they were in the course in mineralogy, I gave way to irrepressible boredom and fell down. My mind became what I call an educated mind, that is to say a mind systematically unified, because of my relative defect in brightness of response. I was easy to educate. [36]

He goes on to argue that 'vivid writers' like Conrad, Stephen Crane and Henry James remained in this sense uneducated because their 'abundant and luminous impressions' were more difficult to subdue to a disciplined, synthesising view of the world.[37] This, he suggests, is because most literary artists are interested only in the concrete instance. As an example, Wells cites a conversation with Conrad:

> I remember a dispute we had one day as we lay on the Sandgate beach and looked out to sea. How, he demanded, would I describe how that boat out there, sat or rode or danced or quivered on the water? I said that in nineteen cases out of twenty I would just let the boat be there in the commonest phrases possible. Unless I wanted the boat to be important I would not give it an outstanding phrase and if I wanted to make it important then the phrase to use would depend on the angle at which the boat became significant. But it was all against Conrad's over-sensitized receptivity that

a boat could ever be just a boat. He wanted to see it and to see it with a vividness of his own. But I wanted to see it and to see it only in relation to something else – a story, a thesis. And I suppose if I had been pressed about it I would have betrayed a disposition to link that story or thesis to something still more extensive and that to something still more extensive and so ultimately to link it up to my philosophy and my world outlook. [38]

Conrad's tendency is to particularise, to focus on the concrete instance, Wells's is to look for wider connections. Wells does not deny that Conrad's type of mind has 'superiorities in many directions',[39] but he clearly believes that his own strong inclination towards rational associations and system has built-in advantages. In *World Brain* (1938), Wells again insists on the way in which this way of thinking has influenced his general approach to his work: 'My particular line of country has always been generalization and synthesis [...] I like my world as coherent and consistent as possible. So far at any rate my temperament is that of a scientific man'.[40]

The link with scientific thinking is significant because Wells's argument in these passages surely owes a great deal to William James's chapter on reasoning in *The Principles of Psychology* which aims to distinguish how 'the peculiar thinking process called reasoning differs from other thought-sequences which may lead to similar results'.[41] James argues that out of a vast number of sense impressions all creatures receive, they single out and attend to the features or 'characters' of any situation which relate to their own practical or instinctive interests. Because man has enormously varied instincts and wants, he attends to far more characters than any other creature. He seeks to discover in what the precise likeness or difference between the two objects lies by transferring his attention rapidly, backwards and forwards, from one to the other; this, he suggests, is what the scientist does when he looks for the reason or law embedded in a phenomenon and 'succeeds in detaching from the collection the peculiarity he was unable to formulate in one alone' (II, 346). Indeed, argues James, it is 'man's superior association by similarity' (II, 345) that determines his position in the animal kingdom and is at the same time the basis of his capacity for reasoning.

James sees language as a paradigm for this process: 'Language is a system of *signs*, different from the things signified but able to suggest them' (II, 356). Animals can be taught to recognise and respond to a number of signs and it is possible therefore that they are, occasionally, consciously aware of the sign as different from the thing signified, in which case this is, says James, 'a true manifestation of language' (II, 356). With man, however, it is very different, because '*He has a deliberate intention to apply a sign to everything.* The linguistic impulse is with him generalized and systematic. For things hitherto unnoticed and unfelt, he desires a sign before he has one' (II, 356). Human language exists, therefore, because, to a far greater degree than other animals, human beings are able to recognise and to extract from a number of concrete instances of signification the one factor they have in common, which is that they have the same use – to function as signs, to stand for something more important than themselves. 'This reflection made, the gulf is passed. Animals probably never make it, because the bond of similarity is not delicate enough' (II, 357).[42] James gives the example of a dog which discovers that yelping at a door or begging for food produce certain responses; to the extent that it deliberately repeats these to achieve a desired result, the dog has learned to recognise particular signs. To become a sign-maker or speaker in the human sense, however, the dog would first have to dissociate the sign from 'the delicate bond of their subtle similarity of use' (II, 357) which exists between them; only then would it be able to use this knowledge to create other signs with the aim of producing similar responses. Animals, James suggests, are unable to associate ideas by similarity because 'characters, the abstraction of which depends on this sort of association, must in the brute always remain drowned, swamped in the total phenomenon which they help constitute, and never use to reason from' (II, 360). Man's capacity for this kind of abstraction is therefore the basis of his reasoning power and it is exemplified by his capacity for language.

In the next section of the chapter, James goes on to apply this distinction to different kinds of mind and to two different kinds of genius. He begins by stating that 'since nature never makes a jump, it is evident that we should find the lowest man occupying in this respect an intermediary position between the brutes and the highest man. And so we do' (II, 360). Genius can be seen as 'identical with the possession of similar association to an extreme degree' (II, 360). What is more, in every field of human endeavour, 'in the arts, in literature, in practical affairs, and in science, association by similarity is the prime condition of success' (II, 360). James then goes on to distinguish between two stages of reasoned thought:

> One where similarity merely operates to call up cognate thoughts, and another farther stage, where the bond of identity between the cognate thoughts is *noticed*; so *minds of genius may divided into two main sorts: those who notice the bond and those who merely obey it.* The first are the abstract reasoners, properly so called, the men of science and philosophers

– the analysts, in a word; the latter are the poets, the critics – the artists, in
a word, the men of intuitions (II, 361)

He is adamant that abstract reasoning '*represents* the higher stage' because
human beings learn to reason by analogy long before they learn to reason
by abstraction (II, 363). Thus, in evolutionary terms intuitive thinking
precedes the higher stage of thinking, and it persists to some extent in all
of us. Whenever we make a judgement for which we are unable to advance
a reason we are, James insists, 'still, all of us, in the savage state.' (II,
365). It is further true, he acknowledges, that the analytical capacity not
only derives out of the earlier stage of thinking, it develops at its expense:
'There must be a penury in one's interest in the details of particular form
in order to permit the forces of the intellect to be concentrated on what is
common to many forms' (II, 361). Thus, the analytic mind is likely to be
less interested in the particular instance which called up the analogy: 'A
certain richness of the æsthetic nature may therefore, easily keep one in
the intuitive stage' (II, 361), and James quotes passages from Homer to
support his contention that the artist need not be judged as intellectually
the inferior of 'a man of the drier mind, in whom the ground is not as
liable to be eclipsed by the general splendour' (II, 362).

It seems very likely that the seeds of Wells's thinking about what he
defines as educated and uneducated minds are to be found in James's
analysis, and although both men emphasise that the æsthetic interest in the
concrete instance should not be judged inferior to the analytic approach,
both are convinced that the latter is a more advanced way of thinking.
What is more, James stresses that it is very rare for both sorts of intellect,
the 'splendid' and the 'analytic', to be found in the same person (II, 362).
It is easy to see, therefore, how Wells, given his respect for William James
as a philosopher and psychologist, and his deeply-held belief in
evolutionary progress, should have been impressed by such statements.
What is more, it gives a new perspective on his repeated insistence that he
did not regard himself as a literary artist.

Since Wells believes that men and women not only can but must
exercise control over their environment and thus over their future, the idea
of movement forward through the exercise of human effort is central to his
philosophy, and this requires the constant refinement of human thinking.
To make such adaptations, men and women must strive to see life
coherently, to relate the individual to the general, to see the concrete
instance as part of a larger whole, and, if this is to be achieved, the kind of
thinking which James categorises as the higher stage of reasoning is a
prerequisite. This view of language and its relation to man's reasoning
power, exalting the analytic above the æsthetic, plays a central role in

shaping the form and expression of Wells's work, both in fiction and non-fiction. It is noticeable, too, that Wells always links himself with systematic, scientific ways of thinking and firmly dissociates himself from what he sees as the artistic mind, with its susceptibility to vivid sense impressions rather than general analytic or synthesizing principles. Admittedly, James is careful to stress that the analytic mind is not cognitively superior to the artistic, but since he *does* maintain in *The Principles of Psychology* that in evolutionary terms it '*represents* the higher stage' because it requires the capacity to abstract the general principle from the concrete instance, then 'Men, taken historically, reason by analogy long before they have learned to reason by abstract characters' (II, 363).

A Modern Utopia, the book which prompted James's first letter to Wells in 1905, exemplifies this distinction. Individualities are respected in utopia 'since every being is unique', nonetheless, for political and social purposes some kind of classification of temperaments is necessary – albeit one which is 'rough' and 'provisional'.[43] Utopians, therefore, are identified according to four types of 'mental individuality', the Poietic, the Kinetic, the Dull and the Base, and the former two 'constitute the living tissue of the state' by providing the governing class, the Samurai.[44] Although both Poietic and Kinetic classes are distinguished by the range and quality of their imagination, there are important differences between them. Poietic types of mind are highly creative and innovative, 'possessing imaginations that range beyond the known and accepted',[45] whilst Kinetic types are more restricted in their thinking: 'They are often very clever and capable people, but they do not do, and they do not desire to do, new things'. It is significant, however, that within these limitations, the Kinetic utopians may imagine 'as vividly or more vividly than members of the former group'.[46] This surely recalls James's distinction between the 'analytic' mind, which focuses on the larger picture – represented in utopia by the Poietic – and the less advanced, intuitive mind – possessed by the Kinetic utopian – which, because it recognises similarities but fails to abstract the bond which links them, cannot see beyond the concrete instance. In *A Modern Utopia*, therefore, Wells is, in James's terms, distinguishing between 'those who notice the bond' of identity between cognate thoughts, and 'those who merely obey it'.[47] It is not surprising that James describes the account of the Samurai as 'magnificent'.[48]

It seems likely, too, that the theory of higher reasoning had an effect on Wells's subsequent writing in a number of less direct ways – most fundamentally, on whether he should convey his ideas through fiction or non-fiction. As early as 1901, Wells writes, in a footnote to *Anticipations*, that fiction would be a less effective way of presenting a serious forecast of the future:

> Fiction is necessarily concrete and definite; it permits of no open alternatives; its aim of illusion prevents a proper amplitude of demonstration, and modern prophecy should be, one submits, a branch of speculation, and should follow with all decorum the scientific method. The very form of fiction carries with something of disavowal.[49]

Fiction has to convey its meaning by way of analogy (this person in this situation is *like* similar persons in similar situations) rather than by following the scientific approach (in James's words, 'abstracting the reason embedded in them all').[50] This means that although a fictional narrative may be equally persuasive, it represents, by definition, a less advanced form of reasoning. But Wells continued to write fiction because, as he stresses in his 1911 lecture on the contemporary novel, he believed that the novel has moral consequences that make it indispensable in a modern world of shifting values.[51] He was always prepared to advance social effectiveness as a justification for literary texts, and after 1918 he regarded it as a moral imperative. In the 1924 Preface to *The Research Magnificent* he cites the onset of the First World War as the end of 'the phase of imaginative play' in his fiction:

> Thereafter there are no more books that turn on a man asking what he shall do with life. The following volumes reflect the onset of the great storm of the world war, and after that war work for the world state ceased to be a subject for discussion and exalted resolution and became as a matter of course the general form of life for a reasonable man of good will.[52]

Wells's commitment to his ideal of the world state has often been cited as an explanation for a change in the style of his fiction, a change which is usually dated around 1910 – Raymond Williams, for instance, declared that 'Wells emigrated to World Government as clearly as Lawrence to New Mexico'[53] – and it is argued that an obsessive, messianic desire to convey his message led Wells to disregard the requirements of his art.[54] I would suggest, however, that it is not 'commitment' in itself that determined the more didactic, discursive form of much of Wells's later fiction so much as the conflict between his belief in the effectiveness of the novel as an agent of social change, and his equally strong conviction that the fictional mode exemplified a 'lower' form of reasoning which precluded the logical presentation of general relationships and system. This conflict led to a search for a fictional form which *could* bring together the concrete example and the generalised principle, the story and the idea. In 1905, Wells set out to marry these two components in *A Modern Utopia* via the interplay of two created characters who comment on what they see, a device which he describes in a Note to the Reader as: 'a sort of shot-silk texture between philosophical discussion on the one hand and imaginative narrative on the other'.[55] A vision of Utopia, argues the narrator, the Owner of the Voice, requires that the immediate vision of the individual human-being be brought together with that of 'a synthetic wider being, the great State, mankind, in which we all move and go, like blood corpuscles'.[56] It is impossible, he adds, to focus on both at the same time:

> *Nevertheless, I cannot separate these two aspects of human life, each commenting on the other. In that incongruity between great and individual inheres the incompatibility I could not resolve, and which therefore, I have had to present in this conflicting form .[57]*

Arguably, this is an incompatibility which Wells never fully resolves. In his autobiography, he claims that it took some years of 'experiments and essays in statement' before he realised that he was feeling his way 'towards something outside any established formula for the novel altogether'.[58] Wells sometimes refers to this new form as the novel of ideas, sometimes as the discussion or dialogue novel:

> In all these novels the interest centres not upon the individual character, but upon the struggles of common and rational motives and frank enquiry against social conditions and stereotyped ideas. The actors in them are types rather than acutely individualized persons. They could not be other than types. [59]

'Types', for Wells, are characters who can represent 'the great' – the general ideas of the book – whilst at the same time retaining their individuality. In 'The Novel of Ideas,' the introduction to his 1939 novel, *Babes in the Darkling Wood*, Wells defends the dialogue novel as one of the oldest forms of literary expression – 'Plato's dramas of the mind *live* to this day'[60] – and he claims that the 'types' he has chosen for this novel are appropriate to its philosophical material – the heroine is a Newnham graduate, her lover an Oxford man who writes for a highbrow weekly, their mentor a psycho-therapeutist: 'I could not devise a more favourable assemblage of personalities for a modern symposium, or I would have done so'.[61] This novel provides ample scope for 'higher reasoning', the discussion of ideas between what William James terms 'minds of a higher order, interested in kindred subjects'.[62]

But if H. G. Wells was influenced so profoundly by William James's ideas, why is it that the philosopher is seldom mentioned in his writings after the First World War, and is conspicuous by his absence in the 1930s and '40s? In *The Science of Life* (1931), James is cited as the 'dominant, liberating personality' of his generation of psychologists, but there are only two brief references to his theories.[63] In *Experiment in Autobiography* there is no reference at all to his psychological or philosophical work, merely an amusing anecdote about Wells and James's first meeting, whilst in *The Conquest of Time*, published in 1942 as a replacement for *First and Last Things*, there is only one dismissive comment. The new book was necessary, Wells claims, because he was 'still mentally adolescent' in 1908. He had never even heard of psychoanalysis, and, he adds, 'Under the influence of William James (*The Will to Believe*), I exaggerated the wilful element in belief.'[64]

Wells was, of course, obliged to draw on the most up-to-date psychological theories in his scientific writings, and in the 1920s and '30s he greeted the new science of psychoanalysis with enthusiasm, declaring in *The Science of Life* that 'Sigmund Freud's name is as cardinal in the history of human thought as Charles Darwin's – the ultimate accolade he had once accorded to William James.[65] But the extent to which Wells was ever strongly influenced by the psychoanalysts is open to question. Although he makes copious use of their terms, he redefines and adapts them to fit his own purposes. As a biologist, he shows a marked preference for those theories about mental processes which can be related to physiological functions and observable behaviour, and, most important of all, he was never able to accept the idea of a unified personality. In his doctoral thesis, submitted to London University in 1942, Wells argues that the notion of a consistent, integrated personality is merely 'a biologically convenient delusion', therefore the expression 'psycho-analysis' is misleading because 'It implies an original mental unity which can undergo an analytic process'.[66] Since, for Wells, the personality has never been and never will be unified, he goes on to offer an account of the psyche which is much closer to the ideas expressed in James's chapters on the stream of thought and the consciousness of self in *The Principles of Psychology* than it is to psychoanalytic theory.

Perhaps the answer to the question I raised earlier is a straightforward one. In 1936, a German philologist who was translating *A Modern Utopia*, wrote to ask why Wells had not said anything about William James and Pragmatism in *Experiment in Autobiography*.[67] Wells replied that he had got bored tracing every step in his mental development, and in any case: 'I assimilated Pragmatism so completely that I failed to do justice in the

Autobiography to William James. I had paid my tribute already. The omission was not deliberate. It is an incompleteness. I took him for granted.'[68] Exactly.

Notes

[1]   William James, *The Principles of Psychology*, 2 vols (London: Macmillan, 1891). Wells's copy is in the Wells Archive, University of Illinois, Urbana Champaign, Ilinois, USA. Although it is impossible to be sure exactly when Wells read these volumes, it seems likely that he had read them by the time he wrote *Anticipations* (1901). Here he describes how amazed he had been 'to discover three copies of a translation of that most wonderful book, the *Text-book of Psychology* [the first edition of *Anticipations* includes an erratum slip correcting "Text-book" to "Principles"] of Professor William James, in a shop in l'Avenue de l'Opera – three copies of a book that I have never seen anywhere in England outside my own house, – and I am an attentive student of bookshop windows!' H. G. Wells, *Anticipations* (London: Chapman & Hall, 1902) p. 238.
[2]   Gerald E. Myers, *William James: His Life and Thought* (New Haven and London: Yale University Press, 1986), p. 2.
[3]   H. G. Wells, *God the Invisible King* (London: Cassell, 1917) p. 203.
[4]   Geoffrey West, *H. G. Wells: A Sketch for a Portrait* (London: Gerald Howe, 1930), p. 178.
[5]   Letter from William James to Reid, dated 30 May, [no year is cited, but James writes that he has just completed the Gifford Lectures at Edinburgh University and is about to return to America, so the letter was written in 1902], University of Illinois at Urbana-Champaign, Wells Archive, Wells-1, J-30.
[6]   Letter to H. G. Wells, dated 6 June 1905, *Selected Letters of William James*, ed. by Henry James, 2 vols (London: Longmans, Green and Co., 1920), II, 231.
[7]   Letter to John Jay Chapman, dated 18 May 1906, James, *Letters*, II, 257.
[8]   Letter to H. G. Wells, dated 28 November 1908, James, *Letters*, II, 316.
[9]   Recounted by William James's next door neighbour, J. Graham Brooks, in a letter to H. G. Wells dated 5 September 1920, Wells Archive, Wells 1, B-505.
[10]   H. G. Wells, 'Scepticism of the Instrument,' *Mind*, n. s. 13 (1904), 379-393 (p. 379). An amended version was reprinted in 1905 in *A Modern Utopia*. Wells had been reading F.C.S Schiller's *Personal Idealism*, sent to him by Henry Sturt, organiser of the Oxford Philosophical Society programme.
[11]   Wells, 'Scepticism', p. 385.
[12]   Wells, 'Scepticism', p. 386. Wells explored this idea in his first published essay, 'The Rediscovery of the Unique', *Fortnightly Review*, n. s. 50 (1891), 106-111.
[13]   H. G. Wells, *First and Last Things: A Confession of Faith and a Rule of Life* (London: The Knickerbocker Press; New York: G.P. Putnam's Sons, 1908), p. 57.
[14]   Wells, *First and Last Things*, pp. 57-8.
[15]   William James, Lecture VI, 'Pragmatism's Conception of Truth', *Pragmatism* (1907) (Indianapolis Cambridge: Hackett Publishing, 1982), pp. 91-105 (p. 92).

---

[16] H. G. Wells, *A Modern Utopia* (London: Chapman & Hall, 1905), p. 5.

[17] Wells, *First and Last Things*, p. 58.

[18] James, Lecture II, 'What Pragmatism Means', in *Pragmatism*, pp .25-39 (p. 28).

[19] H. G. Wells, *Marriage* (London: Macmillan, 1912) p. 514.

[20] Wells, *Marriage*, p. 521.

[21] Wells, *First and Last Things*, p. 46.

[22] Wells, *First and Last Things*, p. 46

[23] H. G. Wells, *Tono-Bungay* (London: Macmillan, 1909) p. 8.

[24] Wells, *Tono-Bungay*, p. 6.

[25] James, Lecture I, 'The Present Dilemma in Philosophy', *Pragmatism*, pp. 7-21, (p. 14)

[26] H. G. Wells, *Christina Alberta's Father* (London: Jonathan Cape, 1925), pp. 292-93.

[27] H. G. Wells, *Babes in the Darkling Wood* (London: Secker & Warburg, 1940), pp. 52-53.

[28] James, Lecture I, *Pragmatism*, pp. 10-18.

[29] James, Lecture II, *Pragmatism*, pp. 54-57.

[30] Myers, *William James*, pp. 46, 531 n. 55.

[31] T. H Huxley, 'Evolution and Ethics', in *Collected Essays*, 9 vols (London: Macmillan, 1893), IX, pp. 46-116 (pp. 81-83).

[32] Wells, *First and Last Things*, p. 71.

[33] Wells, *First and Last Things*, p. 73.

[34] H. G. Wells, *The Time Machine* (1895), in *The Scientific Romances of H. G. Wells* (London: Victor Gollancz, 1933) p. 76.

[35] H. G. Wells, *Experiment in Autobiography: Discoveries and Conclusions of A Very Ordinary Brain (since 1866)*, 2 vols (London: Gollancz and Cresset Press, 1934), II, p. 619.

[36] Wells, *Experiment in Autobiography*, II, 619-20.

[37] Wells, *Experiment in Autobiography*, II, 620.

[38] Wells, *Experiment in Autobiography*, II, 619.

[39] Wells, *Experiment in Autobiography*, II, 619.

[40] H. G. Wells, *World Brain* (London: Methuen, 1938), p. 1.

[41] James, II, 325. Subsequent references to this chapter will be given in the text.

[42] William James's views about language as a uniquely human possession accord with those of contemporary thinkers like the scientist T. H. Huxley, the psychologist Conwy Lloyd Morgan and the linguist, Friedrich Max Müller. Müller was categorical on this issue: 'Where then is the difference between brute and man? What is it that man can do, and of which we find no signs, no rudiments, in the whole brute world? I answer without hesitation: the one great barrier between the brute and man is *Language*. Man speaks, and no brute has ever uttered a word. Language is our Rubicon, and no brute will dare to cross it'. F. M. Müller, *The Science of Language: Founded on the Lectures Delivered at the Royal Institution in 1861 and 1863*, 2 vols (London: Longman, 1899), I, 489-90. On Wells's intervention in debates over animal language, see Steven McLean's discussion in Chapter 2 of this collection.

[43] Wells, *A Modern Utopia*, p. 265.

[44] Wells, *A Modern Utopia*, p. 266.

[45] Wells, *A Modern Utopia*, pp. 265-66

[46] Wells, *A Modern Utopia*, p. 267

[47] James, *Principles,* II, 361-62.

[48] Letter to Wells dated 6 June 1905, James, *Letters* II, 231.

[49] Wells, *Anticipations*, p. 2 n.

[50] James, *Principles*, II, 364.

[51] H. G. Wells, 'The Contemporary Novel' (1911), in *An Englishman Looks at the World: Being a Series of Unrestrained Remarks upon Contemporary Matters* (London: Cassell, 1916), pp. 148-169 (pp. 158-159).

[52] Introduction, *The Research Magnificent, The Atlantic Edition of the Works of H. G. Wells*, 24 vols (London: Fisher Unwin, 1924-27) XIX, ix.

[53] Raymond Williams, *The English Novel from Dickens to Hardy* (St Albans: Paladin, 1974), p. 104.

[54] See Norman and Jeanne Mackenzie, *The Time Traveller: The Life of H. G. Wells* (London: Weidenfeld and Nicolson, 1973) pp. 276-77; Michael Draper, *H. G. Wells* (Houndmills: Macmillan, 1987) pp. 97, 102; Patrick Parrinder, *H. G. Wells* (Edinburgh: Oliver and Boyd, 1970) p. 86; John Batchelor, *H. G. Wells* (Cambridge, London, New York, 1985), p. 94.

[55] H. G.Wells, 'A Note to the Reader', *A Modern Utopia,* p. viii.

[56] Wells, *A Modern Utopia*, p. 372.

[57] Wells, *A Modern Utopia*, p. 373.

[58] Wells, *Experiment in Autobiography* II, 497.

[59] Wells, *Experiment in Autobiography* II, 477.

[60] Wells, 'The Novel of Ideas', *Babes in the Darkling Wood*, p. 7.

[61] Wells, 'The Novel of Ideas', *Babes in the Darkling Wood*, p. 9.

[62] James, *Principles*, II, 370.

[63] H. G.Wells, Julian Huxley, G.P Wells, *The Science of Life* (London: Cassell, 1931), p. 793.

[64] H. G. Wells, *The Conquest of Time,* The Thinker's Library, 92 (London: Watts, 1942), p. 1. Interestingly, James himself came to regret the title of that essay: 'All the critics, neglecting the essay, pounced upon the title. Psychologically it was impossible, morally it was iniquitous'. James, Lecture VII, 'Pragmatism and Humanism,' *Pragmatism*, pp. 109-120 (p. 116)

[65] Wells, *The Science of Life*, p. 814.

[66] H. G. Wells, 'A thesis on the quality of illusion in the continuity of the individual life in the higher metazoa, with the particular reference to the species *homo sapiens,*' in H. G. Wells, *'42-'44: A Contemporary Memoir upon Human Behaviour During the Crisis of the World Revolution* (London: Secker & Warburg, 1944), pp. 169-196 (p. 169). Wells always insisted on 'sub-conscious' for 'unconscious' and spelt 'psychoanalysis' as 'psycho-analysis' with a hyphen because he advocated what he called 'psycho-synthesis' as a cure for psychological disorders. Psycho-synthesis (a kind of Behaviourist Therapy) is explored fictionally in *Babes in the Darkling Wood.*

[67] Letter from Dr Fritz Krog to H. G.Wells, 1 May, 1936, Wells Archive, Wells-1, K161.
[68] Letter from H. G. Wells to Dr Fritz Krog, 4 May, 1936. Copy typed on the back of Krog's letter, Wells Archive, Wells-1, K161.

H. G. WELLS AND WINSTON CHURCHILL: A REASSESSMENT

RICHARD TOYE

In October 1941, *Time* magazine highlighted the differences of opinion between 'two of the world's great mooters', H. G. Wells and Winston Churchill, on a key question of war strategy. This was the issue of whether Britain should act quickly to open a Second Front against the Nazis in Europe in order to assist the USSR. 'These two were the most thunderous writers and talkers about the art of warfare in the years of peace', the article noted. 'Both saw that war would come again, both dared to shout warnings when such shouting was unpopular. Wells, the dreamer, seeing how bad the war would be, was for avoiding it by organizing a new and better world. Churchill, the doer, urged military action.' Now, the article suggested, it seemed their positions were reversed, as a close comparison of a recent Churchill speech and a newspaper article by Wells appeared to demonstrate. Whereas Wells confidently spoke of German weakness, and urged a swift invasion of the Continent, Churchill cautiously warned against premature relaxation and rejoicing.[1] Superficially, this contrast might appear to confirm the expectation that Wells, the socialist internationalist, and Churchill, the Tory imperialist, would inevitably find themselves taking opposite sides in any given political debate. Yet it also illustrates that there was more to each man than common stereotypes suggest. Wells, 'the dreamer', was no pacifist, nor was he unconcerned with the here-and-now; whereas Churchill, 'the doer', could at times urge consolidation and restraint. Although, during their long association, they found themselves in conflict more than once, they had much more in common than one might think.

It is well known that Wells and Churchill had a long acquaintance. It dated from just after the turn of the Twentieth Century, and they remained in touch until not long before Wells's death in 1946. It is also well known that Churchill admired Wells – he once claimed that he could 'pass an examination' in his work.[2] A number of episodes in their relationship have captured the attention of historians, perhaps most notably Wells's support for Churchill in the 1908 Manchester North-West by-election, and the two men's later public controversy over British intervention in the Russian civil war. The fact that Wells satirised Churchill in his novels, most famously in *Men Like Gods* (1923), may have contributed to the dominant impression that they were political antagonists.[3] Thus, although their personal friendship has been thoroughly documented, most fully in a 1989 essay by Wells's biographer David C. Smith, there is no suggestion that Wells had a significant influence on Churchill's social and political thought.[4] (Paul K. Alkon goes furthest, acknowledging that the two men's 'views sometimes coincided', especially when it came to the impact of science on warfare. But even for Alkon, the connection they had was 'a matter of imaginative affinities rather than influence'.)[5] There is a partial exception: Stephen Bungay has observed, in passing, that some phrases in Churchill's famous 1940 speeches may have been inspired by passages in Wells's writings.[6] It would seem, however, that Bungay perceives Wells's influence on Churchill as primarily linguistic, rather than being a matter of ideas.

This chapter argues that Wells did have an intellectual influence on Churchill. The latter's borrowing of Wells's language and ideas was most pronounced during the Edwardian period, and can be seen most clearly in his reaction to *A Modern Utopia* (1905), but there are also traces of it later on. The two men's mutual sympathy in the years prior to World War One makes Wells's support for Churchill in the 1908 by-election, which is usually seen as an example of his 'maverick' tendencies, quite explicable. A full understanding of this, however, requires us to reappraise Wells's own political position and to consider the much-neglected Liberal aspect of his political identity. The chapter begins with a brief narrative of the Wells-Churchill relationship, which provides the context needed for the detailed analysis that follows. Sometimes it is possible to show that Wells's writings had a clear causal impact on Churchill's thinking. At other times we can merely note strong linguistic and intellectual similarities, without there being evidence of direct influence. The fact of the similarities is interesting, even in the absence of proof of what brought them about, for they demonstrate that, to a considerable extent, the two men were swimming in the same intellectual currents.

I

Wells was born in 1866, Churchill twelve years later. In 1931 the latter recalled coming across Wells's early works, including *Select Conversations With an Uncle* (1895), at around the time of their first publication: 'and when I came upon *The Time Machine* [1895], that marvellous philosophical romance [...] I shouted with joy. Then I read all his books.'[7] The first personal contact between the two came in 1901, when Wells's publishers sent Churchill a copy of *Anticipations*, his book of futurological predictions. Churchill (who had recently been elected as a Conservative MP) sent Wells a long letter in response. 'I read everything you write', he told him, and added that there was much in the book with which he agreed, although he felt that Wells put too much faith in government by experts, and argued that society would not change as quickly as the book claimed.[8] Wells thanked him – although he wrote, 'I really do not think that you people who gather in great country houses realize the pace of things [i.e. change]'.[9] After a further exchange of letters – in which Wells admitted that he found Churchill to be 'a particularly interesting and rather terrible figure' – they met at the House of Commons early in 1902.[10] They may well have continued to meet, but their next significant exchange was in 1906, after Churchill joined the Liberal Party, over *A Modern Utopia*. (This episode will be discussed in depth below, as will the circumstances of Wells's endorsement of Churchill in the Manchester by-election.) In 1907, Churchill visited Africa, and the account he published on his return shows that he continued to give thought to Wells's work. He wrote of Uganda: 'A class of rulers is provided by an outside power [i.e. Britain] as remote from, and in all that constitutes fitness to direct, as superior to the Baganda as Mr Wells's Martians would have been to us.'[11] It was more than a little ironic that Churchill should have used this illustration: in *The War of the Worlds* (1898) the Martians ultimately fail in their war of conquest because of their maladaptation to the earth's environment.

It is interesting to note that Churchill was well aware of some of the more controversial aspects of Wells's private life. In 1909, he heard (somewhat belatedly) of Wells's affair with Amber Reeves, and wrote to his wife Clementine that 'Wells has been behaving very badly with a young Girton girl of the new emancipated school'. Although, in this letter, he noted that 'v[er]y serious consequences' (i.e. Reeves's pregnancy) had followed, his concluding remark on the matter suggested amusement rather then wholehearted condemnation. He wrote: 'These literary gents!!'[12] It is unclear whether the two men had many more contacts prior to the Great War, but it seems likely that Churchill continued to read Wells's books and articles, apparently with the encouragement of Lord Northcliffe, owner of *The Daily Mail*.[13] In October 1916 he wrote to Wells to congratulate him on his recently published novel *Mr. Britling Sees It Through*. In the same letter he credited Wells's short story *The Land*

Ironclads (1903) as the inspiration for the concept of the tank, which by this point had been successfully trialled – although, as he later pointed out in his memoirs, no single person could be said to have 'invented' it.[14]

During the post-war period the men moved apart politically. In 1920 Wells visited Bolshevik Russia. On his return he publicly called for the great powers, and in particular the USA, to give assistance to the Soviets to help them establish 'a new social order'.[15] Churchill – now Secretary of State for War in Lloyd George's coalition government – was a strong advocate of military intervention in order to assist the anti-Bolshevik 'Whites'. He responded to Wells with an article riddled with sarcasm and invective: 'We see the Bolshevik cancer eating into the flesh of the wretched being [...] And now Mr Wells, that philosophical romancer, comes forward with the proposition that the cancer is the only thing that can pull the body round; that we must feed that and cultivate that.'[16] Wells hit back with further articles in which he described his antagonist as 'the running sore of waste in our Government [...] He has smeared his vision with human blood, and we are implicated in the things he abets.'[17] In 1923, after the fall of the coalition, the two men engaged in further public debate, this time about the British Empire.[18] Wells described Churchill as his friend, but added: 'There are times when the evil spirit comes upon him and when I can think of him only as a very intractable little boy, a mischievous, dangerous little boy, a knee-worthy little boy. Only by thinking of him in that way can one go on liking him.'[19]

1923 was also the year of *Men Like Gods*, in which Wells satirised Churchill as 'Rupert Catskill'. Projected accidentally into a future Utopia, together with a group of other interlopers, Catskill finds his surroundings boring and attempts to start a war in order to liven things up. In *Meanwhile* (1927) one character repeatedly criticises Churchill's conduct during the 1926 General Strike.[20] (Churchill's return to the Conservatives in the mid-1920s had put further political distance between him and Wells.) In *The Autocracy of Mr. Parham* (1929) the character of Sir Bussy Woodcock is an amalgam of Churchill and Lord Beaverbrook, the press magnate. Churchill seems to have taken all of this in good part – he was perhaps more annoyed about the caricature of his friend Eddie Marsh ('Freddy Mush') in *Men Like Gods* than he was about the one of himself.[21] Although he and Wells continued to clash politically, personal relations appear to have remained cordial.[22] In 1934 Churchill invited Wells to join the 'Other Club', the dining society he had co-founded prior to World War One.[23] Three years later, 'on a sudden impulse', Wells dedicated his novel *Star Begotten* 'to my Friend Winston Spencer Churchill'.[24]

During World War Two relations again became vexed. In May 1940, Wells welcomed Churchill's replacement of Neville Chamberlain as Prime Minister in typically double-edged fashion: 'He is the best war captain possible at the present time but for all that he is dangerous.' It was, he thought, better to risk 'being shot in a Churchill adventure than face the certainty of national decay and disgrace under a Chamberlain regime.'[25] Later that year, Churchill was irritated by Wells's public criticisms of the army leadership.[26] And, as was seen earlier, the two men took very different attitudes to war strategy in connection with the Soviet Union. According to the diary of Jock Colville, Churchill's private secretary, Wells wrote to Churchill just prior to the German invasion 'suggesting measures to relieve German pressure on Russia'. Colville noted: '"Russia is his religion," the P.M. said to me with contempt.'[27] All the same, Churchill did appear to take some of Wells's military suggestions seriously, and the relationship did not descend into unrelieved acrimony, at least in private.[28] Nevertheless, Wells published an article in December 1944, headlined 'Churchill Must Go'. It described the Prime Minister as 'the present would-be British Fuehrer'.[29] As the war ended, Robert Bruce Lockhart recorded in his diary:

> Gave luncheon to-day at the Carlton Grill to Moura Budberg. She has been seeing daily H.G. Wells who is in poor shape. [...] Recently he has been attacking Mr. Churchill in articles and letters. The other day he received a magnificent [present] of flowers from the P.M. H.G. said rather grimly: 'I must issue a notice "no flowers to be sent" '. But Moura said he was purring with pleasure. [30]

This was, perhaps, the authentic note of the relationship in the later years. Wells was more than happy to disparage Churchill – and vice versa – but an element of mutual affection remained.

II

We should not, of course, gloss over the men's political differences. Some of these, such as Churchill's antipathy to Wells's Republicanism, were profound. But nor should these differences blind us to some intriguing areas of ideological similarity. In May 1901, during a speech on army reform, Churchill warned that modern wars, in which 'the resources of science and civilisation' were deployed, would be more ruinous than those of past days: 'The wars of peoples will be more terrible than those of kings.'[31] It is therefore unsurprising that he should have been receptive to *Anticipations*, with its predictions of scientifically driven total war.[32] It is, moreover, possible to show, in a very concrete way, that one of Wells's subsequent works, *A Modern Utopia*, influenced Churchill directly. The book sought to apply the insights of biological evolution to human society – although it must be noted that Wells was no harsh individualist, and was concerned to reconcile collectivism with personal freedom. He described a Utopia ruled over by 'voluntary noblemen' known as 'Samurai'. He rejected the idea of creating a permanent blueprint for a new society in the way that he claimed that Utopian writers had always done 'before Darwin quickened the thought of the world.' Much of the emphasis was on experiment and progressive development; this was to be a 'kinetic' not a 'static' Utopia. In Wells's new society, moreover, 'the State will insure the children of every citizen, and those legitimately dependent upon him, against the inconvenience of his death [...] and it will insure him against old age and infirmity.'[33]

Wells, or his publisher, sent Churchill a copy of the book soon after it was published. However, he did not find time to read it until his holidays the following year. On 9 October 1906 he wrote to Wells about it:

> You have certainly succeeded in making earth a heaven; but I have always feared that heaven might be a v[er]y dull place *à la longue*. Still there is so much in your writing that stimulates my fancy that I owe you a great debt, quite apart from the courtesy & kindness of your present. Especially did I admire the skill and courage with which the questions of marriage & population were discussed.[34]

Two days after writing to Wells, Churchill gave a speech in Glasgow.[35] In it he declared boldly that 'The cause of the Liberal Party is the cause of the left-out millions', and spoke of the need of the state to concern itself with the care of children, the sick and the aged. Like Wells, he used the terminology of evolution: 'The existing organisation of society is driven by one mainspring – competitive selection.' There were also direct verbal similarities with Wells's work. Some of these may have been no more than commonplaces. For example, Wells argued that 'To the onlooker, both Individualism and Socialism are, in the absolute, absurdities [...] the way of sanity runs, perhaps even sinuously, down the intervening valley.'[36] Churchill likewise noted that 'It is not possible to draw a hard-and-fast line between individualism and collectivism.'[37] There were also more striking similarities. Wells wrote: 'The State will stand at the back of the economic struggle as the reserve employer of labour'.[38] Churchill said: 'I am of the opinion that the State should increasingly assume the position of the reserve employer of labour.'[39] Wells argued: 'Whatever we do, man will remain a competitive creature [...] no Utopia will ever save him completely from the emotional drama of struggle, from exultations and humiliations, from pride and prostration and shame. [...] But we may do much to make the margin of failure endurable.'[40] Churchill said: 'I do not want to see impaired the vigour of competition, but we can do much to mitigate the consequences of failure.' Furthermore, it may be significant that Churchill explicitly used the term 'Utopia':

> I am sure that if the vision of a fair [i.e. beautiful] Utopia which cheers the hearts and lights the imagination of the toiling multitudes, should ever break into reality, it will be by developments through, and modifications in, and by improvements out of, the existing competitive organisation of society; and I believe that Liberalism mobilised, and active as it is to-day, will be a principal and indispensable factor in that noble evolution.[41]

We may also note – especially given Churchill's explicit approval of Wells's treatment of 'marriage & population' questions – that the book may have played a part in his becoming 'a strong eugenist'.[42] Wells suggested that in Utopia people would only be allowed to have children if they met certain conditions, including physical fitness and financial independence. He implied that those who broke the rules would be subject to compulsory sterilisation, especially if 'if it is disease or imbecility you have multiplied'.[43]

Churchill was, of course, open to a wide array of intellectual influences and political pressures, and it is important not overstate Wells's impact on him. All the same, on the evidence presented here, there seems to be a strong case for saying, at the very least, that Wells's ideas did have a significant direct effect on the way that he articulated his views on social reform during this formative period. If so, Wells's decision to support Churchill, rather than the socialist candidate, in the 1908 North-West Manchester by-election, is rendered more explicable.

At that point Churchill, having joined the Liberals in 1904, had just been promoted to Cabinet as President of the Board of Trade (Asquith having replaced Campbell-Bannerman as Prime Minister). He was therefore obliged to stand for re-election, as was then customary. He was opposed by William Joynson-Hicks, a Conservative, who had been his opponent in 1906, and by a socialist, Dan Irving, who was backed by the Social Democratic Party.[44] Wells weighed in publicly on Churchill's side, with a letter to the *Daily News*, in which he urged voters to support him rather than Irving. The typical explanation for this is that Wells was motivated by his deep animus against Joynson-Hicks, who had earlier criticised him as an advocate of free love, and/or by personal regard for Churchill. As Smith puts it: 'His support for Churchill was clearly an example of a maverick tendency, but as with many Wellsian moves, it also had a personal quirk, as it enabled him to settle some old disputes of a related but nevertheless different origin.'[45]

Personal factors cannot, it is true, be dismissed entirely. But more importantly, as the 1906 Glasgow speech demonstrated, Wells had good reason to believe that Churchill was sympathetic to his own views. Moreover, his letter to the *News* demonstrates that he was particularly impressed by a recent article Churchill had written in *The Nation*, which argued for the establishment of a 'Minimum Standard' of living through state action.[46] Wells was also acting consistently with the view he had laid out the previous year, i.e. that for socialists to compete electorally with the established parties would antagonise the 'very wide borderland of tepid believers and the half-converted'.[47] Even though the Liberal Party was 'strongly tainted by the memories of Victorian individualism' Churchill could be supported because his of his 'active and still rapidly developing and broadening mind' and because he had demonstrated 'a spirit entirely in accordance with the spirit of our [socialist] movement.'[48] This last remark was clearly wishful thinking, but Wells's overall line was consistent with his own previous thinking, and was part of a considered strategy. Wells, indeed, frequently identified himself as a Liberal, and viewed socialism as an integral part of liberalism, not as antagonistic to it. He was no conventional party Liberal, but – like Churchill at this time – he wanted to reformulate liberalism in a new, collectivist direction.[49]

III

There are further traces of possible Wellsian influence on Churchill, even in the post-Edwardian era, and in spite of their political fallings-out. Some of the similarities are purely verbal. In June 1940, Churchill predicted that if Britain could stand up to Hitler, the world might 'move forward into broad, sunlit uplands.'[50] Bungay argues that this 'was probably an echo' of Wells's *The Discovery of the Future* (1902), in which he spoke of 'the uplands of the future'.[51] In an equally famous speech of August 1940, Churchill spoke of Britain's airmen: 'Never in the field of human conflict was so much owed by so many to so few.'[52] Bungay suggests that 'the thought of describing fighter pilots as "the few" may also have been triggered by a passage in Wells's novel *The War in the Air* [1908], where Wells observed that in air warfare the balance of military efficiency was shifting back "from the many to the few."'[53] Here we need to be cautious, because Churchill had used a similar trope in various different contexts prior to 1908.[54] Nevertheless, he may have got from Wells the idea of applying it to the airmen. There are also other examples. The phrase 'the gathering storm' appears twice in *The War of the Worlds* (1898), and this became the title of the first volume of Churchill's Second World War memoirs.[55] In *The Food of the Gods* (1904), the phrase 'iron curtain' crops up twice, when a character is temporarily imprisoned.[56] Churchill, of course, applied the term to the division of cold war Europe in 1946.[57] Clearly, one should not make too much of such likenesses. Wells did not originate all these phrases himself, and there was often a long delay between his use of them and Churchill's. Churchill could have picked at least some of them up from other sources - for example, in 1920 Ethel Snowden wrote of going behind the Soviet Union's 'iron curtain'.[58] But we do at least know for certain that he read Wells, and, as Bungay notes, 'Churchill kept a store of phrases in his encyclopedic memory like fragments of tunes in the mind of a composer, and at some point they would emerge in full form.'[59] And even if direct influence cannot be proven conclusively in these instances, the elements of shared language are clear, which perhaps can to some extent be attributed to literary heritage that the men had in common.

The respective use that they made of the concept of 'the English-speaking peoples' is another sign of the overlap in their thinking. In *Anticipations* Wells predicted the political unification of 'the English-Speaking states' and that there would develop 'a great federation of white English-speaking peoples'. He also mentioned the idea (already mooted elsewhere) of 'interchangeable citizenship', under which British citizens could become US citizens - and vice versa – if they changed domicile.[60] Churchill too often argued for to the 'fraternal association' or 'unity' of the English-speaking peoples, and in retirement published a four volume *History of the English-Speaking Peoples*. In 1943, as he recalled in his memoirs, he proposed to US officials that 'There might even be some common form of citizenship, under which citizens of the United States and of the British Commonwealth might enjoy voting privileges after residential qualification'.[61] Did Wells's ideas influence Churchill here? It cannot be ruled out, but again, caution is required. Others, including Joseph Chamberlain and Charles Dilke, had used the term 'English-speaking peoples' before Wells did, and Churchill was undoubtedly familiar with ideas of Anglo-American unity.[62] Churchill did not declare publicly in favour of 'the unity of the English-speaking races' until 1911, and it did not become one of his major themes until the 1930s, other prominent politicians having used similar language in the meantime.[63] And Wells and Churchill's 1923 debate shows that, by that stage at least, the two men differed substantially over how the British Empire fitted into a future world order. All the same, one cannot help but be struck by a 1930 Churchill essay, in which he speculated about what would have happened if Lee had won the battle of Gettysburg. In his version, the wise statesmen of Britain, the rump USA, and the Confederacy narrowly avert a renewal of the civil war in 1905 by signing 'the Covenant of the English-speaking Association.' As a consequence, 'Hundreds of millions of people suddenly adopted a new point of view. [...] they gave birth in themselves to a new higher loyalty and a wider sentiment.' The Great War, in turn, was averted.[64] Clearly, there was more than a degree of playfulness here, but the device of a world crisis triggering a moral and psychological awakening is a major theme of much of Wells's fiction. It seems credible to imagine that Churchill borrowed it with the aim of using a work of the imagination – as Wells so often did himself – to make a serious point.

Certainly, when Churchill let his imagination roam over the shape of the future, the results had much in common with Wells's vision. In his essay 'Mass Effects in Modern Life' (1931) Churchill predicted that, once it became possible for major cities to be eliminated at the push of a button, 'The idea of war will become loathsome to humanity.'[65] This is strongly reminiscent of the plot of *The World Set Free* (1914) – as was his suggestion, made in the 1920s, that 'a bomb no bigger than an orange' might contain enough power to destroy a town.[66] In 'Fifty Years Hence' (also 1931) – a piece that includes a quotation from *The War in the Air* on the inevitability of progress – he argued that dramatically improved communications would render superfluous the concentration of populations in cities. 'The cities and the countryside would become indistinguishable', he wrote.[67] Similar ideas can be found in *Anticipations* and elsewhere in Wells's work. Churchill's question 'Are There Men in the Moon?' – the title of an essay written before World War Two but only published in 1942 – may well have been a nod to Wells's *The First Men in the Moon* (1901). (Churchill did not think life on the moon was probable, but he did not rule it out elsewhere in the universe.)[68] Of course, Wells was not Churchill's sole source of influence on such questions; Alkon demonstrates that he was familiar with the work other science fiction writers, notably Karel Čapek and Olaf Stapledon.[69] Churchill also had sources of conventional scientific advice. But although the thoughts he articulated may have been, by the time he wrote, little more than the standard stuff of science fiction and futurology, it must be remembered that these were genres that Wells himself had done much to create and develop.

IV

This chapter has shown that Wells's had a clear and demonstrable influence on Churchill's social thought before 1914. Wells shared a number of beliefs with many of the collectivist oriented 'New Liberals' of the day, of whom Churchill was one. This explains both his fascination with and support for Churchill prior to the Great War and his ability to have an impact on his thinking. Subsequent echoes of Wells in Churchill's speeches and writings appear to be more than coincidence, but it is difficult if not impossible to prove a causal link in any given case. Nevertheless, there was an unmistakeable overlap between their respective world-views.

Of course, it is important not to exaggerate: after all, Wells cast his final vote, in 1945, for Labour and against Churchill's government.[70] There was much about the views of each that the other found difficult to stomach. In his most sustained appreciation of his novelist friend, Churchill wrote that Wells was an 'unquestionably great English writer' and a 'seer'. However, he thought that he nursed a grievance against the British Empire, the United Kingdom, and England. 'Few first-class men of letters have more consistently crabbed and girded at the nation, society and social system in which they have had their being', he wrote. 'Fewer still have owed so much to its ample tolerances and its magnificent complications.'[71] Wells's mature critique of Churchill was equally ambivalent. In his autobiography, he claimed to have grown out of his own war fantasies 'somewhen between 1916 and 1920'; whereas Churchill and other politicians, retaining a 'puerile' outlook, failed to think about war as responsible adults should.[72] Churchill's life, he judged in 1944, consisted of 'a remarkable series of alternating phases of gallantry and sheer self-indulgent stupidity'.[73] But the men's mutual fascination cannot be denied. Only one of them, Churchill, was a 'doer'; but both of them were, in their different ways, prophets and dreamers, wandering on different parts of a shared imaginative landscape.

Notes

I am grateful to the participants at the 'H. G. Wells: New Directions' conference for their comments and suggestions. I owe a particular debt to Patrick Parrinder and to John S. Partington. The latter has provided me with a wealth of valuable information. Michele Gemelos also made some stimulating observations. Any errors that remain are of course my own responsibility.

[1] 'The Great Debate', *Time*, 13 October 1941 [available online at http://www.time.com/time/, consulted 14 May 2007].

[2] Winston Churchill, 'H.G. Wells', *Sunday Pictorial*, 23 Aug. 1931, in *The Collected Essays of Sir Winston Churchill*, ed. by Michael Wolff, 4 vols (London: Library of Imperial History, 1976), III, 50-4 (p. 53).

[3] See, for example, Randolph S. Churchill, *Winston S. Churchill, vol. II: Young Statesman, 1901–1914* (London: Heinemann, 1967), p. 255; Paul Addison, *Churchill on the Home Front, 1900–1955* (London: Pimlico, 1993), pp. 265, 440; Henry Pelling, *Winston Churchill* (London: Macmillan, 1974), pp. 110, 336, 342-3, 634.

[4] David C. Smith, 'Winston Churchill and H.G. Wells: Edwardians in the Twentieth Century', *Cahiers Victoriens et Edouardien*, 30 (1989), 93-116. See also Manfred Weinhorn, *A Harmony of Interests: Explorations in the Mind of sir Winston Churchill* (Cranbury, NJ: Associated University Presses, 1992), pp. 25-30, 40-44.

[5] Paul K. Alkon, *Winston Churchill's Imagination* (Lewisburg: Bucknell University Press, 2006), pp. 167-8.

[6] Stephen Bungay, 'His Speeches: How Churchill Did It', *Finest Hour*, 112 (Autumn 2001), available online at www.winstonchurchill.org, consulted 30 January 2007. C.P. Snow once gave an interesting hint of Wells's influence on Churchill, but did not develop it. See his book *Variety of Men* (London: Macmillan, 1967), p. 57.

[7] Churchill, 'H.G. Wells', pp. 52-3.

[8] Winston Churchill to H.G. Wells, 17 Nov. 1901, H.G. Wells Papers, University of Illinois, C-238-3a.

[9] H.G. Wells to Winston Churchill, 19 Nov. 1901, in *The Correspondence of H.G. Wells*, edited by David C. Smith, 4 vols (London: Pickering & Chatto, 1998), I, 457.

[10] H.G. Wells to Winston Churchill, 21 Nov. 1901, in *The Correspondence of H.G. Wells*, I, 458.

[11] Winston Churchill, *My African Journey* (London: The Holland Press/Neville Spearman Ltd., 1962, originally published 1908), p. 84.

[12] Winston Churchill to Clementine Churchill, 17 Oct. 1909, in *Winston S. Churchill Vol. II Companion Part 2* (London: Heinemann, 1969), edited by Randolph S. Churchill, p. 914. In fact, Reeves went to Newnham, not Girton.

[13] See Lord Northcliffe to Churchill, 8 April 1913, and Churchill's reply of the following day, Winston Churchill Papers, Churchill College, Cambridge, CHAR 28/117/111-2.

[14] Churchill to Wells, 1 Oct. 1916, Wells Papers, C-238-7a; Winston Churchill, *The World Crisis 1911-1918*, 2 vols (New York: Barnes & Noble, 1993, originally published 1923-7), I, 514-5. See also 'High Court Of Justice., King's Bench Division., A Claim For The Invention Of Tanks., Bentley v. The King', *The Times*, 26 Nov. 1925.

[15] Wells's articles on the USSR appeared in the *Sunday Express* and, after revision, were published as *Russia in the Shadows* (London: Hodder & Stoughton, 1920). Quotation at p. 148.

[16] Winston Churchill, 'Mr. Wells and Bolshevism', *Sunday Express*, 5, Dec. 1920, in *Collected Essays*, III, 79-84 (p. 83).

[17] Quoted in Smith, 'Winston Churchill and H.G. Wells', p. 102.

[18] H.G. Wells, 'The Future of the British Empire', *The Empire Review*, 38: 273, Oct. 1923, 1071-9; Winston Churchill, 'Mr. H.G. Wells and the British Empire', *The Empire Review*, 38: 274, Nov. 1923, 1217-1223.

[19] H.G. Wells, 'Winston', 10 Nov. 1923, in *A Year of Prophesying* (London: T. Fisher Unwin, 1924), pp. 52-6 (p. 54).

[20] H.G. Wells, *Meanwhile: The Picture of a Lady* (London: Ernest Benn, 1927), esp. p. 178.

[21] Winston Churchill to Edward Marsh, 27 Sept. 1923, in *Winston S. Churchill Volume V: Companion Part I*, edited by Martin Gilbert (London: Heinemann, 1979), p. 61.

[22] See, for example, Winston Churchill, message to the Southend electorate, 11 Nov. 1927, in ibid., p. 1098; Churchill to Wells , 9 June 1927, Wells Papers, C-238-8.

[23] Churchill to Wells, 1 March 1934, Wells Papers, C-238-9.

[24] Wells to I.M. Parsons, 30 April 1937, in *The Correspondence of H.G. Wells*, IV, p. 149.

[25] H.G. Wells, 'The New Captain And His Crew', *Reynolds News*, 19 May 1940, p. 6.

[26] Martin Gilbert, *Winston S. Churchill, vol. VI: Finest Hour, 1939–1941* (London: Heinemann, 1983), pp. 830-1.

[27] John Colville, *The Fringes of Power: Diaries 1939-55* (London: Hodder & Stoughton, 1985), p. 479 (entry for 20 June 1941).

[28] Gilbert, *Finest Hour*, p. 1123.

[29] H.G. Wells, 'Churchill Must Go', *Tribune*, 15 Dec. 1944, p. 9.

[30] Kenneth Young (ed.), *The Diaries of Sir Robert Bruce Lockhart Vol. 2, 1939-1965* (London: Macmillan, 1980), pp. 431-2 (entry for 10 May 1945).

[31] Speech of 13 May 1901. All Churchill's speeches cited are to be found in *Winston S. Churchill: His Complete Speeches, 1897–1963*, 8 vols, edited by Robert Rhodes James (New York: Chelsea House, 1974).

[32] H.G. Wells, *Anticipations of the Reaction of Mechanical and Scientific Progress Upon Human Life and Thought* (1901) (New York: Dover Publications, 1999, reproducing the text of the revised 1902 edition), Chapter 6, 'War in the Twentieth Century'.

[33] H.G. Wells, *A Modern Utopia* (London: Thomas Nelson and Sons, n.d. but 1905), pp. 16, 99-100.

[34] Winston Churchill to H.G. Wells, 9 Oct. 1906, H.G. Wells Papers, University of Illinois, C-238-2.

[35] Speech of 11 October 1906.

[36] Wells, *A Modern Utopia*, p. 92.

[37] Speech of 11 October 1906.

[38] Wells, *A Modern Utopia*, p. 141.

[39] Speech of 11 October 1906.

[40] Wells, *A Modern Utopia*, p. 139.

[41] Speech of 11 October 1906.

[42] Wilfrid Scawen Blunt, *My Diaries: Being a Personal Narrative of Events 1888-1914: Part Two [1900-1914]* (London: Martin Secker, n.d), p. 399 (entry for 20 Oct. 1912). Churchill's eugenic beliefs are well documented. See Addison, *Churchill*, pp. 123-6.

[43] Wells, *Modern Utopia*, pp. 182-3.

[44] I.e. the recently renamed Social Democratic Federation.

[45] Smith, 'Winston Churchill and H.G. Wells', p. 99. See also Lisanne Radice, *Beatrice and Sidney Webb: Fabian Socialists* (London: Macmillan, 1984), p. 178, and Michael Foot, *H.G.: The History of Mr. Wells* (London: Doubleday, 1996) pp. 88-9. Anthony West, however, differs from this standard interpretation, correctly noting Wells's view that Churchill was 'open-minded and educable': *H.G. Wells: Aspects of a Life* (London: Hutchinson, 1984), p. 315.

[46] Winston Churchill, 'The Untrodden Field in Politics', *The Nation*, 7 March 1908, 812-3.

[47] Wells, 'The Socialist Movement and Socialist Parties', *The New Age*, 13 June 1907, 105-6.

[48] H.G. Wells, 'An Open Letter to an elector in N. W. Manchester', *Daily News*, 21 Apr. 1908.

[49] Richard Toye, 'H.G. Wells and the New Liberalism', *Twentieth Century British History*, 19:2 (2008, forthcoming). See also Steven McLean, ' "The Fertilising Conflict of Individualities": H. G. Wells's *A Modern Utopia*, John Stuart Mill's *On Liberty* and the Victorian Tradition of Liberalism', *Papers on Language and Literature*, 43:2 (May 2007), 166-89.

[50] Speech of 18 June, 1940.

[51] Bungay, 'How Churchill Did It'; H.G. Wells, *The Discovery of the Future* (London: A. C. Fifield 1913, first published in *Nature*, 6 Feb. 1902).

[52] Speech of 20 Aug. 1940.

[53] Bungay, 'How Churchill Did It'; H.G. Wells, *The War in the Air and particularly how Mr. Bert Smallways fared while it lasted* (London: George Bell and Sons, 1908), p. 181.

[54] Ronald Hyam, 'Winston Churchill before 1914', *The Historical Journal*, 12 (1969), 164-173 (p. 173).

[55] *A Critical Edition of The War of the Worlds: H.G. Wells's Scientific Romance*, edited by David Y. Hughes and Harry M. Geduld (Bloomington: Indiana University Press, 1993), pp. 83, 104.

[56] H.G. Wells, *The Food of the Gods and How it Came to Earth* (1904) (New York: Dover Publications, 2006), pp. 167, 172.

[57] Speech of 5 March 1946.

[58] Henry B. Ryan, 'A New Look at Churchill's "Iron Curtain" Speech', *Historical Journal*, 22 (1979), 895-920 (p. 897).

[59] Bungay, 'How Churchill Did It'.

[60] Wells, *Anticipations*, pp. 146, 148

[61] Winston Churchill, *The Collected Works of Sir Winston Churchill, Volume XXV: The Second World War Volume Four: The Hinge of Fate* (London: Library of Imperial History, 1975, first published 1951), p. 522.

[62] Weidhorn, *Harmony*, p. 134.

[63] Paul Addison, 'Winston Churchill's Concept of "The English-Speaking Peoples"', in *The Fabric of Modern Europe: Essays in Honour of Éva Haraszti Taylor*, edited by Attila Pók (Nottingham: Astra Press, 1999), pp. 103-117 (pp. 105-6); Jason Tomes*, Balfour and Foreign Policy: The international thought of a Conservative statesman* (Cambridge: Cambridge University Press, 1997), esp. p. 190; Philip Williamson, 'The doctrinal politics of Stanley Baldwin' in *Public and Private Doctrine: Essays in British History presented to Maurice Cowling*, edited by Michael Bentley (Cambridge: Cambridge University Press, 1993), pp. 181-208 (p. 199).

[64] Winston Churchill, 'If Lee had not won the Battle of Gettysburg', *Scribner's Magazine*, Dec. 1930, in *Collected Essays*, IV, 73-84 (p. 82).

[65] 'Mass Effects in Modern Life', in Winston Churchill, *Thoughts and Adventures* (London: Odhams Press, 1947, first published 1932), pp. 192-202 (p. 201).

[66] 'Shall We All Commit Suicide?', in ibid., pp. 184-191 (pp. 188-9).

[67] 'Fifty Years Hence', in ibid., 203-214 (pp. 203, 209).

[68] Winston Churchill, 'Are There Men in the Moon?', *Sunday Dispatch*, 5 Apr. 1942, in *Collected Essays*, IV, pp. 493-503. Wells had speculated about the existence of 'Intelligence on Mars' in the *Saturday Review* in 1896: Gordon N. Ray, 'H. G. Wells's Contributions to the *Saturday Review*', Library, XVI (1961), 29-36.

[69] Alkon, *Churchill's Imagination*, pp. 162-3.

[70] Young, *Bruce Lockhart Diaries*, p. 480 (entry for 3 Aug. 1945).

[71] Churchill, 'H.G. Wells', pp. 50-51.

[72] H.G. Wells, *Experiment in Autobiography: Discoveries and Conclusions of a Very Ordinary Brain (Since 1866)*, 2 vols (London: Faber & Faber, 1984, originally published 1934), I, 102.

[73] Wells, 'Churchill Must Go'.

BIBLIOGRAPHY

1. Wells's writings

a) Fiction

Apropos of Dolores (London: Cape, 1934)

Babes in the Darkling Wood (London: Secker & Warburg, 1940)

'A Bardlett Romance', *Truth*, 8 March 1894, pp. 555-8

The Book of Catherine Wells (London: Chatto and Windus, 1928)

Brynhild (London: Methuen, 1937)

The Bulpington of Blup (London: Hutchinson, 1932)

Christina Alberta's Father (London: Jonathan Cape, 1925)

A Critical Edition of The War of the Worlds: H. G. Wells's Scientific Romance, ed. by David Y. Hughes and Harry M. Geduld (Bloomington, Indianapolis: Indiana University Press, 1993)

'The Crystal Egg' (1897), in *The Complete Short Stories of H. G. Wells*, ed. by John Hammond (London: Phoenix Press, 1998), pp. 267-80

The Dream (London: Cape, 1924)

The First Men in the Moon (1901) (London: Penguin, 2005)

The Food of the Gods and How it Came to Earth (1904) (New York: Dover Publications, 2006)

God the Invisible King (London: Cassell, 1917)

The History of Mr Polly (1910) (London: Penguin, 1948)

Hoopdriver's Holiday, ed. by Michael Timko (Lafayette: English Literature in Transition, 1964)

'How Gabriel Became Thomson', *Truth*, 26 July 1894, pp. 208-211

'In the Abyss', *Pearson's Magazine*, August 1896, pp. 154-66

'In the Avu Observatory' (1894), in *The Complete Short Stories of H. G. Wells*, ed. by John Hammond (London: Phoenix Press, 1998), pp. 16-21

The Island of Doctor Moreau (1896), ed. by Patrick Parrinder (London: Penguin, 2005)

'The Land Ironclads' (1903), in *The Complete Short Stories of H. G. Wells*, ed. by John Hammond (London: Phoenix Press, 1998), pp. 603-20

Marriage (London: Macmillan, 1912)
Meanwhile: The Picture of a Lady (London: Ernest Benn, 1927)
A Modern Utopia (London: Chapman & Hall, 1905)
—. (London: Thomas Nelson and Sons, n.d., first published 1905)
—. (1905) (London: Penguin, 2005)
Mr Blettsworthy on Rampole Island (London: Ernest Benn, 1928)
'The Rajah's Treasure', *Pearson's Magazine*, July 1896, pp. 39-47
The Scientific Romances of H. G. Wells (London: Victor Gollancz, 1933)
'The Star' (1897), in *The Complete Short Stories of H. G. Wells*, ed. by
    John Hammond (London: Phoenix Press, 1998), pp. 281-89
'The Stolen Body', *Strand Magazine*, November 1898, pp. 567-76
'A Story of the Days to Come' (1897), in *The Complete Short Stories of
    H. G. Wells* (London: St. Martin's Press, 1974), pp. 715-806
The Time Machine (1895), in *The Scientific Romances of H.G Wells*
    (London: Victor Gollancz, 1933)
—. (1895) (London: Penguin, 2005)
—. (1895) (New York: Barnes and Noble, 2006)
Tono-Bungay (London: Macmillan, 1909)
The War in the Air (1908) (Harmondsworth: Penguin, 1975)
*The War in the Air and particularly how Mr. Bert Smallways fared while it
    lasted* (London: George Bell and Sons, 1908)
—. (1908) (London: Penguin, 2005)
The War of the Worlds (serialisation), *Pearson's Magazine*, April-
    December 1897
The War of the Worlds (1898) (London: Heinemann, 1898)
—. (1898) [abridged], with illustrations by Johan Briedé, *Strand
    Magazine*, February 1920, pp. 154-63
—. (1898) (London: Penguin, 2005)
The Wheels of Chance (London: Dent, 1896)
—. (London: Dent, 1901)
The Works of H. G. Wells: Atlantic Edition, 28 vols (London: Fisher
    Unwin, 1924-7), XXIII, *Joan and Peter*
—. VIII, *Kipps*
—. XIX, *The Research Magnificent*
—.VII, *The Wheels of Chance, Love and Mr Lewisham*
When the Sleeper Wakes (1899) (London: Dent, 1994)
—. (1899) (New York: Random House, 2003)
You Can't Be Too Careful (London: Secker and Warburg, 1941)

b) Non-Fiction

'An Open Letter to an elector in N. W. Manchester', *Daily News*, 21 Apr. 1908

Anticipations of the Reaction of Mechanical and Scientific Progress Upon Human Life and Thought (London: Chapman & Hall, 1902)

—. (New York: Dover Publications, 1999, reproducing the text of the revised 1902 edition)

'Churchill Must Go', *Tribune*, 15 Dec. 1944, p. 9

'The Contemporary Novel' (1911), in *H. G. Wells's Literary Criticism* (see *H. G. Wells's Literary Criticism*), pp. 192-205

—. *An Englishman Looks at the World: Being a Series of Unrestrained Remarks upon Contemporary Matters* (London: Cassell, 1914), pp. 148-69

The Conquest of Time, The Thinker's Library, 92 (London: Watts, 1942)

The Discovery of the Future (London: A.C. Fifield 1913, first published in *Nature*, 6 Feb. 1902)

First and Last Things: A Confession of Faith and a Rule of Life (London: The Knickerbocker Press; New York: G. P. Putnam's Sons, 1908)

'From an Observatory' (1894), reprinted in *Certain Personal Matters* (London: Lawrence and Bullen, 1898), pp. 262-6

'The Future of the British Empire', *The Empire Review*, 38 no. 273, Oct. 1923, pp. 1071-9

'Human Evolution, An Artificial Process', *Fortnightly Review*, 60 (1896), 590-5

'Huxley', *Royal College of Science Magazine*, 13 (1901), 209-211

'The Influence of Islands on Variation' (1895), reprinted in *The Island of Doctor Moreau: A Critical Text*, ed. Leon Stover (Jefferson, NC and London: McFarland, 1996), pp. 246-9

'Intelligence on Mars' (1896), reprinted in *Early Writings in Science and Science Fiction* (see *Early Writings*), pp. 175-8

'Jude the Obscure' [review of Thomas Hardy's novel], *Saturday Review*, 81 (1896), 153-4

'The Lost Stevenson' (1896), in *H. G. Wells's Literary Criticism* (see *H. G. Wells's Literary Criticism*), pp. 99-103

'The Man of the Year Million: A Scientific Forecast' (1893), reprinted in H. G. Wells *Journalism and Prophecy*, ed. by W. Warren Wagar (London: Bodley Head, 1965), pp. 3-8

'The Mind in Animals', *Saturday Review*, 78 (1894), 683-4

This Misery of Boots: Reprinted with Alterations from The Independent Review, December 1905 (London: Fabian Society, 1907)

'Mr Wells on the Habitability of the Planets', *Science Schools Journal*, 15 (1888), 57-8

'The New Captain And His Crew', *Reynolds News*, 19 May 1940, p. 6.

'The Novel of Types' (1896), in *H. G. Wells's Literary Criticism* (see *H. G. Wells's Literary Criticism*), pp. 67-70

'On a Tricycle', *Select Conversations with an Uncle with Two Hitherto Unreprinted Conversations*, ed. by David C. Smith and Patrick Parrinder (London: University of North London Press, 1992), pp. 54-57

The Outline of History: Being a Plain History of Life and Mankind, 2 vols (London: George Newnes, 1920)

'A Perfect Gentleman on Wheels', in *The Humours of Cycling: Stories and Pictures* by Jerome K. Jerome, H. G. Wells, L. Raven-Hill, Barry Pain etc., (London: Bowden, 1897), pp. 5-14

'Popular Writers and Press Critics' (1896), in *H. G. Wells's Literary Criticism* (see *H. G. Wells's Literary Criticism*), pp. 74-77

'The Rediscovery of the Unique', *Fortnightly Review*, n.s. 50 (1891), 106-11

Russia in the Shadows (London: Hodder & Stoughton, 1920)

'The Sawdust Doll' (1895), in *H. G. Wells's Literary Criticism* (see *H. G. Wells's Literary Criticism*), pp. 44-47

'Scepticism of the Instrument', *Mind*, n.s. 13 (1904), 379-93

[With Julian Huxley, G.P Wells] *The Science of Life: A Summary of Contemporary Knowledge about Life and its Possibilities*, 3 vols (London: Waverley Book Co. 1930)

The Science of Life (London: Cassell, 1931)

'The Shopman', in *Certain Personal Matters* (London: Unwin, 1901), pp. 80-84

'The So-Called Science of Sociology' (1905), in *An Englishman Looks at the World: Being a Series of Unrestrained Remarks upon Contemporary Matters* (London: Cassell, 1914), pp. 192-206

'The Socialist Movement and Socialist Parties', *The New Age*, 13 June 1907, pp. 105-6

'Specimen Day [From a Holiday Itinerary]', *Science Schools Journal*, 33 (1891), 17-20

Text-Book of Biology, 8 vols (London: W.B. Clive/University Correspondence College Press, 1892-93)

'A thesis on the quality of illusion in the continuity of the individual life in the higher metazoa, with the particular reference to the species *homo sapiens*', in H. G. Wells, *'42-'44: A Contemporary Memoir upon*

Human Behaviour During the Crisis of the World Revolution (London: Secker & Warburg, 1944), pp. 169-196

'Through a Microscope' (1894), reprinted in *Certain Personal Matters* (London: Lawrence and Bullen, 1898), pp. 238-45

'The Visibility of Change in the Moon', *Knowledge*, 18 (1894), 230-1

World Brain (London: Methuen, 1938)

A Year of Prophesying (London: T. Fisher Unwin, 1924)

'Zoological Retrogression', *Gentleman's Magazine*, 271 (1891), 246-53

c) Collected Writings

Certain Personal Matters (London: Lawrence and Bullen, 1898)

—. (London: Fisher Unwin, 1901)

The Complete Short Stories of H. G. Wells, ed. by John Hammond (London: Phoenix Press, 1998)

H. G. Wells: Early Writings in Science and Science Fiction, Edited, With Critical Commentary and Notes by Robert M. Philmus and David Y. Hughes (Berkeley and London: University of California Press, 1975)

H. G. Wells's Literary Criticism, ed. by Patrick Parrinder and Robert M. Philmus (Brighton: Harvester Press, 1980)

d) Autobiographical Writings and Letters

Bernard Shaw and H. G. Wells: Selected Correspondence of George Bernard Shaw, ed. by J. Percy Smith (Toronto: University of Toronto Press, 1985)

The Correspondence of H. G. Wells, 4 vols, ed. by David C. Smith (London: Pickering and Chatto, 1998)

Experiment in Autobiography: Discoveries and Conclusions of A Very Ordinary Brain (since 1866), 2 vols (London: Gollancz and Cresset Press, 1934)

Henry James and H. G. Wells: A Record of their Friendship, their Debate on the Art of Fiction and their Quarrel, ed. by Leon Edel and Gordon Ray (London: Hart-Davis, 1958)

2. Primary Texts

Adorno, Theodor W. and Max Horkheimer, *Dialectic of Enlightenment*, trans. by John Cumming (London: Verso, 1997)

Allen, Grant, *The British Barbarians* (London: John Lane, 1895)

—. 'The Thames Valley Catastrophe', *Strand Magazine*, December 1897, pp. 674-84

Anonymous, 'The Great Debate', *Time*, 13 October 1941 [available online at http://www.time.com/time/]

Anonymous, 'A Strange Light on Mars', *Nature*, 50 (1894), 319

Anonymous, 'The Tragedies of a Camera', *Strand Magazine*, November 1898, pp. 545-52

Bellamy, Edward, *Looking Backward 2000-1887* (1888) (New York: Dover, 1996)

—. (Toronto: Dover, 1996)

Booth, Charles, *Life and Labour of the People in London* (London: 1902-03)

Burns, Robert, *The Canongate Burns*, ed. by Andrew Noble and Patrick Scott Hogg (Edinburgh: Canongate, 2001)

Caine, Hall, 'The New Watchwords of Fiction', *Contemporary Review*, 57 (1890), 479-88

Churchill, Winston, *The Collected Essays of Sir Winston Churchill*, ed. by Michael Wolff, 4 vols (London: Library of Imperial History, 1976)

—. *The Collected Works of Sir Winston Churchill, Volume XXV: The Second World War Volume Four: The Hinge of Fate* (London: Library of Imperial History, 1975, first published 1951)

—. 'Mr. H. G. Wells and the British Empire', *The Empire Review*, 38 no. 274, Nov. 1923, 1217-23

—. *My African Journey* (1908) (London: The Holland Press/Neville Spearman Ltd., 1962)

—. *Thoughts and Adventures* (1932) (London: Odhams Press, 1947)

—. 'The Untrodden Field in Politics', *The Nation*, 7 March 1908, 812-13

—. *Winston S. Churchill: His Complete Speeches, 1897–1963*, 8 vols, edited by Robert Rhodes James (New York: Chelsea House, 1974)

—. *Winston S. Churchill Vol. II Companion Part 2*, edited by Randolph S. Churchill (London: Heinemann, 1969)

—. *Winston S. Churchill Volume V: Companion Part I*, edited by Martin Gilbert (London: Heinemann, 1979)

—. *The World Crisis 1911-1918*, 2 vols (New York: Barnes & Noble, 1993, originally published 1923-7)

Cole, Robert W., *The Struggle for Empire: A Story of the Year 2236* (1900), reprinted in *Sources of Science Fiction*, ed. by Locke (see Locke)

Colville, John, *The Fringes of Power: Diaries 1939-55* (London: Hodder & Stoughton, 1985)

Conrad, Joseph, *Heart of Darkness* (1902) (London: Penguin, 2000)

Donne, John, *Complete Poetry and Selected Prose*, ed. by John Hayward (London: Nonesuch, 1962)

Flammarion, Camille, *La Fin du Monde* (Paris: Ernest Flammarion, 1894)

—. *Lumen* (1886), authorised translation (London: Heinemann, 1897)

Garner, R. L., 'The Simian Tongue [I]', in *The Origin of Language*, ed. by Roy Harris (Bristol: Thoemmes, 1996), pp. 314-21

—. 'The Simian Tongue [II]', in *The Origin of Language*, pp. 321-27

Gramsci, Antonio, *Selections from the Prison Notebooks*, ed. and trans. by Quintin Hoare and Geoffrey Nowell Smith (London: Lawrence and Wishart, 1971)

Graves, Charles L., and Edward V. Lucas, *The War of the Wenuses* (1898), reprinted in *Sources of Science Fiction*, ed. by Locke (See Locke)

Greg, Percy, *Across the Zodiac*, 2 vols (London: Trübner, 1880)

Griffith, George, *Olga Romanoff, Or The Syren of the Skies: A Sequel to The Angel of the Revolution* (London: Tower Publishing, 1894)

Griffith, M., 'An Electric Eye: The Marvellous Discovery of an Eastern Professor Which Distances the Röntgen Rays As They Distance Photography', *Pearson's Magazine*, December 1896, pp. 749-56

—. 'The Christopher Columbus of Mars', *Pearson's Magazine*, July 1896, pp. 30-37

—. 'The Paris Exhibition of 1900', *Pearson's Magazine*, August 1896, pp. 140-9

Hay, William Delisle, *The Doom of the Great City; Being the Narrative of a Survivor, written A.D. 1942* (London: Newman & Co, 1880)

Hodgson, William Hope, *The Night Land* (1912), in *The House on the Borderland and other novels* (London: Gollancz, 2002)

Howard, Ebenezer, *Tomorrow: A Peaceful Path to Real Reform* (London: Swan Sonnenschirm, 1898)

Hudson, W. H., *A Crystal Age* (1887) (London: Fisher & Unwin, 1906)

—. *A Crystal Age* (1887), in *The Collected Works of W.H. Hudson* (London: J.M. Dent, 1922)

Huxley, T. H., 'Evolution and Ethics' (1893) in *The Collected Essays of T. H. Huxley, IX* (London: Macmillan, 1894), 46-86

—. 'Evolution and Ethics' (1893), reprinted in T.H. Huxley and Julian Huxley, *Evolution and Ethics 1893-1943* (London: Pilot Press, 1947), pp. 60-102

—. 'Prolegomena' in *The Collected Essays of T. H. Huxley* (see 'Evolution and Ethics', *Collected Essays*), 1-45

'The Struggle for Existence in Human Society' (1888), in *Collected Essays IX* (see 'Evolution and Ethics', *Collected Essays*), 195-236

Hyam, Ronald 'Winston Churchill before 1914', *The Historical Journal*, 12 (1969), 164-173

James, Henry, ed., *Selected Letters of William James*, 2 vols (London: Longmans, Green and Co., 1920)

James, William, *Pragmatism* (1907) (Indianapolis Cambridge: Hackett Publishing, 1982)

—. *The Principles of Psychology*, 2 vols (London: Macmillan, 1891)

Jean-Aubry, G., ed., *J. Conrad: Life and Letters* (New York: Doubleday, 1927)

Jefferies, Richard, *After London; or, Wild England* (London: Cassell, 1885)

—. *After London; or Wild England* (1885) (Oxford: Oxford University Press, 1980)

Keun, Odette, 'H. G. Wells –The Player', *Time and Tide*, 15 (1934), 1249, 1307-9, 1346-8

Kipling, Rudyard, 'The White Man's Burden' (1899), in *Rudyard Kipling's Verse: Definitive Edition* (London: Hodder and Stoughton, 1973), pp. 323-24

Lankester, E. Ray, *Degeneration: A Chapter in Darwinism* (London: Macmillan, 1880)

Lasswitz, Kurd, *Two Planets (Auf Zwei Planeten)* (1897), abridged by Erich Lasswitz and trans. Hans. H. Rudnick (Carbondale and Edwardsville: Southern Illinois University Press; London and Amsterdam: Feffer and Simons, 1971)

Laurie, André (pseudonym of Paschal Grousset), *The Conquest of the Moon: A Story of the Bayouda* (London: Sampson, Low, Marston, Searle and Rivington, 1889)

Locke, George, ed., *Sources of Science Fiction: Future War Novels of the 1890s* (London: Routledge/Thoemmes Press, 1998)

Lowell, Percival, *Mars* (1895) (London and Bombay: Longman's Green, 1896)

More, Sir Thomas, *Utopia* (1516) (London: Dent, 1974)

Morgan, C. Lloyd, 'The limits of animal intelligence', *Fortnightly Review*, 54 (1893), 223-39

Morris, William, *News From Nowhere* [1890], *News From Nowhere and Other Writings* (Harmondsworth: Penguin Classics, 1993), pp. 43-228

—. *News From Nowhere* (1890) (Oxford: Oxford World's Classics, 2003)

Mouton, Eugène, *Fantasies* (Paris: Charpentier, 1883)

Müller, F. M., *The Science of Language: Founded on the Lectures Delivered at the Royal Institution in 1861 and 1863*, 2 vols (London: Longman, 1899)

Nordau, Max, *Degeneration* (1892) (New York: Appleton, 1895)

Plato, *The Dialogues, Volume 3: Timaeus and Other Dialogues*, trans. Benjamin Jowett, ed. by R. M. Hare and D. A. Russell (London: Sphere, 1970)

Pope, Gustavus W., *Journey to Mars. The Wonderful World: Its Beauty and Splendor; Its Mighty Races and Kingdoms; Its Final Doom* (1894) (Westport, CN: Hyperion Press, 1974)

Popper, Karl, *The Logic of Scientific Discovery* (London: Hutchinson, 1959)

Proctor, Richard, 'The Photographic Eyes of Science', *Longman's Magazine*, February 1883, pp. 439-62, also reprinted in *Literature and Science in the Nineteenth Century: An Anthology*, ed. by Laura Otis (Oxford: Oxford University Press, 2002), pp. 84-87

Serviss, Garret P., *Edison's Conquest of Mars* (1898), reprinted in *Sources of Science Fiction*, ed. by Locke (see Locke)

—. *Other Worlds: Their Nature, Possibilities and Habitability in the Light of the Latest Discoveries* (New York and London: Appleton, 1901)

Tupper, Martin, *Stephan Langton*, 2 vols (London: Hurst and Blacket, 1858)

Unsigned Review [*The Island of Doctor Moreau*], *Review of Reviews*, 13 (1896), 374.

Unsigned Review [*The Island of Doctor Moreau*], *The Guardian* (3 June 1896), reprinted in *H. G. Wells: The Critical Heritage*, p. 53

Unsigned Review [*Love and Mr Lewisham*], *Daily Telegraph* (6 June 1900), reprinted in *H. G. Wells: The Critical Heritage*, ed. by Patrick Parrinder (London: Routledge & Kegan Paul, 1972), p.80

Unsigned Review [*Love and Mr Lewisham*], *Saturday Review* (16 June 1900), reprinted in *H. G. Wells: The Critical Heritage*, p.82

Unsigned Review [*The War of the Worlds*], *Spectator*, 80 (29 Jan. 1898), 168-9

Young, Kenneth, ed., *The Diaries of Sir Robert Bruce Lockhart Vol. 2, 1939-1965* (London: Macmillan, 1980)

Zamyatin, Yevgeny, *We* (1924) (Harmondsworth: Penguin, 1972)

Zola, Emile, 'The Experimental Novel' (1880), in *Documents of Modern Literary Realism*, ed. by George J. Becker (Princeton: Princeton University Press, 1963), pp. 162-96

3. Secondary Texts

Addison, Paul, *Churchill on the Home Front, 1900–1955* (London: Pimlico, 1993)

Aldiss, Brian, with David Wingrove, *Trillion Year Spree: The History of Science Fiction* (Thirsk and Poughkeepsie: House of Stratus, 2001)

Alkon, Paul K., *Winston Churchill's Imagination* (Lewisburg: Bucknell University Press, 2006)

Batchelor, John, *H. G. Wells* (Cambridge: Cambridge University Press, 1985)

Beer, Gillian, *Darwin's Plots: Evolutionary Narrative in Darwin, George Eliot and Nineteenth-Century Fiction* (London: Ark, 1985)

Belsey, Catherine, *Critical Practice* (London: Methuen, 1980)

Bentley, Michael, ed., *Public and Private Doctrine: Essays in British History presented to Maurice Cowling* (Cambridge: Cambridge University Press, 1993)

Beresford, J. D., *H. G. Wells: A Critical Biography* (London: Nisbet, 1915)

Bergonzi, Bernard, *The Early H. G. Wells: A Study of the Scientific Romances* (Manchester: Manchester University Press, 1961)

Bloom, Robert, *Anatomies of Egotism: A Reading of the Last Novels of H. G. Wells* (Lincoln: University of Nebraska Press, 1977)

Blunt, Wilfrid Scawen, *My Diaries: Being a Personal Narrative of Events 1888-1914: Part Two [1900-1914]* (London: Martin Secker, n.d)

Bowen, Roger, '*Mr Blettsworthy on Rampole Island*: "The Story of a Gentleman of Culture and Refinement" ', *The Wellsian*, n.s. 2 (1978), 6-21

Brooks, Van Wyck, *The World of H. G. Wells* (New York and London: T Fisher Unwin, 1915)

Bungay, Stephen, 'His Speeches: How Churchill Did It', *Finest Hour*, No. 112, Autumn 2001, available online at www.winstonchurchill.org

Burrell, Gibson and Karen Dale, 'Utopiary: Utopias, gardens and organization', in *Utopia and Organization,* ed. by Martin Parker (Oxford: Blackwell Publishing, 2002) pp. 106-127

Choi, Yoonjoung, 'Real Romance Came Out of Dreamland into Life: H. G. Wells as a Romancer', Unpublished PhD., Durham University, 2007

Churchill, Randolph S., *Winston S. Churchill, vol. II*: *Young Statesman, 1901–1914* (London: Heinemann, 1967)

Clarke, I. F., *The Tale of the Next War, 1871-1914* (Liverpool: Liverpool University Press, 1995)

—. *Voices Prophesying War, 1763-1984* (1966) (London: Panther, 1970)

Clute, John and Peter Nicholls, eds., *The Encyclopedia of Science Fiction* (New York: St Martin's, 1995)

Cornils, Ingo, 'The Martians Are Coming! War, Peace, Love and Scientific Progress in H. G. Wells's *The War of the Worlds* and Kurd Lasswitz's *Auf Zwei Planeten*', *Comparative Literature*, 55 (Winter 2003), 24-41

Cromie, Robert, *A Plunge into Space* (London and New York: Frederick Warne, 1890)

Derry, Stephen, 'The Time Traveller's Utopian Books and his Reading of the Future', *Foundation*, 65 (1995), 16-24

Draper, Michael, *H. G. Wells* (Houndmills: Macmillan, 1987)

Dryden, Linda, *The Modern Gothic and Literary Doubles: Stevenson, Wilde, and Wells* (Basingstoke: Palgrave Macmillan, 2003)

Ensor, R. C. K., *England 1870-1914* (Oxford: Clarendon Press, 1936)

Ferguson, Niall, *The War of the World: History's Age of Hatred* (London: Allen Lane, 2006)

Fitting, Peter, 'Estranged Invaders: *The War of the Worlds*', in *Learning from Other Worlds: Estrangement, Cognition and the Politics of Science Fiction and Utopia*, ed. by Patrick Parrinder (Liverpool: Liverpool University Press, 2000), pp. 127-45

Foot, Michael, *H. G.: The History of Mr. Wells* (London: Doubleday, 1996)

Fraser, Robert, *Victorian Quest Romance: Stevenson, Haggard, Kipling, and Conan Doyle* (Plymouth: Northcote, 1998)

Freeman, Nick, 'British Barbarians at the Gates: Grant Allen, Michael Moorcock and Decadence', *Foundation*, 83 (2001), 35-47

Gafford, Sam, 'Writing Backwards: the novels of William Hope Hodgson' (1997) <http://alangullette.com/lit/hodgson/gafford.htm> [Accessed 2/05/2006] (originally published in *Studies in Weird Fiction*, 11 (1992), 12-15)

Gilbert, Martin, *Winston S. Churchill, vol. VI: Finest Hour, 1939-1941* (London: Heinemann, 1983)

Greenslade, William, *Degeneration, Culture and the Novel 1880-1920* (Cambridge: Cambridge University Press, 1994)

Guthke, Karl S., *Imagining Other Worlds, From the Copernican Revolution to Modern Science Fiction*, trans. by Helen Atkins (Ithaca and London: Cornell University Press, 1990)

Hammond, J. R., *An H. G. Wells Companion* (London: Macmillan, 1979)

—. *H. G. Wells and the Modern Novel* (New York: St. Martin's, 1988)

—. *H. G. Wells and the Short Story* (London: Macmillan, 1992)

Haynes, Roslynn D., *H. G. Wells: Discoverer of the Future, The Influence of Science on his Thought* (London: Macmillan, 1980)

—. (London: New York University Press, 1980)

Hedgecock, Liz, ' "The Martians are Coming!": Civilisation v. Invasion in *The War of the Worlds* and *Mars Attacks!*', in *Alien Identities: Exploring Difference in Film and Fiction*, ed. by Deborah Cartmell, I.Q. Hunter, Heidi Kaye and Imelda Whelehan (London: Pluto Press, 1999), pp. 104-20

Hillegas, Mark, *The Future as Nightmare: H. G. Wells and the Anti-Utopians* (New York: Oxford University Press, 1967)

Hughes, David Y., and Robert M. Philmus, 'A Selective Bibliography (with Abstracts) of H. G. Wells's Science Journalism 1887-1901', in *H. G. Wells and Modern Science Fiction*, ed. by Darko Suvin and Robert M. Philmus (Lewisburg: Bucknell University Press; London: Associated University Presses, 1977), pp.191-222

—. 'A Queer Notion of Grant Allen's', *Science-Fiction Studies,* 25 (1998), 271-284

—. 'H. G. Wells and the Charge of Plagiarism', *Nineteenth-Century Fiction*, 21 (1966), 85-90

Hurley, Kelly, 'The Modernist Abominations of William Hope Hodgson', in *Gothic Modernisms*, ed. by Andrew Smith and Jeff Wallace (Basingstoke: Palgrave, 2001), pp. 129-149

Israel, Paul, *Edison: A Life of Invention* (New York: John Wiley, 1998)

James, Edward, 'Science Fiction by Gaslight', in *Anticipations*, ed. by Seed (see Seed), pp. 26-45

James, Simon J., 'Pathological Consumption: Commodities and the End of Culture in H. G. Wells's *Tono-Bungay*' in *Consuming for Pleasure,* ed. by Nickianne Moody and Julia Hallam (Liverpool: Liverpool John Moores University Press, 2000), pp. 44-61

—. 'The Truth about Gissing', *The Wellsian*, n.s.24 (2001), 2-21

Jann, Rosemary, 'Sherlock Holmes Codes the Social Body', *English Literature in Transition, 1880-1920*, 57 (1990), 685-708

Keating, P. J., *The Representation of the Working Classes in English Fiction* (London: Routledge and Kegan Paul, 1971)

Kerslake, Patricia, 'Moments of Empire: Perceptions of Kurt [sic] Lasswitz and H. G. Wells', in *The Wellsian*, n.s. 25 (2002), 25-38

Kumar, Krishan, *Utopia and Anti-Utopia in Modern Times* (Oxford: Blackwell, 1991)

Law, Richard, 'The Narrator in Double Exposure in *The War of the Worlds*', *Wellsian*, n.s. 23 (2000), 47-56

Levine, George, *Darwin and the Novelists: Patterns of Science in Victorian Fiction* (Cambridge, MA: Harvard University Press, 1988)

Loing, Bernard, *H. G. Wells à l'Oeuvre (1894-1900)* (Paris: Didier Erudition, 1984)

—. 'H. G. Wells at Work (1894-1900)', *The Wellsian*, n.s. 9 (1986), 23-26

McConnell, Frank, *The Science Fiction of H. G. Wells* (New York: Oxford University Press, 1981)

McGurn, James, *On Your Bicycle: An Illustrated History of Cycling* (London: John Murray, 1987)

Mackenzie, Norman and Jeanne, *The Time Traveller: The Life of H.G Wells* (London: Weidenfeld and Nicolson, 1973)

McLean, Steven, '"The Fertilising Conflict of Individualities": H. G. Wells's *A Modern Utopia*, John Stuart Mill's *On Liberty* and the Victorian Tradition of Liberalism', *Papers on Language and Literature*, 43 (2007), 166-89

Meacham, Standish, *Regaining Paradise: Englishness and the Early Garden City Movement* (New Haven, CT: Yale University Press, 1999)

Miller, Tom 'Wells's Mythological Republic', *H. G. Wells Newsletter*, 5: 11 (Summer 2006), pp. 4-7

Morton, Peter, *The Vital Science: Biology and the Literary Imagination, 1860-1900* (London: Allen, 1984)

Myers Gerald E., *William James: His Life and Thought* (New Haven and London: Yale University Press, 1986)

Pagetti, Carlo, 'Change in the City: The Time Traveller's London and the "Baseless Fabric" of his Vision', in *H .G. Wells's Perennial Time Machine: Selected Essays From the Centenary Conference*, ed. by George Slusser, Patrick Parrinder and Danièle Chatelain (Athens, GA., and London: University of Georgia Press, 2001), pp.122-134

Parrinder, Patrick, 'From Mary Shelley to *The War of the Worlds*: The Thames Valley Catastrophe', in *Anticipations*, ed. by Seed (see Seed), pp. 58-75

—. *H. G. Wells* (Edinburgh: Oliver and Boyd, 1970)

Pelling, Henry, *Winston Churchill* (London: Macmillan, 1974)

Philmus, Robert M., *Visions and Re-Visions: (Re)constructing Science Fiction* (Liverpool: Liverpool University Press, 2005)

Pók, Attila, ed., *The Fabric of Modern Europe: Essays in Honour of Éva Haraszti Taylor* (Nottingham: Astra Press, 1999)

Radice, Lisanne, *Beatrice and Sidney Webb: Fabian Socialists* (London: Macmillan, 1984)

Radick, Gregory, 'Morgan's canon, Garner's phonograph, and the evolutionary origins of language and reason', *British Journal for the History of Science*, 33 (2000), 3-23

Raknem, Ingvald, *H. G. Wells and His Critics* (Oslo: George Allen & Unwin, 1962)

Ray, Gordon N., 'H. G. Wells's Contributions to the *Saturday Review*', Library, 16 (1961), 29-36

—. 'H. G. Wells Tries to be a Novelist', in *Edwardians and Late Victorians*, ed. by Richard Ellmann (New York: Columbia University Press, 1960), pp. 106-229

Reed, John R., 'The Vanity of Law in *The Island of Doctor Moreau*', in *H. G. Wells Under Revision*, ed. by Patrick Parrinder and Robert M. Philmus (London and Toronto: Associated University Presses, 1986), pp. 134-43

Rieder, John, 'Science Fiction, Colonialism, and the Plot of Invasion', *Extrapolation*, 46 (Fall 2005), 373-94

Roberts, Adam, *Science Fiction* (London and New York: Routledge, 2000)

Ryan, Henry B., 'A New Look at Churchill's "Iron Curtain" Speech', *Historical Journal*, 22, 4 (1979), 895-920

Said, Edward, *Orientalism: Western Conceptions of the Orient* (1978) (Harmondsworth: Penguin, 1995)

Sardar, Ziauddin, and Sean Cubitt, eds., *Aliens R Us: The Other in Science Fiction Cinema* (London: Pluto, 2002)

Schiller, F.C.S., 'Axioms and Postulates' in *Personal Idealism*, ed. Henry Sturt (London: Macmillan, 1902)

Seed, David, ed., *Anticipations: Essays on Early Science Fiction and Its Precursors* (Liverpool: Liverpool University Press, 1995)

Shelton, Robert, 'Locating *The Time Machine* within (and beyond) the Bergonzi/Wagar Debate', *The Undying Fire*, 1 (2002), 29-42

Smith, David C, *H. G. Wells: Desperately Mortal* (New Haven: Yale University Press, 1986)

—. 'Winston Churchill and H. G. Wells: Edwardians in the Twentieth Century', *Cahiers Victoriens et Edouardien*, 30 (1989), 93-116

Smith, Jonathan, *Fact and Feeling: Baconian Science and the Nineteenth-Century Literary Imagination* (Madison: University of Wisconsin Press, 1994)

Snow, C.P., *Variety of Men* (London: Macmillan, 1967)

Stokes, John, ed., *Fin de Siècle: Fin du Globe: Fears and Fantasies of the Late Nineteenth Century* (Basingstoke: Macmillan, 1992)

Sussman, Herbert L., *The Victorians and the Machine: The Literary Response to Technology* (Cambridge, Mass: Harvard UP, 1968)

Tomes, Jason, *Balfour and Foreign Policy: The international thought of a Conservative statesman* (Cambridge: Cambridge University Press, 1997)

Toye, Richard, 'H .G. Wells and the New Liberalism', *Twentieth Century British History*, 19 (2008), 156-85

Vernier, Jean-Pierre, *H. G. Wells et son Temps* (Rouen: Publications de l'Université de Rouen, 1971)

Wagar, W. Warren, *H. G. Wells and the World State* (New Haven: Yale University Press, 1961)

—. *H. G. Wells: Traversing Time* (Middletown, CT: Wesleyan University Press, 2004)

Weinhorn, Manfred, *A Harmony of Interests: Explorations in the Mind of sir Winston Churchill* (Cranbury, NJ: Associated University Presses, 1992)

West, Anthony, 'H. G. Wells', in *Principles and Persuasions: The Literary Essays of Anthony West* (London: Eyre and Spottiswoode 1958), pp. 4-20

—. *H .G. Wells: Aspects of a Life* (London: Hutchinson, 1984)

West, Geoffrey, *H. G Wells: A Sketch for a Portrait* (London: Gerald Howe, 1930)

Westfahl, Gary, *Science Fiction, Children's Literature and Popular Culture: Coming of Age in Fantasyland* (Westport, CN, and London: Greenwood Press, 2000)

—. 'Space Opera', in *The Cambridge Companion to Science Fiction*, ed. by Edward James and Farah Mendlesohn (Cambridge: Cambridge University Press, 2003), pp. 197-208

Williams, Keith, *H. G. Wells, Modernity and the Movies* (Liverpool: Liverpool University Press, 2007)

Williams, Raymond, *The English Novel from Dickens to Hardy* (St Albans: Paladin, 1974)

Williamson, Philip, 'The doctrinal politics of Stanley Baldwin' in *Public and Private Doctrine: Essays in British History presented to Maurice Cowling*, edited by Michael Bentley, (Cambridge: Cambridge University Press, 1993), pp. 181-208

4. Films

Independence Day. Dir. Roland Emmerich. TCF/Centropolis. 1996
Mars Attacks! Dir. Tim Burton. Warner Bros. 1996
The War of the Worlds. Dir. Byron Haskin. Paramount. 1953
The War of the Worlds. Dir. Steven Spielberg. Paramount. 2005

5. Archives

Winston Churchill Papers, Churchill Archives Centre, Cambridge
H. G. Wells Papers, University of Illinois

CONTRIBUTORS

Editor

Steven McLean is a former Secretary of the H. G. Wells Society and the author of *The Early Fiction of H. G. Wells: Fantasies of Science* (Basingstoke and New York: Palgrave Macmillan, 2009). He has published articles, reviews and encyclopaedic entries on Wells and annotated three Wells titles in Penguin Classics.

Contributors

Emily Alder graduated with a degree in English Literature from Newcastle University and has recently completed her PhD in the School of Arts & Creative Industries at Edinburgh Napier University. Her thesis investigates 'William Hope Hodgson and the borderlands of the fin de siècle'.

John R. Hammond is the founder and President of the H. G. Wells Society. He is the author of *H. G. Wells and the Modern Novel* (1988), *H. G. Wells and the Short Story* (1992) and *The Time Machine: A Reference Guide* (2004). He is a former Research Fellow at Nottingham Trent University.

Sylvia Hardy is a former lecturer, now a Visiting Fellow at the University of Northampton, and a Vice-President of the H. G. Wells Society. She has written on Wells and language, and is currently writing on H. G. Wells and film.

Simon J. James is Senior Lecturer in Victorian Literature in the Department of English Studies at Durham University. He is the author of *Unsettled Accounts: Money and Narrative Form in the Novels of George Gissing* (Anthem, 2003), and of articles on George Gissing, H. G. Wells and Charles Dickens. He has edited Gissing's *Charles Dickens: A Critical Study* (Grayswood, 2004) and four Wells novels in Penguin Classics. He is currently working on a study of Wells and high culture.

Bernard Loing is chairman of the H. G. Wells Society and a former professor of English literature and linguistics at the universities of Caen and Tours in France. He is the author of *H. G. Wells à l'Oeuvre (1894-1900)* (Paris: Didier Erudition, 1984). Bernard is President of the International Conference of NGOs at UNESCO.

Formerly a pharmacist, **Sylvia A. Pamboukian**, Ph.D. is an assistant professor of English Studies at Robert Morris University in Pittsburgh, Pennsylvania. Her research interests include literature and medicine, the Gothic, and nineteenth-century century science fiction. She is currently completing a book on medical practitioners in nineteenth-century fiction.

Patrick Parrinder is Professor of English at the University of Reading and author of numerous books and articles on H. G. Wells, science fiction, and nineteenth-and twentieth-century fiction and criticism. He is a Vice-President of the H. G. Wells Society and is general editor of the H. G. Wells texts published in Penguin Classics. His most recent book is *Nation and Novel: The English Novel From Its Origins To The Present Day*, and he is general editor of the forthcoming multi-volume *Oxford History of the Novel in English*.

Richard Toye is a Senior Lecturer in the Department of History at the University of Exeter. He is the author of *The Labour Party and the Planned Economy, 1931-1951* (2003) and *Lloyd George and Churchill: Rivals for Greatness* (2007).

Keith Williams is Senior Lecturer in English at the University of Dundee. He is the author of *H. G. Wells, Modernity and the Movies* (Liverpool UP, 2007) and is currently writing a monograph on *James Joyce and Cinematicity*. He also chairs the Scottish Word and Image Group.

INDEX

Unless otherwise indicated, all books, articles and short stories indexed below are by H. G. Wells.